T0214955

Communications in Computer and Information Science 1394

More information about this series at http://www.springer.com/series/7899

Ashish Kumar Luhach ·
Dharm Singh Jat · Kamarul Hawari Bin Ghazali ·
Xiao-Zhi Gao · Pawan Lingras (Eds.)

Advanced Informatics for Computing Research

4th International Conference, ICAICR 2020
Gurugram, India, December 26–27, 2020
Revised Selected Papers, Part II

 Springer

Editors
Ashish Kumar Luhach
Papua New Guinea University
of Technology
Lae, Papua New Guinea

Dharm Singh Jat
Namibia University of Science
and Technology
Windhoek, Namibia

Kamarul Hawari Bin Ghazali
Universiti Malaysia Pahang
Pekan, Pahang, Malaysia

Xiao-Zhi Gao
University of Eastern Finland
Kuopio, Finland

Pawan Lingras
Saint Mary's University
Halifax, NS, Canada

ISSN 1865-0929   ISSN 1865-0937 (electronic)
Communications in Computer and Information Science
ISBN 978-981-16-3652-3   ISBN 978-981-16-3653-0 (eBook)
https://doi.org/10.1007/978-981-16-3653-0

This Springer imprint is published by the registered company Springer Nature Singapore Pte Ltd.
The registered company address is: 152 Beach Road, #21-01/04 Gateway East, Singapore 189721,
Singapore

Preface

This book "Advanced Informatics for Computing Research" contains selected and edited papers from the Fourth International Conference on Advanced Informatics for Computing Research (ICAICR 2020), targeting state-of-the-art as well as emerging topics pertaining to advanced informatics for computing research and its implementation for engineering applications. The objective of this international conference is to provide opportunities for researchers, academicians, industry professionals, and students to interact and exchange ideas, experience, and expertise in the current trends and strategies for information and communication technologies. Moreover, ICAICR aims to enlighten participants about the vast avenues, and current and emerging technological developments, in the field of advanced informatics and its applications, which are thoroughly explored and discussed.

The Fourth International Conference on Advanced Informatics for Computing Research (ICAICR 2020) was held during December 26–27, 2020, in Gurugram, India, in association with the Namibia University of Science and Technology, Namibia, and technically sponsored by the Mata Raj Kaur Institute of Engineering and Technology, Haryana, India, and Leafra Research Pvt. Ltd., Haryana, India.

We are extremely grateful to our valuable authors for their contributions and our Technical Program Committee for their immense support and motivation in making this edition of ICAICR a success. We are also grateful to our keynote speakers for sharing their precious work and enlightening the delegates of the conference.We express our sincere gratitude to our publication partner, Springer, for believing in us.

January 2021

Ashish Kumar Luhach
Dharm Singh Jat
Kamarul Hawari Bin Ghazali
Xiao-Zhi Gao
Pawan Lingras

Organization

Conference Chairs

Kamarul Hawari Bin Ghazali	Universiti Malaysia Pahang, Malaysia
Dharm Singh Jat	Namibia University of Science and Technology, Namibia
Ashish Kumar Luhach	The PNG University of Technology, Papua New Guinea

Publicity Chair

Aditya Khamparia	Lovely Professional University, Punjab, India

Technical Program Chairs

Pawan Lingras	Saint Mary's University, Canada
Xiao-Zhi Gao	University of Eastern Finland, Finland

Technical Program Committee

K. T. Arasu	Wright State University, USA
Rumyantsev Konstantin	Southern Federal University, Russia
Syed Akhat Hossain	Daffodil International University, Bangladesh
Sophia Rahaman	Manipal University, Dubai
Thippeswamy Mn	University of KwaZulu-Natal, South Africa
Lavneet Singh	University of Canberra, Australia
Pao-Ann Hsiung	National Chung Cheng University, Taiwan
Mohd Helmey Abd Wahab	Universiti Tun Hussein Onn, Malaysia
Shireen Panchoo	University of Technology, Mauritius
Sumathy Ayyausamy	Manipal University, Dubai
Kamarul Hawari Bin Ghazali	Universiti Malaysia Pahang, Malaysia
Dharm Singh Jat	Namibia University of Science and Technology, Namibia
Abbas Karimi	Islamic Azad University, Arak, Iran
Upasana G. Singh	University of KwaZulu-Natal, South Africa
Ritesh Chugh	Central Queensland University, Melbourne, Australia
Pawan Lingras	Saint Mary's University, Canada
Poonam Dhaka	University of Namibia, Namibia
Ashish Kumar Luhach	The PNG University of Technology, Papua New Guinea

Indra Seher	Central Queensland University, Sydney, Australia
Sugam Sharma	Iowa State University, USA
T. G. K. Vasista	King Saud University, Saudi Arabia
Akhtar Kalam	Victoria University, Australia
Ioan-Cosmin Mihai	Alexandru Ioan Cuza Police Academy, Romania
Abhijit Sen	Kwantlen Polytechnic University, Canada
R. B. Mishra	Indian Institute of Technology (BHU) Varanasi, India
Bhaskar Bisawas	Indian Institute of Technology (BHU) Varanasi, India

Contents – Part II

Security and Privacy

Contents – Part I

Hardware

Design and Simulation of a Coaxial Fed Slotted Wide-Band Rectenna for Wireless Power Transmission

Raghav Tola[✉] and Asmita Rajawat

Amity University, Noida, Uttar Pradesh, India
arajawat@amity.edu

Abstract. There has been an ever-increasing demand for efficient and reliable method of power transmission and energy harvesting. There has been increasing demand for wireless power transmission which can provide renewable free energy. Energy harvesting devices such as Rectenna caters to this purpose due to its significant improvement over the disadvantages of the conventional method of power transfer. The concept of wireless power transmission was first proposed over a century ago, but the real-world application still face a no. of challenges. Employing rectenna as energy harvesting device for portable electronic devices presents advantages which include reducing the cost factor, having consistent and robust transfer system, no affect under different environmental factors. The design proposed in here is a wide band rectenna which can be utilised at frequencies of 5.46 GHz and 5.75 GHz. The rectifier circuit had been implemented using a HSMS-285C Schottky diode, Greinacher voltage doubler has been selected. While designing the antenna Duroid substrate was implemented as it has a dielectric permittivity of 2.2, this substrate possesses various advantages over conventional FR-4 substrate including minimal electrical losses and low moisture absorption hence efficiency of the antenna design improves significantly. For the designing of the rectifier circuit ADS software was used. Designing of the antenna was done on HFSS software and Proteus design software has been used for the PCB designing of the proposed model. The designed rectifier yielded a conversion efficiency of 70.905% and 68.307% for 5.46 GHz and 5.75 GHz, respectively. The gain of the proposed antenna achieved was 7.46 dB, the directivity achieved was 7.55 dB. The proposed design can be useful under ample number of applications and provides an alternate power source for small wireless electronic devices.

Keywords: Rectenna · Energy harvesting · Wide band slotted antenna · Wireless power transmission · Conversion efficiency · Return loss

1 Introduction

1.1 Related Work

Elimination of wires from the power transmission techniques has made everything much simpler rendering various advantages. Rectenna is a device capable of capturing RF

© Springer Nature Singapore Pte Ltd. 2021
A. K. Luhach et al. (Eds.): ICAICR 2020, CCIS 1394, pp. 3–14, 2021.
https://doi.org/10.1007/978-981-16-3653-0_1

signals and converting them to DC signal. A Rectenna is known to have high efficiency and its compact design makes it suitable replacement for battery dependencies of portable devices. Antenna captures electromagnetic radiation and converts it to electrical signals. A slot antenna is designed from a metal plate in which different slots are cut out. The radiation pattern of the antenna is determined in accordance to shape and size of the slots. A feed line joins the transmission end and receiving end of the antenna. Coaxial cables are widely used for feed lines. They do not induce unwanted currents in them even when attached to a conductive support. In ideal coaxial cables, the signal from the electromagnetic field does not exist other than the space between inner and outer conductors. An Antenna has truncated edges due to which they lack continuity, and it causes radiation hence to make antenna resonant the length of the transmission line is kept half of the wavelength. In [1] focus is laid on nano systems on how they can put an impact on health, infrastructure. They operate with external energy and focus is laid on energy harvesting systems upon how these nano systems can be utilised to be used as an energy harvester. the designed microstrip patch antenna resonated at a frequency of 5 GHz. It has been observed in this paper that when the width of the patch reduces the gain enhances and the return loss diminishes [2]. [3] describes a RF power transmission system for a wireless sensor network to reduce battery dependency of such wireless networks. [4] describes a fully integrated wireless power transfer system which has a convergence efficiency of 35%, this system demonstrated that it could support wireless communication of a sensor node up to 0.15-m distance. [5] describes about 2.45 GHz rectenna capable of wireless power transfer. In this paper a high-power rectification system is portrayed. This paper explains how RF power transmission can co-exist with pre-existing communication function. Attempt to maximise gain of patch antenna, a frequency selective substrate has been employed to increase the efficiency and minimise the thickness of substrate [6]. The research work in [7] is done for the fabrication of a rectifier circuit for wireless energy transfer at 5.8 GHz frequency which gives conversion efficiency of 66% at 100 mW power. In [8] a rectifier circuit is introduced which is based on Voltage doubler circuit which consist of Schottky diode which yields a conversion efficiency of more than 50%. In [9] Energy Harvesting based on WLAN is focussed upon. The frequencies taken is 2.4 GHz and hence providing an alternate energy source. It achieves a return loss of -26.46 dB with impedance of 52.45 Ω. [10] A wide band sierpinski fractal antenna has been designed, moreover the geometry is modified using circular shape. The usage of fractal pattern provides efficient method for compactness.

1.2 Contribution

The research carried out for Rectenna designing has been done into two parts. The first part includes designing of the rectifier circuit with the help of a Greinacher voltage doubler and a Schottky diode. The second part includes designing of a wide band slotted antenna. The main fixation is laid at achieving a high conversion efficiency for the rectifier circuit and attaining high-level antenna directivity and gain.

1.3   Organisation of the Paper

This paper is organised as follows- The Sect. 2 comprises of the intended rectenna design which has been additionally segregated into 2 different subsections covering the design of Wide Band Antenna and the intended model of the Rectifier Circuit. Section 3 illustrates the results achieved from the design of the intended model. Further, Sect. 4 cites the conclusion and finally wrap up of the paper.

2   Proposed Rectenna Design

2.1   Slotted Antenna Design

The patch of the slotted antenna presents a complex shape consisting of different sizes of slots. The substrate Duroid having a dielectric permittivity of 2.2 is chosen for being a less lossy dielectric in comparison of the conventional FR-4 designs. It has a thickness of 3.2 mm. Following formulas will define the proportions of the patch-

The formula for the patch width is calculated with-

$$w = \frac{C}{2f_0\sqrt{\frac{\varepsilon r + 1}{2}}} \tag{1}$$

where, ε_r is the Dielectric Constant having a value of 2.2.

$$w = \frac{3 \times 10^8}{2 \times 5.46 \times 10^9 \sqrt{1.6}} \tag{2}$$

This yields a width of 17.2 mm. And the length of the patch is calculated by-

$$L = \frac{c}{2f_0\sqrt{\varepsilon_{eff}}} - 2\Delta L \tag{3}$$

After calculations, the length is obtained to be 19 mm (approx.). Co-axial method of feeding is applied here by using Teflon as the primary material for the feed cylinder. The radius of the inner conductor and outer conductor are 0.65 mm and 2.35 mm, respectively. To minimise effects of losses during the transmission process, the length of feed line was taken to be 8.62 mm. Thus, the final dimensions of the patch along with the feeding point are given below-

$$(L, W, H) = (17.2, 19, 3.2)$$

Position of the feed point from the centre of the patch-

$$(X, Y) = (-3.4, 0)$$

Figure 1(a) shows the dimensions of the patch antenna and illustrates the slots integrated on the antenna. Figure 1(b) illustrates a cross-section of the design which highlight the coaxial feeding technique.

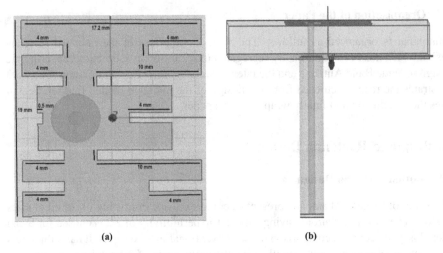

Fig. 1. (a) Dimensions of the patch and the slots (b) Co-axial method of feeding

Initially an E-shaped design was presented by cutting the two parallel slots with lengths 10 mm and widths 1 mm. However, this produced a small value of Return Loss due to high inductive behaviour of the slots. Another rectangular slot was cut between these two slots having dimensions of 6.2 mm length and 2.8 mm width to increase the capacitive behaviour. This improved the results and the Return Loss decreased below −10 dB. Figure 2(a) presents the initial E-shaped design making use of only three slots. In order to make band wide, two more slots on the opposite sides of the parallel slots were cut. Their lengths were varied from 1 mm to 5 mm keeping widths constant at 1 mm. Optimized results were obtained for 4 mm length. Similar procedure was followed for cutting the capacitive slot having dimensions 6.2 mm length and 1.5 mm width. Figure 2(b) presents the double E-shaped patch. In the next step two slots were incorporated in the capacitive gaps and their lengths were varied from 0.5 mm to 5 mm keeping width constant at 1 mm. The Return Loss improved significantly at this point. Figure 2(c) represents the design consisting of centrally cut slots. However, the width of the band still needed improvement to cover lower frequencies in the 5–6 GHz range. For this purpose, four slots were incorporated adjacent to the previously cut parallel slots. For the left side lengths obtained were 4 mm and for the right side these were 5 mm. Figure 2(d) displays the four incorporated slots which gives the final shape of the patch.

2.2 Greinacher Voltage Doubler Iinspired Rectifier Circuit

A Voltage Doubler circuit is a circuit which uses input voltage to charge capacitors in such a way that the output voltage generated is twice the amount of the input voltage. This circuit forms a rectifier; hence the incoming RF signals are rectified to produce DC signal output. To increase the efficiency of the rectifier circuit, impedance matching process is adopted.

Following design is based on Greinacher voltage doubler because it has significant advantages over existing conventional circuits which includes elimination of ripples

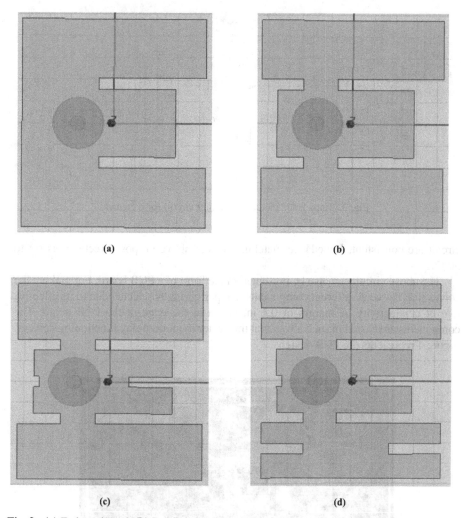

Fig. 2. (a) E-shaped patch (b) Parallel slots incorporated (c) Central slots in capacitive(d) Final design with adjacent slots

which therefore influences the level of current drawn from the circuit. The impedance of the circuit varies for different range of frequencies which are to be tested, hence impendence matching is performed to solve this hindrance. When the doubler circuit is directly coupled to the power source, conversion efficiency of the designed circuit is significantly low. To improve the efficiency a ladder network comprising of inductors and capacitors was employed which considerably improved the efficiency of the designed circuit. Impedance matching rectifier circuit is shown in Fig. 3.

A load of 1500 Ω is considered at the output terminal of the rectifier circuit across which the output voltage will be measured, impedance matching of the rectifier circuit is done so that the output impedance of the antenna and input impedance of the rectifier

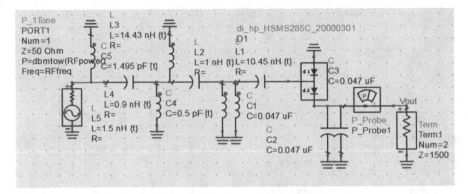

Fig. 3. Impedance matching rectifier circuit for rectenna

circuit are consistent. Impedance matching for the above proposed rectenna is set to 50 Ω.

The above circuit can also be presented in the form of a PCB board. For making the connection between different components, copper wiring is selected due to its effective rate of conductivity. A margin of 0.1 in. is left at the edge of the PCB board. The components are casted in such a way that they cater to modern-day functioning devices. Figure 4 represents the PCB design.

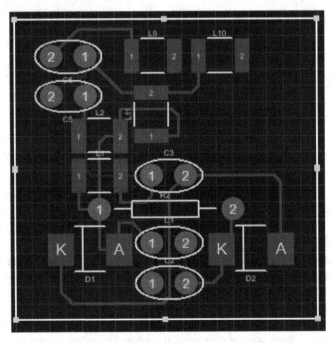

Fig. 4. PCB design of the matching circuit

Dark blue layer in the above figure represents the ground layer on the PCB board. A 3D representation of the design has been presented in Fig. 5. This helps to visualize the circuit better and give a better understanding to the circuit.

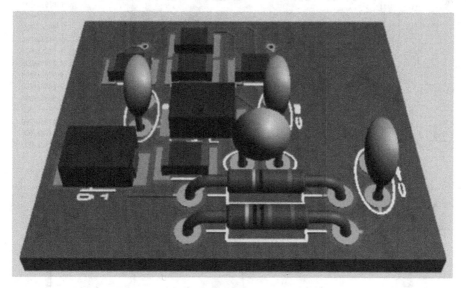

Fig. 5. 3D visualisation of the matched circuit

3   Results and Discussions

3.1   Results of Slotted Antenna

For a better performance of the co-axial fed slotted rectenna, an antenna with high gain is required. Additionally, the S11 plot should have significant values lower than $-10\,\text{dB}$ causing its wide band operation. To study and identify the flow of current, an analysis of the patch surface is performed. The direction of the flow of current on the surface of the patch is presented in Fig. 6(a). The movement is indicated from higher slot width towards the lower slot width on the left side of the patch. Higher current density values are depicted by Converging arrows. Figure 6(b) shows a similar model of the flow of current. This indicates lower density values at the edges of the slot and comparatively higher values at the centre and the opposite edges of the patch. A minimum value of 0.747 A/m is observed.

Return Loss of the Antenna was analysed. Figure 7 shows S11 graph of Return Loss with simulated values. At a frequency of 5.25 GHz the plot plummets below the crucial $-10\,\text{dB}$ mark. Minimum value of $-39.46\,\text{dB}$ was obtained for 5.46 GHz and $-28.46\,\text{dB}$ was obtained for 5.75 GHz. The trace climbs back towards $-10\,\text{dB}$ at 5.81 GHz.

Essential Antenna parameters such as the overall Antenna Gain have been observed by the simulation results. A peak value of 7.46 dB has been obtained for the overall

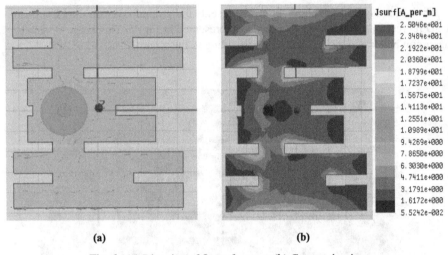

(a)   (b)

Fig. 6. (a) Direction of flow of current (b) Current density

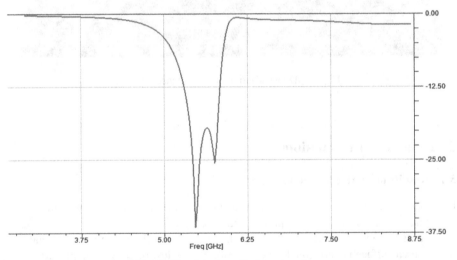

Fig. 7. Simulated results for return loss

gain with the peak value of directivity being 7.55 dB. Figure 8(a) and (b) present the three-dimensional plots for the overall Antenna Gain. As per the conventional method for calculating gain,

$$G = kD \tag{4}$$

Where 'G' is the Antenna Gain, 'D' is the Directivity and 'k' is the efficiency of the Antenna. Thus, performance of the Antenna can be assessed as followed-

$$k = G/D \tag{5}$$

By putting in the peak values,

$$k = 7.46/7.55 \tag{6}$$

$$k = 0.988 \text{ or } 98.8\%$$

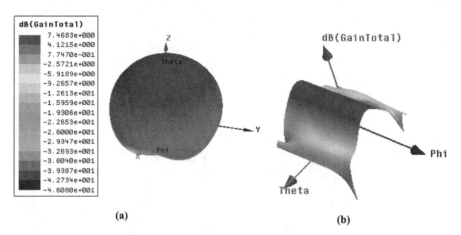

(a)   (b)

Fig. 8. (a) 3D polar plot for gain (b) 3D rectangular plot for gain

Figure 9(a) and (b) display the radiation patterns at 5.46 GHz and 5.75 GHz, respectively. Both patterns are broad sided and similar in their operational aspects.

Proposed rectenna can be employed for Wireless Energy Transfer (WET) for the GSM band, since the design of the rectenna supports wide band operation between 5 to 6 GHz. Figure 9(c) provides the radiation pattern for the antenna at 5.8 GHz which is in accordance with the previous results.

3.2   Results for Rectifier Circuit

The results obtained for the rectifier circuit were optimised for two different frequencies which are 5.46 GHz and 5.75 GHz. For each frequency two different plots are obtained, respectively. The graph for output voltage was observed and the graph for conversion efficiency was observed. The above-mentioned graphs were observed against a range of 0–10 dBm of input RF power.

For the frequency of 5.46 GHz the maximum output voltage achieved at 10 dBm of input RF power is 3.261 V. Figure 10(a) represents a graph for output voltage against input RF power. At input power of 10 dBm, the maximum conversion efficiency obtained is 70.905%.

The conversion efficiency can be determined using following formulas -

$$P_{out} = (V_{out})^2/R_L \tag{7}$$

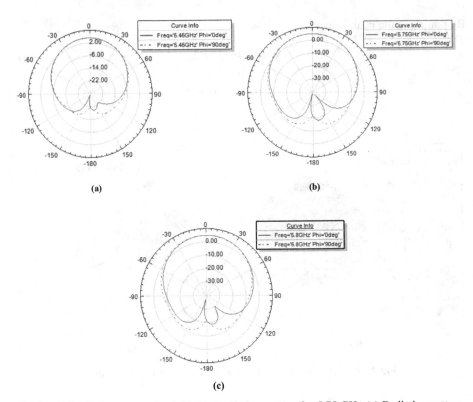

Fig. 9. (**a**) Radiation pattern for 5.46 (**b**) Rradiation pattern for 5.75 GHz (**c**) Radiation pattern for 5.8 GHz

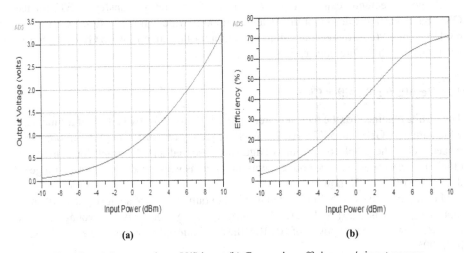

Fig. 10. (a) Output voltage V/S input (b) Conversion efficiency v/s input power

$$\eta = P_{out}/P_{in} \tag{8}$$

P_{out} implies the output power whereas V_{out} indicates the output voltage achieved. The impedance is taken to be 1500 Ω across which the output is obtained. Figure 10(b) illustrates the graph between the conversion efficiency versus the input Radio Frequency power.

The proposed rectifier circuit for the wide band rectenna, yields maximum output voltage of 3.201 V at input power of 10 dBm resonant at 5.75 GHz. the output voltage is represented by Fig. 11(a). The maximum conversion efficiency achieved for the above input power is 68.307% which is represented by Fig. 11(b).

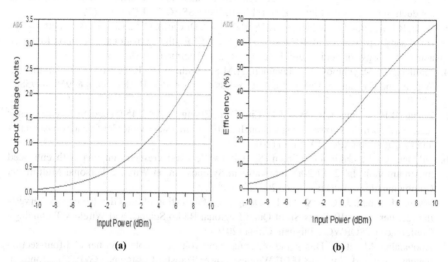

(a)   (b)

Fig. 11. (a) Output voltage V/S input power. (b) Conversion efficiency v/s input power

4 Conclusion

The proposed rectenna yields suitable results for the application of wireless energy transfer. The rectifier simulations were performed using ADS software, the designed rectifier was able to achieve an output voltage of 3.261 V at a frequency of 5.46 GHz and a maximum conversion efficiency of 70.905%. And when simulated for the frequency of 5.75 GHz the result for maximum output voltage was 3.201 V and 68.307% for the maximum conversion efficiency. The Wide Band Antenna simulations were performed using HFSS software, maximum efficiency of the designed antenna achieved was 98.8%.

The proposed design can be employed as a suitable energy providing replacement of batteries which are currently being used for portable devices.

5 Future Work

In future, work will be done to improve the present conversion efficiency of the proposed rectenna design, the design of the antenna will be optimised to improve the wide band capability of the antenna which will allow it to capture more radiation.

References

1. Wang, Z.L., Wu, W.: Nanotechnology-Enabled Energy Harvesting for Self- Powered Micro-/Nano Systems, Angewandte Chemie (International ed.) (2013)
2. Jain, S.K.: Performance analysis of rectangular patch antenna using variation in width of conducting patch. SSRG Int. J. Electr. Electr. Eng. (SSRG-IJEEE) **3**(11) (2016)
3. Rosa, R.L., Zoppi, G., Di Donato, L., Sorbello, G., Di Carlo, C.A., Livreri, P.: A battery-free smart sensor powered with RF energy. In: 2018 IEEE 4th International Forum on Research and Technology for Society and Industry (RTSI), Palermo (2018)
4. Malik, B.T., Doychinov, V., Hayajneh, A.M.S., Zaidi, A.R., Robertson, I.D., Somjit, N.: Wireless power transfer system for battery-less sensor nodes. IEEE Access **6**, 95878–95887 (2020)
5. Zhang, B.H., Zhang, J.W., Wu, Z.P., Liu, C.G., Zhang, B.: A 2.45 GHz dielectric resonator rectenna for wireless power transmission. In: 2017 Sixth Asia-Pacific Conference on Antennas and Propagation (APCAP), Xi'an (2017)
6. Dikmen, C.M., Cakir, G., Cimen, S.: Ultra-wide band crescent antenna with enhanced maximum gain. In: 2017 20th International Symposium on Wireless Personal Multimedia Communications (WPMC), Bali (2017)
7. Wang, M., Chen, J., Cui, X., Li, L.: Design and fabrication of 5.8 GHz RF energy harvesting rectifier. In: 2019 Cross Strait Quad-Regional Radio Science and Wireless Technology Conference (CSQRWC), Taiyuan, China (2019)
8. Aboualalaa, M., et al.: Dual-band rectenna using voltage doubler rectifier and four-section matching network. In: 2018 IEEE Wireless Power Transfer Conference (WPTC), Montreal, QC, Canada (2018)
9. Chaour, I., Fakhfakh, A., Kanoun, O.: Patch antenna array for RF energy harvesting systems in 2.4 GHz WLAN frequency band. In: 2018 15th International Multi-Conference on Systems, Signals & Devices (SSD), Hammamet (2018)
10. Kirubavathy, P.S., Ramprakash, K.: Design of Sierpinski fractal antenna for wideband applications. In: 2017 International Conference on Innovations in Information, Embedded and Communication Systems (ICIIECS), Coimbatore (2017)

Optimised Multi Energy System (OMES)
for Electric Vehicle

Sheeja Nair[1]($\boxtimes$), Avinash More[2], and Ionut Cristian Scurtu[3]

[1] Dwarkadas J Sanghvi College of Engineering, Mumbai 400056, India
Shreeja.nair@djsce.ac.in
[2] Mukesh Patel School of Technology Management and Engineering, NMIMS University,
Mumbai 400056, India
avinash.more@nmims.edu
[3] Mircea Cel Batran, Naval Academy, Constanta, Romania

Abstract. Air pollution due to carbon emission is a perennial problem faced
globally and causing a big threat to the environment and health in particular.
Thus, it becomes essential to explore and interface different types of electrical
energy to develop an optimized system. Hence, renewable energy resources have
been widely acknowledged as a viable option to override this issue along with
other viable energy sources. In order to handle this we have proposed, Optimized
Multi Energ System (OMES) which consists of a battery, fuel cell and solar energy
to improve the overall efficiency of the electric vehicles while reducing carbon
emission.

Keywords: Electric vehicle · Optimized Multi Energy System (OMES) ·
Renewable energy · Fuel cell · Solar energy · Lithium ion battery

1 Introduction

The lifestyle and demand in today's world is raising the concerns and impact of global
warming in the present and for the future to come [1]. Experts analyze the prime reasons of the same being carbon emissions from vehicles and factories followed by the
deforestation which has led to steady increase of carbon dioxide. The levels of Carbon
dioxide has been on a steady increase from 1959 at a rate 315 ppm and post 50 years the
same stands at 385 ppm which is further believed to reach 1000 ppm by the year 2100
[2]. Carbon emission is causing a big threat to the environment and badly impacting
human health in particular. It's significantly observed that maximum amount of carbon
is emitted by China, 28% and US, 15% whereas only 21% is emitted from rest of the
world. Figure 1 shows the worldwide carbon dioxide emission [3]. Thus, it becomes
essential to explore energy resources which have the least carbon content.

Internal combustion engines (ICE) are the most commonly used heat engines; they
are used majorly in vehicles. ICE has been dominating since the mid-20th century, which
has caused higher carbon emissions and in turn has led to the global warming. Also due to
increase in usage of fossil fuels the future consequences with substantial anthropogenic

© Springer Nature Singapore Pte Ltd. 2021
A. K. Luhach et al. (Eds.): ICAICR 2020, CCIS 1394, pp. 15–26, 2021.
https://doi.org/10.1007/978-981-16-3653-0_2

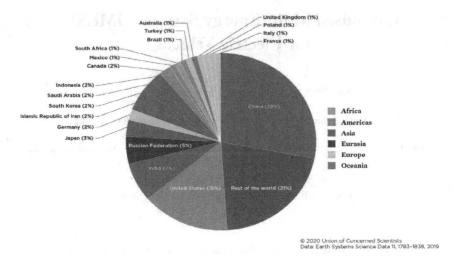

Fig. 1. Worldwide carbon dioxide emission [3]

climate changes and constant depletion in fossil fuel has been identified as a future challenge. Hence, it has become important to shift from internal combustion engines to least fuel consumption vehicles. To incentivize Electric Vehicles (EVs) [4] are used instead of internal combustion engine. EVs operate on an electric motor along with li-ion batteries to store energy.

Hybrid energy system can control different parameters such as efficiency; reliability and system complexity pose a challenge in designing and devising energy storage systems [5]. The single storage device made of lithium ion batteries are widely used for powering laptop, smart devices, mobile phones, electric vehicles and many more devices. Single storage device is well established and its usages to store electrical energy are very high. However, the ageing process of li-ion batteries are fast and it emits carbon emission while operating frequently. Hence, this paper proposes OMES to overcome all the difficulties caused by single battery storage system. The main objective of research work is to bring the best of both and incorporate the same in an effective manner. Different combinations of energy sources are used and comparative analysis is done to understand the limitations of each proposed model. The OMES consists of lithium ion battery, fuel cell interfaced with the solar energy resource along with the dc-dc converter circuits, filter circuits and loads. The organization of paper is as follows: Sect. 2 presents the literature overview. We have Presented our proposed mechanism OMES in Sect. 3. Section 4 discussed about result analysis and concluding remark is presented in Sect. 5.

2   Literature Overview

In the last few years, Electric Vehicles (EVs) [6] are in great demand and the market is drastically shifting from Internal Combustion Engine (ICE) to Electric Vehicles. ICE where the fuel is ignited inside the engine to produce power and ignite vehicle. Due to constant increase in harmful gases, depletion of reservoirs and fuels, variation in climate forces to shift focus to no fuel vehicles. As EVs are legitimately associated with electric signal, many of its features like easy control, systematic monitoring, and energy exchange are easy to obtain [7]. It is also useful to monitor the state of the battery like charging and discharging time, protect overcharging and alert if inadequate charging is observed. Energy can be exchanged between renewable resources, storage system and load [8]. For uninterruptable supply, charging, discharging and storage of the battery need higher priority to optimize the system and minimize the losses [9]. Since, the discharge rate of batteries used in electric vehicles are comparatively faster than conventional vehicles, they run out of charge before reaching the designated destination or charging station. Thus, it becomes essential to focus on efficient energy system along with rechargeable capabilities. The energy system [10], does not just track the amount of charge left in a battery, but also manages the charging and prevents the battery from overcharging. If the cell is fully charged, the voltage rises and if the rise is detected, then charging should be ceased beyond it. It even provides communication mechanism between the battery and other electronic devices interfaced with the vehicle.

Using li-ion batteries will not only decrease the cost significantly but will also increase the efficiency of the battery; it carries powerful electrical energy supplies at mobile applications [11]. However, the major drawbacks with the standalone system like battery storage are degradation at high temperature, difficulty in fast charging, current leakages, loss of energy during braking, needs protection to prevent thermal runaway at increased stress. Hence, BESS needs multiple storage system along with renewable energy resources [12]. The rapid growth of electric vehicles globally requires Hybrid Energy Storage System (HESS). Solar power is the fastest growing source of energy due to abundance and free availability, combining this energy resource with the energy storage device, will yield better and carbon free result. The energy system that can successfully store the electrical energy extracted from solar on operation [13].

Nowadays, fuel cell technologies are developing which have promising outcomes in terms of emissions and efficiency. The hybrid system consists of solar power systems, fuel cell type Polymer Type Electrolyte (PEM) and diesel engine with synchronous machine. Fuzzy logic controller is used to control the fuel cell operation with respect to battery state of charge [14]. The author describes about the switching between solar panel and fuel cell depending upon the state of charge to result in continuous operation for electric vehicle. A novel HESS [15] proposed here has better acceleration and driving range of the electric vehicle. The conventional HESS sourced vehicles required a higher rating of dc-dc converters whereas the novel HESS maintains constant voltage due to which it enhances the life of the battery.

3 Proposed Mechanism Using Solar Energy and MESS

A solar energy source integrates into the modern power systems to meet the ever-increasing worldwide energy demands as well as to reduce the harmful gas emissions. Along with solar optimized Energy System (OMES) is used in order to provide continuous supply to the Electric Vehicle (EV). Figure 2 shows a viable circuit diagram for HESS using multiple energy sources. The circuit incorporates solar renewable energy sources along with the conventional energy sources li-ion batteries along with fuel cells.

Different power converters help to achieve the desired output. The proposed work is to provide uninterruptable and continuous power supply. A boost converter is used to step up the renewable voltage which can be supplied to the load as well as storage system. Boost converter is a dc-dc power converter which steps up the dc input voltage. It consists of active and passive switches like IGBT switches and diode along with energy storage element which is used to step-up the voltage. The bidirectional dc-dc converter is used for charging and discharging of energy storage devices. The bidirectional inverter converts dc power into ac power. IGBT switches are more economical which combine high efficiency and fast switching. LC filter circuits are used to provide ac voltage and current at the load. The paper describes and calculates various parameters consisting of energy distribution, various losses, improved efficiency, power allocations and carbon emission. Optimal power split for different energy distributions and different loads will minimize the losses of HESS, improve the overall efficiency, and maximize the travelled distance.

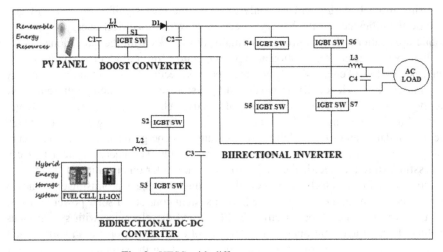

Fig. 2. HESS with different energy sources

The Optimized Multi Energy Storage System OMES will work in different modes of operation as mentioned below [16]:

Mode 1: Charging Conventional Energy Source and Powering Load
In this mode, when solar energy is available then the dc input voltage from solar is stepped up using boost converter which passes the stepped up voltage to the inverter circuit to produce ac supply which is supplied to the ac load, which will drive the electric vehicle. Also it charges the Hybrid Energy Storage System (HESS). During this

mode of operation, the bi-directional dc-dc converter circuit acts as a buck converter that accepts energy from solar.

Mode 2: Discharging Energy from Conventional Energy Source (Fuel Cell) to Load
In this mode, when solar energy is not available then the fuel cell gives the energy to the load. During this mode of operation, the bi-directional dc-dc converter circuit acts as a boost converter that dissipates energy to the load known as discharging state.

Mode 3: Discharging Energy from Conventional Energy Source (Li-ion) to Load.
In this mode, when solar energy is not available, and the fuel cell too does not have energy then li-ion battery feeds the energy to the load. Battery management system is used to monitor the energy charging and dissipation. During this mode of operation, the bi-directional dc-dc converter circuit acts as a boost converter that dissipates energy to the load known as discharging state.

Mode 4: Regenerating Braking System.
If excess energy passes to the ac load then it will dissipate its energy to the li-ion battery in order to reduce wastage of energy. Regenerative braking energy conversion mechanism where kinetic energy of an object in motion is transferred to the store energy using electromagnetic, flywheel, spring, hydraulic and so on. Solar energy alone is not capable to supply continuous energy to the load. Hence, conventional energy resources along with solar energy are the prime requirement.

Using different combinations of energy resources we have proposed, the different models and their analysis:

Model 1: Solar and Li-ion Batteries
As shown in Fig. 3, solar cell combines with li-ion batteries. If solar is available, then the energy dissipates to the load and due to the bidirectional converter, li-ion battery gets charged.

Block 1 (PV and Li-ion Energy Resources): Lithium batteries are rechargeable energy storage which can be paired with solar energy to store excess solar energy and use it when solar is unavailable. If solar is available, then energy is dissipated through solar and simultaneously used to charge li-ion batteries and if load demands energy in the absence of solar then li-ion battery is used to dissipate energy to the load.

Block 3 (Boost Converter): Boost converter is a dc-dc converter which mainly consists of IGBT switch, diode, l-c circuit which is used to step up the dc voltage. Boost converter takes input dc from solar and step up the voltage using energy storage device like inductor and semiconductor devices like diode and IGBT switch which helps to dissipate the stepped up voltage to the load.

Block 4 (Dc-dc Converter): Bidirectional dc-dc converters are used such that energy can flow in both the direction. When energy is absorbed by the battery from solar then it's called buck converter and if energy dissipates from the battery to the load it's called boost converter.

Block 5 (Inverter Circuit):   It consists of IGBT switches to convert dc supply to ac load along with l-c circuit to provide ac voltage and current with reduced voltage losses.

Block 2 (Result Analysis):   The scope represents the input and output voltage, current, power and efficiency.

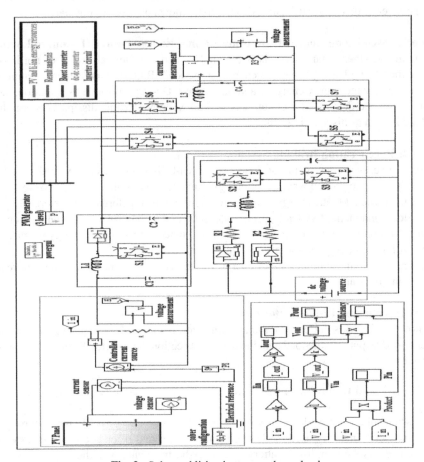

Fig. 3.   Solar and li-ion battery to the ac load

Model 2: Solar and Fuel Cell

In the conventional energy source li-ion is replaced with fuel cell to understand the efficiency, output power and carbon emission produced. The design aimed to reduce the use of fossil fuel and increase the renewable energy system penetration and main focus is to reduce carbon emission. When solar is available the dc supply is fed to the electric vehicle through solar via boost converter. In the absence of solar the energy is fetched from the fuel cell. In model2 Li-ion is replaced by fuel cell rest all the blocks are similar as discussed in the earlier block diagram [refer page no. 7 and figure no. 3] (Fig. 4).

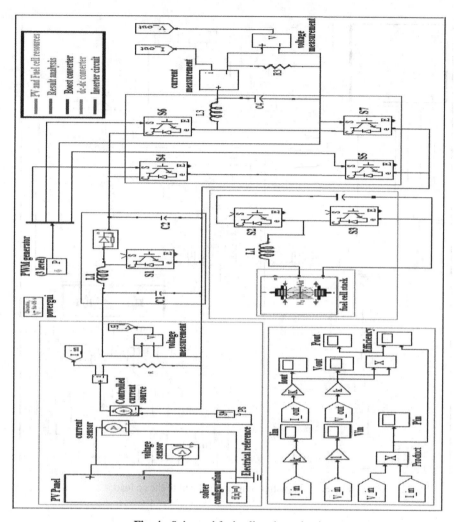

Fig. 4. Solar and fuel cell to the ac load

Model-3

This model is the combination of model 1 and model 2 which consists of solar energy along with li-ion batteries and fuel cell which is designed to understand the efficiency of the system. This design is proposed to run efficiently over long duration and also to understand carbon emission. The dc supply is stepped up using boost converter and fed to the ac load and in the absence of solar energy, energy is taken from fuel cell and further if required then fetched from li-ion battery which has the ability to store energy for long duration (Fig. 5).

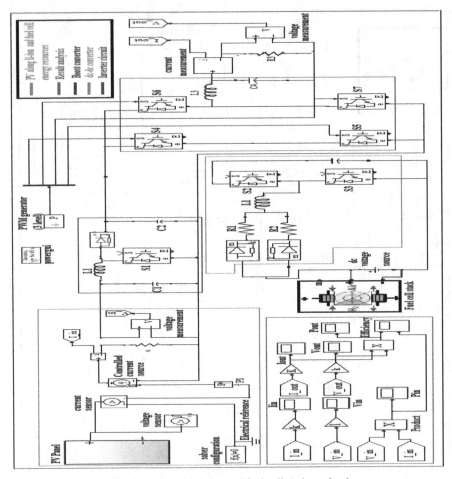

Fig. 5. Solar with li-ion and fuel cell to the ac load

4 Result Analysis

Model 1: Solar and Li-ion Batteries

An average electric car consumes 200 W. Hence, considering 30 W as input power from the solar energy which is stepped up to 200 W using boost converter which is then fed to the load. If solar is unavailable then lithium ion battery is used to dissipate energy to the load. The efficiency, ratio of output power to the input power is applied and carbon emission analyses are done based upon the power rating. When 200 W power is supplied from the li-ion batteries to the load, the overall output power as well as efficiency obtained is 165 W and 82.5% as obtained and shown in the Fig. 6. Carbon emission obtained is (65–75) % which is huge due to high rating of li-ion battery used (200 W) which needs to be controlled.

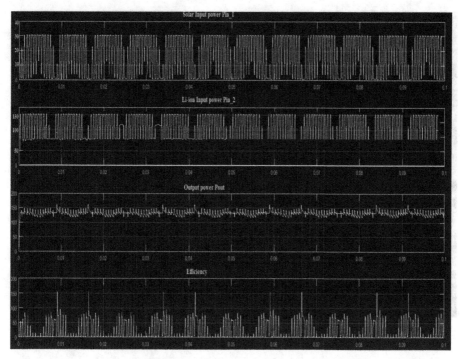

Fig. 6. Input-output waveforms of solar and li-ion batteries to the ac load

Model 2: Solar and Fuel Cell

When solar is generating 30 W of power and using boost converter it is stepped up to 200 W and fuel cell is producing 200 W of power then the output obtained is 130 W which though reduced the overall efficiency of the system to 65% shown in Fig. 7 but the carbon emission was reduced drastically. For long run this type of model generates least carbon less than 10% as fuel cell emits water which can be used as coolant for electric vehicle and emits 0% carbon.

Model 3: Solar with Li-ion Batteries and Fuel Cell

When Li-ion and fuel cell is combined then the rating of li-ion is reduced as fuel cell is used. When 30 W solar power is stepped up to 170 W which is obtained from the boost converter and is fed to the load. In the absence of solar combine 170 W power is obtained from li-ion and fuel cell it helps to reduce the carbon emission drastically maintaining the efficiency of the system to 77.14%. The output obtained is 135 W as shown in Fig. 8. Whereas the carbon emission is reduced to less than 30%. It's observed that the output is optimized and efficiency obtained as well as carbon emissions are satisfactory.

Table 1 shows the overall efficiency and carbon emission obtained due to different models. It eases to compare the different models and understand the better performance characteristics.

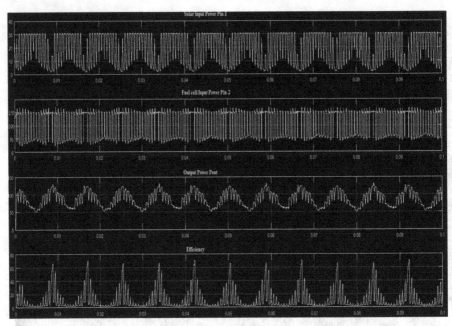

Fig. 7. Input-output waveforms of solar and fuel cell to the ac load

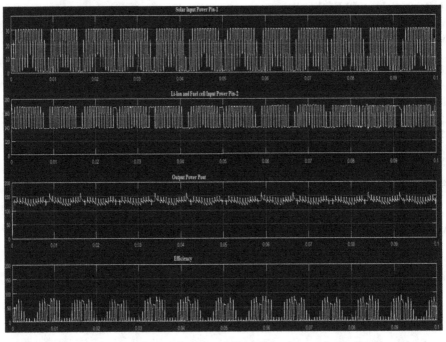

Fig. 8. Input-output waveforms of solar with li-ion batteries and fuel cell to the ac load

Table 1. Efficiency and carbon emission

Type	P (Solar)	Pin-1 boost converter	Pin-2 (conventional)	Pin-1 or Pin-2	Pout	Efficiency = Pout/Pin	Carbon emission
Model 1	30 W	200 W	200 W	200 W	165 W	82.5%	(65–75)%
Model 2	30 W	200 W	200 W	200 W	130 W	65.0%	(5–10)%
Model 3	30 W	200 W	200 W	190 W	150 W	78.94%	(25–30)%

5 Conclusion

The electric vehicle has many advantages and benefits over the internal combustion engine. The research paper is focused on the different models which are compared to analyze the overall efficiency and carbon emissions. It is observed that in Model 1 when solar is combined with high rated li-ion battery the efficiency obtained is better but not better in terms of carbon emission and in Model-2 when solar is combined with fuel cell it is less efficient but has got a reduced carbon emission whereas in Model-3 when solar is combined with li-ion battery and fuel cell the overall efficiency was at 75% with 30% less carbon emission. To improve the overall efficiency as well as reduce carbon emission, the renewable energy resources along with Optimized Multi Energy System (OMES) will be a definite approach.

References

1. Tsitomeneas, S.Th., Kokkosis, A.I., Charitopoulos, A.G.: Natural or anthropogenic is the unbalance of the radiation on earth and the related global warming-climate change? Parameters, answers and practices. In: IEEE Xplore, 13th September 2020
2. Jafar, H., Nurulhaiza, U., Amran, N.A., Abdullah, A., Hadi, M.A., Halim, Z.A.: A low cost approach of multisensor device for global warming studies. In: 2014 International Symposium on Technology Management and Emerging Technology (ISTMET 2014), Indonesia, 27–29 May 2014 (2014)
3. Each country share of Carbon dioxide emission. https://www.ucsusa.org/resources/each-cou ntrys-share-CO2_emissions. Accessed 12 Aug 2020
4. Jayluke Malatji, M., Daniel Chowdhury, S.P.: Comparative study on improvement in battery management system of hybrid batteries. In: 2019 IEEE PES/IAS Power Africa. IEEE Xplore, 16th September 2020
5. Baker, J.N., Collinson, A.: Electrical energy storage at the turn of the millennium. Power Eng. J. **6**, 107–112 (1999)
6. Abhin, A., Vijaya Chandrakala, K.R.M.: Hybrid energy storage system for an electric vehicle powered by brushless DC motor. In: 2018 International conference on Control, Power, Communication and Computing Technologies. IEEE (2018)
7. Huang, Q., Li, J., Chen, Y.: University of Electronic Science and Technology of China, P.R. China. Control of Electric Vehicles, Sciyo, Croatia, p. 192, September 2010. https://www.sciyo.com. ISBN 978-953-307-100-8
8. Prajeesh, K., Waheeda Beevi, M.: An efficient regenerative braking system for BLDCM driven electric vehicles. In: 2018 4th International Conference for Convergence in Technology (I2CT) SDMIT, Ujjre, India. IEEE (2018)

9. Handbook on 'Energy Storage System' Dec2018 by Asian development bank
10. Pirienko, S., Balakhontsev, A., Beshta, A., Albu, A., Khuoliy, S.: Optimization of hybrid energy storage system for electric vehicles. Power Electron. Drives **1**(36), no. 2 (2016). https://doi.org/10.5277/PED160206
11. Weiss, H., Winkler, T., Ziegerhofer, H.: Large lithium ion battery powered electric vehicles-from idea to reality. 978-1-5386-4759-2/18/\$31.00 ©2018 IEEE
12. Obaid, W., Hamid, A-K., Ghenai, C.: Hybrid PEM fuel-cell-diesel-solar power system design with fuzzy battery management system and weather forecasting for electric boats. IEEE Xplore. 978-1-7281-1182-7/18
13. Rizoug, N.: Teacher-researcher at ESTACA Lab on "Hybrid Energy Storage System for Electric Vehicles". 29 May 2018
14. Habibur, Md., Barua, K., Annis-Uz-Zaman, Md., Razak, M.A., Islam, N.: Simulation of a solar power system with fuel cell backup source for hybrid power system application. IEEE Xplore, 17 September 2020
15. Katuri, R., Gorantla, S.: Modelling and comparative analysis of ANN and PID controllers with MFB applied to HESS of electric vehicle. SN Appl. Sci. **1**(11), 1–16 (2019). https://doi.org/10.1007/s42452-019-1502-4
16. Dominic Savio, V., Lakshmi, G.R.P.: Automative engine/battery hybrid power generation using BDC. Int. J. Pure Appl. Math. **118**(16), 1149–1161 (2018)

Modeling of Microstrip Patch Antenna Using Artificial Neural Network Algorithms

M. V. V. Prasad Kantipudi[1(✉)], Sailaja Vemuri[2], S. Sreenath Kashyap[3], Rajanikanth Aluvalu[4], and Y. Satish Kumar[1]

[1] Department of ECE, Sreyas Institute of Engineering and Technology, Hyderabad, India
{mvvprasad,satishkumar.y}@sreyas.ac.in
[2] Department of ECE, Pragati Engineering College, Surampalem, India
sailaja.v@pragati.ac.in
[3] Department of ECE, Kommuri Pratap Reddy Institute of Technology, Hyderabad, India
sreenathkashyap@kpritech.ac.in
[4] Department of CSE, Vardhaman College of Engineering, Hyderabad, India

Abstract. In this paper, a novel method of approach of designing the microstrip antenna operating at Industrial, Scientific and Medical band is being analyzed and simulated. As the resonant frequency of the antennas configuration is dependent on the geometrical confinement and dimensions of the antenna the analysis and synthesis of the resonant frequency is carried out using the Artificial Neural Network (ANN) model. The physical dimensions like width (W), Length (L), Height (h), Dielectric permittivity are taken into consideration for the ANN algorithms Radix Basic Function Model (RBF) and Multilayer Perception Algorithm (MLP). The feed forward method and reverse side method is used for the analysis and synthesis of the parameters in determining the resonant frequency (f_r) of the Antenna. The antenna configuration is designed by calculating using conventional formulas for the values of Length, Width and Height for the Operating frequency. A good matching is observed in terms of the values of the geometrical parameters between the RBF, MLP and Conventional formula method. The antenna configuration is analyzed using CST and the electrical parameters namely Return loss (S_{11}), Gain and directivity are determined. Further the same is fabricated. The test and measurement values are also produced and a good agreement is observed in terms of Returnloss (S_{11}). This study and analysis of the ANN Model of designing can be extended further in the design of the RF and Microwave components also. As a future scope this design of Antenna using Artificial Neural Network ANN can be extended to the design of Meta materials antennas for communication applications.

Keywords: CST · Returnloss · Multilayer Perception Algorithm · Radix Basic Function Model

1 Introduction

In this fast growing and ever changing era of science and technology various algorithms and techniques plays a vital role. The design of such systems has inspired various

© Springer Nature Singapore Pte Ltd. 2021
A. K. Luhach et al. (Eds.): ICAICR 2020, CCIS 1394, pp. 27–36, 2021.
https://doi.org/10.1007/978-981-16-3653-0_3

researchers and young aspirants to focus towards the development of wireless communication systems for the wireless systems. In recent days the cost effective and wide bandwidth antenna systems are developed which enhances the overall efficacy and performance of the entire wireless system. A number of methods are available to design antennas which operate for the particular resonant frequency. However the theoretical and experimental investigations are carried out for enhancing the electrical performance parameters and the operation of antenna systems. Various research aspirants focused towards the development of different antenna models. The challenging task is determining the parameters for the particular resonant frequency for a particular application. The frequency of operation or the resonant frequency will be more predominantly dependant on the various mechanical parameters of the antenna system. Enormous amount of work is carried out in determining the mechanical parameters of the antenna system through theoretical and mathematical investigations [1, 2]. However the necessity of extensive analysis for the calculation of the mechanical parameters which determines the frequency of operation is to be carried out using a scientific method or an algorithm. One such interdisciplinary stream of science and technology is Artificial Neural Networks (ANN) [3]. The concept and algorithms of the artificial neural network will help in solving the problem and finding the mechanical parameters of the antennas. This concept of implementation of ANN in the determining the frequency of operation through the mechanical parameters has brought a tremendous change in the ease of the design of the antennas for various frequencies [4]. In this paper the analysis of the problem has been defined to find out the resonant frequency for a given substrate material which have the dielectric coefficient and the geometric model.

2 Antenna Configuration

Antennas play a crucial role in the Wireless systems. The performance of the wireless systems depends on the antenna design and its performance [2, 5]. In recent days Microstrip patch antenna has gained the attention of the research community. Patch antenna configuration consists of a radiating structure mounted on the dielectric substrate on one side and the metallic ground on the other side [8]. The substrate layers are generally isotropic in nature where as the height (h) dielectric permittivity (ε_r), length and width are the mechanical parameters which influence the performance of the antenna system. Anti isotropic substrates can also be considered for the design of microstrip patch antenna. The improvised efficiency and bandwidth is generally obtained by using the substrates of less dielectric permittivity values whereas generally the value of the dielectric permittivity ranges from 2.2 to 12. The below Fig. 1 depict the model of the basic patch antenna configuration.

The modeling of the antenna is carried out by calculating the value of the effective dielectric permittivity of the substrate as stated in Eq. 1, length and width of the radiator as specified in Eq. 2

$$\varepsilon_{eff} = \frac{\varepsilon_r + 1}{2} + \frac{\varepsilon_r + 1}{2}\left[1 + 12\frac{h}{W}\right]^{-\frac{1}{2}} \tag{1}$$

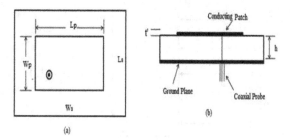

Fig. 1. Antenna structure [1, 2]

$$W = \frac{1}{2f_r\sqrt{\varepsilon_r\mu 0}}\sqrt{\frac{2}{\varepsilon_r + 1}} \tag{2}$$

$$L = \frac{1}{2f_r\sqrt{\varepsilon_{eff}}\sqrt{\varepsilon_0\mu 0}} - 2\Delta L \tag{3}$$

3 ANN Model of a Patch Antenna

In recent times various ANN techniques are developed for the calculation and determination of the resonant frequency of various shapes of patch of the antennas. The evaluation of the frequency of operation of a patch antenna is a prime factor for determining the behavior. The test data sheets used for these models are to be obtained analytically of from the earlier literature work carried out by various research aspirants. The ANN models are also utilized for determining the impedance of the patch antenna. The utilization of the neuro fuzzy networks is one of the fastest techniques of determining the frequency of operation of the patch antenna. The calculations or the analysis is based on the wave number of the domain which results in the spectral analysis to analyze the behavior of the model.

The ANN model is developed to calculate the dimensions of the patch of a microstrip patch antenna. The variables of the patch width (W) and length (L) are considered as a function of the input variables, where as height of the dielectric substrate is (h) and dielectric permittivity (ε_r) of the material is considered in terms of x and y directions namely (ε_x, ε_y) which determines the electrical properties of the substrate material respectively. Figure 2 shows the ANN model of the antenna which provide the details of the input parameters and output parameters of the black box.

The ANN Model usage in determining the parameters of antenna can be done in two different methods. One is through forward method in which the input parameters are used to synthesize to find the output. The synthesis model of the ANN model is as shown in Fig. 2.

The second one is by reverse method in which the output parameter is obtained from the chosen inputs which are at the input side. This method is called as analysis model of the ANN model. To determine the output parameters of th ANN algorithm by these two methods the ANN algorithms are need to be studied which are as described in the next section of this paper.

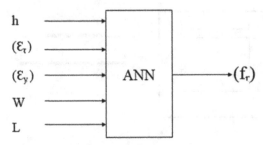

Fig. 2. Input and output parameters analysis using ANN model

4   ANN Algorithms

The artificial neural network model is developed based on the input and out variables for the microstrip patch antenna configuration. In order to determine the parameters on an antenna suing the ANN techniques various algorithms are to studied. One of these algorithms like Radial Basis Fucntion (RBF) and Multilayer Perceptions (MLP) are used for the ANN Model [13]. The brief of these RBF and MLP is a state below.

4.1   RBF Model

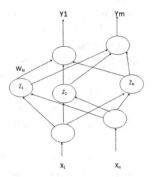

Fig. 3. Radial Basis Function Network of ANN Model

In this model of ANN the feed forward networks are used for a hidden layer which uses the radial function for activating the hidden neurons [14]. A typical structure of the model is shown in Fig. 2. Gaussian and multi-quadratic functions are generally used for activating the radial function in this RBF network (Fig. 3).

In the RBF model of ANN around 45 samples are tested and for five inputs and single output of which number of inputs is 4 and number of outputs is 2 respectively in order to synthesize the ANN.

4.2   MLP Model

MLP models are trained by the backward propagation algorithm. These MLP networks are used to transform the data into a desired response which will be highly useful in modeling the pattern classifications. In the MLP model which consists of a single unit of a neuron is composed of the weight which will be sum of the input and threshold value for activating the function. As the name itself specifies the multilayer perception which means the output of one neuron unit will act as an input for the next presiding layer.

The configuration of an MLP will be of four input neurons which consist of 10 and 5 neurons in the hidden layer. The rate of learning will be 0.1 with a goal estimation of 0.01 for approximately 450 echos. The accuracy level will be best in the range of the value of spread is 0.01 appropriately.

5 Determining the Parameters of Patch Antenna Using ANN

The training is performed by using the 45 data sets which comprises of the various mechanical parameters of the patch namely width, length, height, dielectric permittivity will act as input and the resonant frequency of operation will be the output of the ANN model. The ANN network is trained for a good network convergence condition [7]. The ANN model was tested for input frequencies the entire range. The Multilayer perception model consists of layers which are namely MLP1 and MLP2 and MLP3 which uses scaled conjugate, Resilient and Levenberg Marquardt algorithms for optimizing the values in the ANN model [9, 10]. The accuracy of the synthesis ANN model for the designed 4 networks is being synthesized and Analyzed as specified in the Table 1. The RBF is found to be the best approximation with the structure of the antenna. The synthesized results are shown in the Table 2 respectively (Tables 3 and 4).

Table 1. ANN synthesis and its comparison with the targets

Height (cm)	Permittivity	Frequency (GHz)	Width (cm)	Width – RBF (cm)	Length (cm.)	L RBF (cm.)
0.3250	2.33	2.320	5.6300000e+000	5.5945405e+000	3.9000000e+000	3.856472e+000
0.3250	2.33	2.980	4.4800000e+000	4.4451162e+000	3.0800000e+000	3.040534e+000
0.3250	2.33	4.210	2.9200000e+000	4.4174521e+000	1.9100000e+000	1.900053488e+000
0.3250	2.33	5.740	1.9500000e+000	1.9347063e+000	1.4000000e+000	1.295348658e+000
0.3250	2.33	6.750	1.6900000e+000	1.6523145e+000	1.1000000e+000	1.103542580e+000
0.3250	2.33	7.600	1.3900000e+000	1.3300561e+000	8.000000e−001	9.52145683e−001
0.3250	2.33	8.170	1.0500000e+000	1.0352471e+000	6.000000e−001	6.87589405e−001
0.3250	2.33	9.150	1.7000000e+000	1.7005635e+000	7.000000e−001	7.01865487e−001
0.9425	2.33	4.630	6.9800000e+000	6.9845726e+000	1.2000000e+000	1.25798458e+000
0.4100	2.55	7.134	8.9700000e+000	8.9502548e+000	1.3550000e+000	1.35874587e+000
0.4500	2.55	6.090	1.0000000e+000	1.0325489e+000	1.3500000e+000	1.35645821e+000
0.4670	2.55	5.820	8.1300000e+000	8.1765896e+000	1.4200000e+000	1.4105879e+000
0.4870	2.55	6.280	7.8000000e+000	7.8356789e+000	1.3400000e+000	1.3414655e+000
0.5300	2.55	5.970	7.9200000e+000	7.8236548e+000	1.5200000e+000	1.5187655e+000
0.1670	2.33	5.030	1.7300000e+000	1.7156487e+000	1.7600000e+000	1.7643571e+000

Table 2. Accuracy of the ANN synthesis neural networks

ANN model	Accuracy
RBF	99.56
MLP1	97.65
MLP2	94.50
MLP3	93.88

Table 3. ANN analysis and its comparison with the appropriate targets

Height (cm)	Permittivity	Width (cm)	Length (cm)	Frequency-target (GHz)	Frequency-RBF (GHz)
0.3250	2.33	5.63	3.90	2.3200000e+000	2.1008457e+000
0.3250	2.33	4.48	3.08	2.9800000e+000	2.9602547e+000
0.3250	2.33	2.92	1.91	4.2100000e+000	4.2060254e+000
0.3250	2.33	1.95	1.40	5.7400000e+000	5.7584687e+000
0.3250	2.33	1.69	1.10	6.7500000e+000	6.6985657e+000
0.3250	2.33	1.39	8.00	7.6000000e+000	7.7985467e+000
0.3250	2.33	1.05	6.00	8.1700000e+000	8.1264785e+000
0.3250	2.33	1.70	7.00	9.1500000e+000	9.0854678e+000
0.9425	2.33	6.98	1.20	4.6300000e+000	4.5687521e+000
0.4100	2.55	8.97	1.35	7.1340000e+000	7.0638452e+000
0.4500	2.55	1.00	1.35	6.0900000e+000	6.1058765e+000
0.4670	2.55	8.13	1.42	5.8200000e+000	5.8545702e+000
0.4870	2.55	7.80	1.34	6.2800000e+000	6.4265790e+000
0.5300	2.55	7.92	1.52	5.9700000e+000	5.9845875e+000
0.1670	2.33	1.73	1.76	5.030	5.0158689e+000

Table 4. Accuracy of the ANN analysis of the neural networks

ANN model	Accuracy (%)
RBF	99.56
MLP1	97.65
MLP2	94.50
MLP3	93.88

6 Modeling the Patch Antenna in CST

The design of patch antenna is carried out in computer simulation tool and the dimensions are calculated for the antenna designed for the specific frequency of operation. The results obtained in the design are as shown in the Fig. 4 (Figs. 5, 6, 7, 8 and 9).

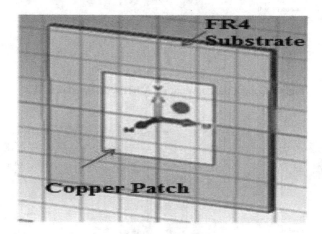

Fig. 4. Conventional MSTPA designed in CST

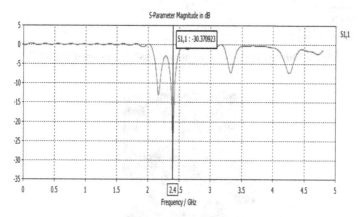

Fig. 5. S_{11} of the conventional MSTPA designed in CST

The Tables 5 and 6 show the comparative analysis of the performance parameters of the microstrip patch antenna. The geometrical parameters are also compared which are determined by using the ANN algorithms and the calculated by using the formulas using conventional method as specified in table. A good matching is found between the geometrical values of the antenna structure determined by using the ANN model and conventional method.

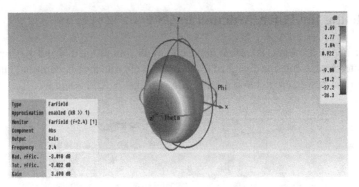

Fig. 6. Gain of the conventional MSTPA designed in CST

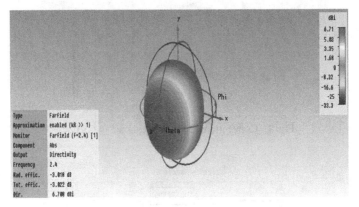

Fig. 7. Directivity of the conventional MSTPA designed in CST

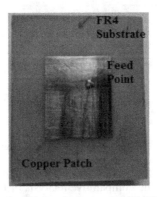

Fig. 8. Fabricated conventional MSTPA

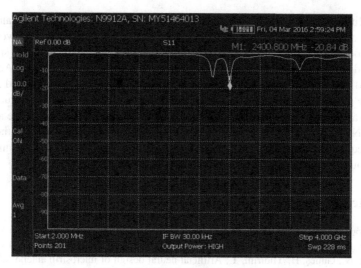

Fig. 9. S11 of the fabricated conventional MSTPA

Table 5. Comparative analysis of geometrical parameters for the Patch Antenna using ANN, conventional formula method simulated in CST and fabricated structure.

Parameter	ANN-RBF	ANN-MLP	Simulated in CST	Fabricated structure in CST
Length	5.63	5.63	5.43	5.43
Width	4.63	6.98	5.23	5.23
Frequency (GHz)	2.33	2.33	2.4	2.4

Table 6. Comparative analysis of electrical performance parameters for the Patch Antenna designed in CST and fabricated structure

Parameter	Simulated in CST	Fabricated structure in CST
Frequency (GHz)	2.4	2.4
Return Loss (S_{11}) (dB)	−30.37	−20.84
Gain (dB)	3.698	−
Directivity (dBi)	6.780	−

7   Conclusion

In this paper, an approach presented for designing of MSTPA (Microstrip patch antenna) using artificial neural network. The synthesis is carried out using the forward scale and analysis by carefully considering reverse side of the problem. The dimensions can be obtained with high accuracy in terms of length, width of the patch which acts as input to the preliminary input layer of the ANN model and the frequency of resonance will act as the output of the ANN model antenna using the Artificial neural network as a tool. A good matching is found between the geometrical values of the antenna structure determined by using the ANN model and conventional method. Almost 98% Accuracy is obtained in determining the geometrical dimensions. The same is fabricated and the acceptable matching is obtained in the electrical performance of the S11 value of the simulated and fabricated structure of the antenna. Further the modeling of the antenna using ANN can be extended for designing the patch antenna of any shape of the patch for the frequency of interest. The ANN modeling can also be used for design of RF devices, multilayered patch antenna, Metamaterials also.

References

1. Karaboga, D., et al.: Neural computation of resonant frequency of electrically thin and thick rectangular microstrip antennas. IEE Proc. Microw. Antennas Propag. **146**(2), 155–159 (1999)
2. Türker, N., Güneş, F., Yildirim, T.: Artificial neural design of microstrip antennas. Turk. J. Electr. Eng. Comput. Sci. **14**(3), 445–453 (2007)
3. Patnaik, A., Mishra, R.K.: ANN techniques in microwave engineering. IEEE Microwave Mag. **1**(1), 55–60 (2000)
4. Narayana, J.L., Sri Rama Krishna, K., Pratap Reddy, L.: Design of microstrip antennas using artificial neural networks. In: International Conference on Computational Intelligence and Multimedia Applications 2007, vol. 1. IEEE (2007)
5. Mishra, R.K., Patnaik, A.: Design of circular microstrip antenna using neural networks. IETE J. Res. **44**(1–2), 35–39 (1998)
6. Wang, Z., et al.: An ANN-based synthesis model for the single-feed circularly-polarized square microstrip antenna with truncated corners. IEEE Trans. Antennas Propag. **60**(12), 5989–5992 (2012)
7. Yao, X.: Evolving artificial neural networks. Proc. IEEE **87**(9), 1423–1447 (1999)
8. Badjian, M.H., et al.: Circuit modeling of an UWB patch antenna. In: IEEE International RF and Microwave Conference 2008, RFM 2008. IEEE (2008)
9. Güney, K., Erler, M., Sagiroglu, S.: Artificial neural networks for the resonant resistance calculation of electrically thin and thick rectangular microstrip antennas. Electromagnetics **20**(5), 387–400 (2000)
10. Washington, G.: Aperture antenna shape prediction by feedforward neural networks. IEEE Trans. Antennas Propag. **45**(4), 683–688 (1997)
11. Ouchar, A., Aksas, R., Baudrand, H.: Artificial neural network for computing the resonant frequency of circular patch antennas. Microw. Optical Technol. Lett. **47**(6), 564–566 (2005)
12. Gupta, V.R., Gupta, N.: An artificial neural network model for feed position of the microstrip antenna. Elektronika ir Elektrotechnika **60**(4), 82–89 (2005)
13. Zhihua, Y.: Artificial neural network models for the return loss of microstrip patch antennas loaded with a short pin. It Age **3**, 006 (2004)
14. Billings, S.A., Zheng, G.L.: Radial basis function network configuration using genetic algorithms. Neural Netw. **8**(6), 877–890 (1995)
15. Sreenath Kashyap, S., Prasad, K.M.V.V., Dabhi, V.M.: Novel microstrip band pass filter for C-band wireless applications. Int. J. Eng. Technol. **7**(4.6), 227–229 (2018)
16. Damaraju, S.S.S., Kantipudi, M.V.V.P.: Multilayered antenna design for smart city applications 56 (7 pp.) (2019). https://doi.org/10.1049/cp.2019.0229
17. Damaraju, S.S.S., Kantipudi, M.V.V.P.: Multilayered swastika antenna design for enhancement of bandwidth. Int. Res. J. Eng. Technol. (IRJET) **06**(05) (2019)

Smart PDM: A Novel Smart Meter for Design Measurement and Data Collection for Smart Grid

Van-Truong Truong[1,2], Anand Nayyar[3,4(✉)], and Dac Binh Ha[1,2]

[1] Faculty of Electrical-Electronic Engineering, Duy Tan University, Da Nang 550000, Vietnam
truongvantruong@dtu.edu.vn, hadacbinh@duytan.edu.vn
[2] Institute of Research and Development, Duy Tan University, Da Nang 550000, Vietnam
[3] Graduate School, Duy Tan University, Da Nang, Vietnam
anandnayyar@duytan.edu.vn
[4] Faculty of Information Technology, Duy Tan University, Da Nang, Vietnam

Abstract. The smart meter is one of the indispensable devices in the Smart Grid (SG). A smart meter is an advanced energy meter that collects user power consumption data and provides information. Several sensors and control units coordinately work in the smart meter. In this research paper, a novel Smart Meter design is proposed for power measurement data collection to assist end-users for energy savings. The proposed system is a wireless monitoring system to measure the power consumption of electrical appliances at home. The system comprises of Node-stations, which are electrical meters at the customer's house, and central data collection system that communicates via RF channel. The software at the master station helps store power in memory ICs and displays them graphically in real-time. The Node stations are built using Atmega328P microprocessor and current-voltage sensors, communicating with the Main station via the NRF24L01 module. The Main station uses the Arduino Mega module and stores information on 24C32 ROM chip and performs real-time management using RTC DS1307 IC. The proposed system operates within a distance of 100 m, a delay of 100 ms, and an accuracy of up to 96%. With the proposed system, users can track how much energy is used as well as the associated cost. Moreover, the Management software provides instructions and recommendations to optimize the time and duration of household electrical appliances.

Keywords: Smart meter · Smart grid · Current sensor · RF transceiver · Smart technology · Arduino

1 Introduction

Nowadays, Vietnam is making a strong effort in Industry 4.0. Internet of Things (IoT) is one of the three main pillars of this revolution and is currently integrated into all aspects of development. IoT is applied in all areas of life: urban management, environmental monitoring, smart shopping, personal device management, smart meters (SM), home automation. IoT development improves the quality of human life, especially in the

© Springer Nature Singapore Pte Ltd. 2021
A. K. Luhach et al. (Eds.): ICAICR 2020, CCIS 1394, pp. 37–58, 2021.
https://doi.org/10.1007/978-981-16-3653-0_4

field of household appliances. However, the emergence of many home appliances using electricity leads to significant challenges of effective power management [1, 22, 23]. Efficient power management helps to save energy resources, assess power consumption to make energy and cost-saving options, monitors power quality, and minimize risks [2, 3]. Moreover, large-scale energy monitoring can provide valuable data resources, improve the reliability and continuity of the electricity system, and is considered an indispensable component in the Smart Grid (SG) system [29, 30, 35, 36]. Therefore, it leads to the urgent need to design a reliable and intelligent electricity collection system.

In recent years, lots of research is conducted towards the modification and enhancement of Smart Meter [4–15, 31–34]. Typically, the study [4] describes the architecture of the smart power measuring system. The metering system must meet standards in terms of programmable following local conditions, measuring and transmitting electrical information, having communication ports with smart devices, reducing the load of power loss for the user. A novel smart monitoring system, i.e., SIGMET, is proposed in this paper comprising Multiplexor, ADC, memory, central processor, PLC communication unit, RF communication unit, and power unit [5]. In [6, 7], the authors proposed a model of measuring power consumption using a AT89S52 processor. The system acquires all electrical parameters in real-time and communicates with other devices using Zigbee or RS485 link. Furthermore, researchers have proposed general models concerning power data measurement that operates efficiently and performs synchronization between hardware and software. Kumari et al. [33] proposed an SG model based on Fog Computing to handle the latency issue, in which advanced sensors and measurement systems are using Next-generation 5G wireless networks. Challenges and solutions on SG are also presented very specifically in the studies [32–34].

However, there is no paper investigate flexibility and scalable in real-time operations. Moreover, the device measuring their power is usually connected one-to-one with the meter. While in reality, switches and sockets for electrical equipment are scattered throughout the house and require a more flexible measuring system. As compared to previous studies, the proposed system has strong edge over the following points:

- Hardware design of proposed power measurement system has attained an accuracy of 95%.
- The system ensures real-time measurement of current, voltage, power, and power factor and is capable of measuring large currents for high powering multiple devices and communicating via RF, providing convenient assembly.
- The system has a mechanism to automatically identify newly connected devices, making it flexible and scalable.
- The system is integrated with building management software installed on PC and Server, visually displaying power usage parameters in real-time.

Structure of Paper

Section 2 elaborates the related terminologies surrounding Smart Meter. Section 3 highlights the novel proposed system, i.e., Smart PDM 1.0 - A Smart Power Data Measurement System for monitoring energy consumption - System model, hardware and software used, and operation. Section 4 gives a preview of Smart PDM 1.0 prototype's real-time results. The paper is concluded in Sect. 5.

2 Smart Meter

2.1 Introduction and Architecture

Smart meters are an essential component of SG, and they enable many "smart" grids functionalities. Smart meter systems include sensors, data management software, consumption displays, and communications [8–10]. The smart meter incorporates many intelligent control and communication technologies to automate many functions: electric meters, identifying error transmission and power outages, detecting fraud and electrical theft, connecting and disconnecting services, and energy monitoring [11–14], as demonstrated in Fig. 1.

Smart meter deployment typically consists of three key components:

- Energy consumption sensing module: SMs installed at the customer's premises, typically collect electricity consumption data at a time interval of 1, 2, 5, 15 min using this module. In addition, the module collects information with regard to current, power consumption, and power factor.
- Communication module: New or upgraded communications module transmits large volume of data from the meter to the utility back offices. SMs can use wireless or wired communication depending on specific conditions, such as Power Line Communication, Zigbee, and Radio Frequency protocol.
- Meter data management system (MDMS): The module stores and processes the interval load data, and integrates meter data with one or more critical information and control systems. This module is usually deployed as a management software on PC/smartphone with an intuitive user interface [24].

2.2 Challenges of Smart Meter

Some practical challenges surrounding Smart Meter [18–21] are:

- Security Threats: SMs have two-way communication with the electrical system and are distributed throughout the SG. Because there are so many unprotected locations, it is easy to exploit these devices' vulnerabilities to mislead data or steal access to more critical parts of the core network.
- Privacy: For traditional grids, data reading is done monthly manually. While on the SG, detailed power consumption data is collected via SMs at much shorter intervals (about 15 min or less). This amount of data is vital for efficient power distribution, on-demand management, load management. However, it has the potential to reveal valuable customer information, such as energy usage habits, information on appliances, and the number of individuals in a home and their specific activities.

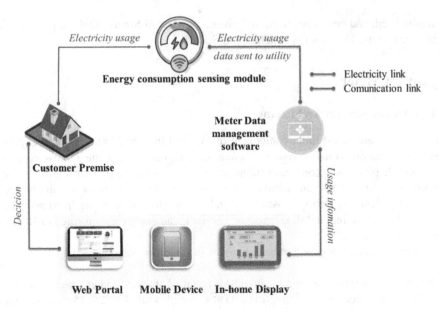

Fig. 1. Standard Smart Meter architecture

- Scalability: Household electrical appliances tend to increase in number over time. Once it is necessary to measure the power consumption parameters of these devices, the system will need a separate line to communicate with them. Connection requirements will be quite complex, as we need to edit the source code to identify new connected devices. For large buildings, the management of equipment will be complex. If it is a wired system, it will cost more, and if the wireless system, the communication distance, and data reliability are required.

3 Smart PDM 1.0 - Smart Power Data Measurement System

3.1 System Model

The system consists of multiple measuring nodes and the central station responsible for collecting and analyzing data.

Every Node designed is highlighted in Fig. 2a, which includes sensors that measure the current and voltage of the device. LCD module and RF module are connected to MCU, respectively, by I2C and SPI protocols. The measured values are displayed on the LCD screen and then sent to the Main station via the RF module. Also, Bluetooth connectivity is built into the Node's to access information from the smartphone. FTDI port enables connectivity to the PC directly, if needed. The system uses a current measuring IC capable of measuring large currents for high power devices such as refrigerators, washing machines...

The Main station is represented in Fig. 2b. Module PZEM-004T measures the total voltage, total current, and power factor. The data is transmitted to Arduino Mega 2560 via the UART connection. The system checks the accuracy of the data collected by comparing the total current measured at the Main station, and the total component flows from the Nodes. If the data is correct, these two parameters will be approximately the same. The main station connects to the RF module via SPI protocol. The system is also equipped with a ROM and RTC module, communicating via I2C. Each data packet at the Main station will be added to real-time information and stored in ROM before being sent to the server ThingSpeak via ESP8266 and management software via USB [27, 28].

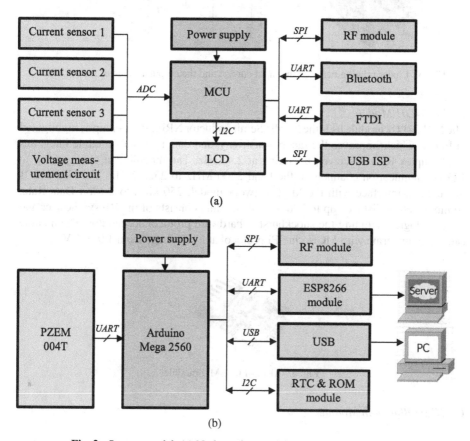

Fig. 2. System model: (a) Node station model, (b) Main station model

I. Hardware

A. Current Sensor ACS712

The alternating current value is measured and calculated using IC ACS712 of Allegro based on the Hall effect. This IC is easily integrated with MCU via an ADC connection with a shallow noise level. Its operating voltage is 5 V, bandwidth is 50 kHz, and the total error is 4% at –40 °C to 85 °C. When the current through the ACS712 IC has a definite value, it generates a corresponding voltage value according to the linear relationship, as shown in Fig. 3. This voltage value is added to an offset voltage of $U_{offset} = V_{CC}/2$

to ensure that in the entire cycle, the measuring signal oscillates completely within the 0-VCC voltage range suitable for the microcontroller's ADC. The sensitivity of ACS712 ranges from 64 to 190 mV/A and depends on the module type.

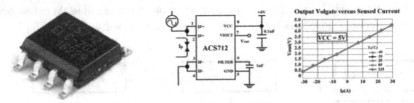

Fig. 3. Linear relation between the input current and the output voltage of the ACS712

B. NRF24L01 Module

The NRF24L01 module uses the Nordic Semiconductor NRF24L01+ chip as highlighted in Fig. 4, which improves the range, sensitivity, and data rate. This module integrates a full-duplex RF transceiver, operating at 2.4 GHz. The module can configure up to 125 communication channels in the band 2400 MHz to 2525 MHz. The NRF24L01 module can interface with the Mesh network model, 250 kbps to 2 Mbit Data Rate, communication distance up to 200 m. This module consists of the RF synthesizer and the base logic, including the shockburst™ hardware protocol accelerator. The module can easily integrate with MCU via SPI protocol at low voltage from 1.9–3.6 V.

Fig. 4. NRF24L01 SMD module

C. HC-05 Bluetooth Module

Fig. 5. HC-05 Bluetooth module

The HC-05 module Fig. 5 is Bluetooth SPP (Serial Port Protocol) module with easy-to-use authentication and encryption mechanism. HC-05 works by default in Slave mode, and we can configure it to work in Master mode if needed. It operates in the 2.4 GHz band with CMOS technology and with AFH (Adaptive Frequency Hopping), Gaussian frequency-shift keying modulation, with selectable Baudrate UART: 1200, 2400, 4800, 9600, 19200, 38400, 57600, 115200, 160 kbps to 2.1 Mbps data rate. The common sensitivity of HC-05 is -80 dBm, RF transmission power up to $+4$ dBm with integrated antenna.

D. PZEM 004T

Fig. 6. PZEM-004T module

The PZEM-004T in Fig. 6 is a multifunctional module designed to measure current, voltage, power, and power factors for AC and DC currents. It can store the accumulated energy data before power off. Using UART TTL MODBUS, it can communicate with various terminals through the pinboard, read and set the parameters. The working voltage of PZEM-004T is 80–260 VAC, and measurement accuracy is 1.0 grade.

E. ESP8266 Module

Fig. 7. ESP8266 module

The ESP8266 module in Fig. 7 uses a Tensilica Xtensa Diamond Standard 106Micro processor and runs at 80 MHz. This is a very cheap module but offers a complete and closed Wi-Fi network solution. In many applications, the ESP8266 module will act as a Client connecting to an MQTT Broker service to perform two main tasks. The first task is to publish data to the MQTT Broker, and the second task is to subscribe to information from the MQTT broker, check the data, and perform command operations. ESP8266 can operate independently or integrated with MCU via SPI protocol. The module supports 64 KB boot ROM, 80 KB user data RAM, and 32 KB instruction RAM. ESP8266 module operates at 2.4 GHz with 3.3 V voltage.

F. RTC and ROM Module

The Tiny RTC I2C modules is integrated two chips, as Fig. 8. The first chip is Maxim's DS1307, which is easily integrated with MCU via the I2C protocol. DS1307 provides

Fig. 8. DS1307 and ROM module

real-time information with seconds, minutes, hours, days, days, months, and years. DS1307 needs to be combined with Lithium coin cell battery (CR1225) to maintain the correct time when the main power of the device is interrupted. The built-in sensor module continuously monitors the status of the V_{CC} to detect power outages and automatically switches to standby power. The second chip is Atmel's EEPROM 24C32, which is used to store data. When communicating with MCU, these two chips are set up with different addresses to avoid transmission conflict.

II. Software

A. Arduino IDE Environment

The Arduino integrated development environment (IDE) is a cross-platform (multi-platform) application written in Java, includes a code editor with functions such as syntax highlighting, automatic brace matching, and automatic alignment, as well as compile and uploads the program to the board with just one click [25, 26].

The Arduino IDE provides an easy-to-use build-in library system. Each library set usually consists of two files: the header file and the source file. In particular, the header file contains definitions, including commands (functions) and needed variables. The source file (.cpp) contains the command line to help the library work. The library manager system of IDE makes adding, deleting, and adjusting libraries very easy. Standard library sets help the Arduino board connect to the sensors via I2C, SPI, ADC, connect to Internet access modules via UART, or connect to other hardware devices via CAN-BUS, Modbus 485 etc. The Arduino IDE also provides compiling capabilities for a variety of hardware: Arduino-supported boards such as Nano, UNO, Mega, Leonardo, ESP8266, ESP32-based boards, other Atmega-based boards, and many more other platforms.

B. Thingspeak.com

ThingSpeak is an open-source cloud service developed by IOBridge that allows users to easily send data and provide graphical interfaces that display data via HTTP and MQTT protocols. This source code supports APIs to store, retrieve data from devices via the Internet or Local Area Network.

C. Visual Studio

Microsoft Visual Studio is an integrated development environment from Microsoft. It is used to develop computer programs for Microsoft Windows, as well as websites, web applications, and web services. Visual Studio uses Microsoft software development platforms such as Windows API, Windows Forms, Windows Presentation Foundation, Windows Store, and Microsoft Silverlight.

3.2 Architecture

Smart PDM 1.0 consists of two Nodes station and one Main station. In this section, we discuss the electronics circuit and architecture of the proposed prototype.

In the proposed model, three ACS712 current sensors are deployed on the Node board and can expand to eight sensors, depicted as Fig. 9. The voltage sensor is made by an isolation transformer combined with a voltage divider bridge. The Atmega328P processor handles all the data. Power parameters are collected every minute, visualized on the LCD screen, and sent to the main station via RF. Node integrates the HC-05 module to transfer data to smartphones via Bluetooth.

The main station diagram is shown in Fig. 10. The Arduino Mega 2560 acts as a centralized processor. The PZEM-004T module is mounted in the main electrical cabinet, which measures the total current and voltage of all electrical equipment. The total current value will be compared with the sum of component streams from data received via the RF module. RTC & ROM module provides real-time value for each packet. The system stores information on ROM every 1 min and sends it to the server via the ESP8266 module.

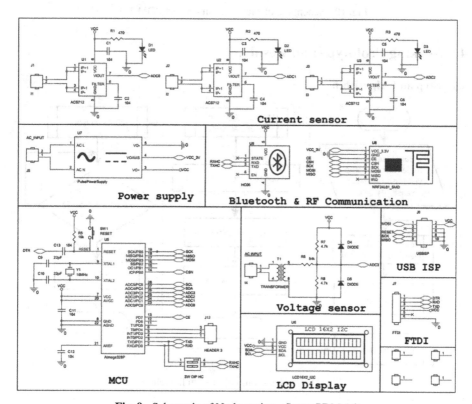

Fig. 9. Schematic of Node station - Smart PDM 1.0

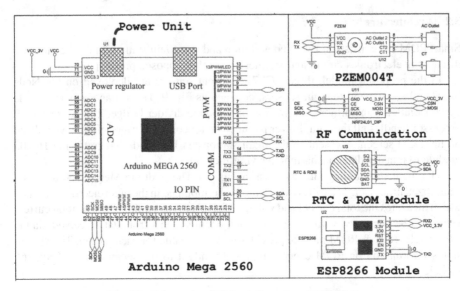

Fig. 10. Schematic of Main station - Smart PDM 1.0

4 Working Prototype and Results

4.1 Step and Algorithm

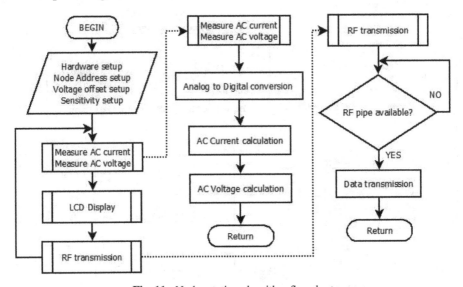

Fig. 11. Nodes station algorithm flowchart

The Node station of Smart PDM 1.0 operation is shown in Fig. 11, specifically as follows:

- First, the mainboard initializes the initial value, such as: I2C, SPI, ADC, UART, the port, node address, offset voltage, and sensitivity value.
- Second, AC current and voltage data will be read. Atmega328P chip has 10bit ADC, corresponding to 1024 ADC steps. The reference voltage value is $V_{CC} = 5$ V $= 5000$ mV. Let Vol be the output voltage of ASC712 going into the ADC, and so on.

$$Vol = \frac{ADC\_number}{1024} * 5000 \, (mV) \tag{1}$$

According to the datasheet of this IC, the value of alternating current is calculated by the formula:

$$I_{AC} = \frac{Vol - V_{offset}/Sensitivity}{\sqrt{2}} * 1000 \, (mA) \tag{2}$$

Each Node station uses ACS712-30A to perform a current device measurement. Node's operating voltage is 5000 mV, so the voltage offset is 2500 mV. The sensitivity of the ACS712-30A module is in the range of 64–68 mV/A, so here the average sensitivity is 66.

From formula (2), we obtain the current value as:

$$I_{AC} = \frac{Vol - V_{offset}/Sensitivity}{\sqrt{2}} * 1000 \, (mA) = \frac{Vol - 2500/66}{\sqrt{2}} * 1000 \, (mA) \tag{3}$$

The actual alternating voltage value is from 80% to 115% of 220 V AC, i.e., the nominal voltage value will be from 176 V to 253 V. To measure this voltage range, we use 220 V–28 V AC voltage transformer and voltage divider R_2, R_3. To ensure a positive voltage level in all cycles, we use analog signal conditioning by adding 2.5 V offset voltage to the AC signal. The waveform result is presented in Fig. 12.

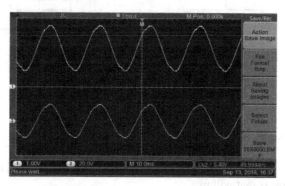

Fig. 12. Actual AC voltage from the transformer (blue) and analog signal conditioning output (yellow) (Color figure online)

For standard 220 V AC voltage taken from the grid, after adjusting to the 0 - VCC voltage range in step a, we use the Arduino UART Terminal to determine two standard peak values are ADCmax and ADCmin. Let k be the corresponding conversion factor from 220 V AC to the standard voltage:

$$k = \frac{220}{ADC_{\max} - ADC_{\min}} \tag{4}$$

So the actual AC voltage is calculated by the formula:

$$V_{AC} = k * (\text{ADC}_{\max} - \text{ADC}_{\min}) \tag{5}$$

– Next, current data is displayed on the LCD and sent to the Main station using the nRF24L01 module. To transmit a signal from every Node, the nRF module must first be given a unique address, not in conflict with other modules, and agreed with the Main station. The current values are stored in an array and attached to the packet for transmission with the specified address. The Main station algorithm flowchart is as Fig. 13.

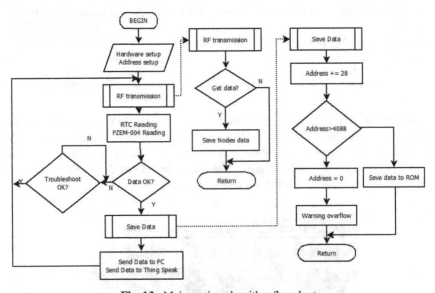

Fig. 13. Main station algorithm flowchart

Main station Smart PDM 1.0 Working:

– First, the main station initializes the initial value, such as SPI, UART, the port, and all of the node address that will use.
– Second, the nRF24L01 module receives data from all the nodes sequentially, with total current and voltage named I_{total1} and V_1, respectively. The PZEM-004T module measures total current I_{total2}, voltage V_2, and power factor θ using UART Modbus-RTU protocol. The command format of the main station reads the measurement result is total of 8 bytes:

Slave Address + 0x04 + Register Address High Byte + Register Address Low Byte + Number of Registers High Byte + Number of Registers Low Byte + CRC Check High Byte + CRC Check Low Byte.

The register of the measurement results is arranged as Table 1:

Table 1. Register of the measurement results

Register address	Description	Register address	Description
0x0000	Voltage value	0x0004	Power value high 16 bits
0x0001	Current value low 16 bits	0x0005	Energy value low 16 bits
0x0002	Current value high 16 bits	0x0006	Energy value high 16 bits
0x0003	Power value low 16 bits	0x0008	Power factor value

The I_{total1} and I_{total2}, V_1 and V_2 values are compared. If they are approximately the same, the system works well. If these values are different, the system has encountered an error and needs to perform calibration checks. Error messages are sent to LCD and PC software as Table 2.

Table 2. Error codes

Error codes	Message	Meaning
0xFF	RF communication error	Do not receive RF signal after 1 min. Need to check status of RF modules
0xFA	Negative signal error	The received signal is a negative value, check the PZEM-004T module and the RF module
0xF8	Voltage error	$\frac{V_1 - V_2}{V_1} > \theta_v = 4\%$. Measurement error greater than 4%
0xF7	Current error	$\frac{I_{total1} - I_{toal2}}{I_{total1}} > \theta_i = 4\%$. Measurement error greater than 4%
0xCC	Serial error	COM port is not connected. Check COM port on PC/Smartphone
0xC8	ROM error	ROM unresponsive
0xC7	ROM overflow warning	ROM overflow
0xC6	ESP8266 error	ESP8266 unresponsive

- Based on the error code, the system will require appropriate troubleshoot actions for the administrator. Once the error has been fixed, the procedure above will repeat.
- If all data received is correct, real-time data will be added to the frame before storing on ROM. The 24C32 memory chip with a memory capacity of 4096 bytes is used

to store data. Each node's current parameters, voltage, power, power factor, time are stored in 2 bytes, totaling 14 values in a data stream and has a capacity of 28 bytes. We use the address from 0 to 4088 to store data corresponding to 146 data lines. Data is also collected by software on the PC. After offline storage, we use ESP8266 to send data to the ThingSpeak server.

4.2 Working of System

The following Fig. 14 highlights the complete ready to use Smart PDM -1.0.

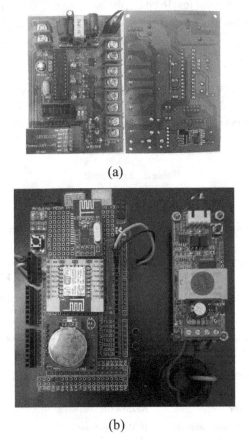

(a)

(b)

Fig. 14. Smart PDM 1.0: (a) Node station board TOP & BOT, (b) Main station board

The management software is as Fig. 15, including the following main functions:

- Connection unit: Contains menu to select COM port, Connect/Disconnect button to make connect/disconnect with COM port, and Exit button to exit the software.

- Control unit: Contains five function buttons, "Run" to start the system, "Pause" to pause, "Clear" to delete data, "Offline" to export stored data, and "Save" to export Generate Excel file with power usage information.
- Display block: Displays operating data of each device in real-time with graphs and statistical lists. Alarm block: Including the meters showing the total value preset and lights, alarm bells when the current and voltage overload.

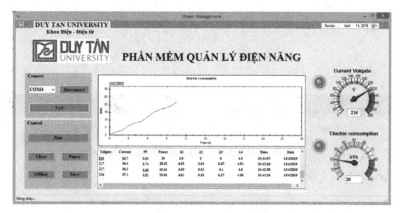

Fig. 15. PC management software

Figure 16 outlines the live working of Smart PDM 1.0 device in the laboratory. Node 1 is connected to 1 bulk. Node 2 is connected to 1 bulk and 1 Laptop charger. Data is displayed on the LCD of each node, as well as on PC software.

Fig. 16. Smart PDM - 1.0

ThingSpeak.com, an IoT analytics platform service, to aggregate, visualize, and analyze live data streams in the cloud, is used. The information is displayed graphically on the server, including AC voltage, AC current, Power, and Power factor as Fig. 17.

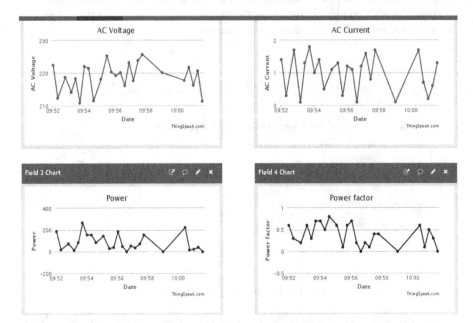

Fig. 17. Live Thingspeak.com results - AC Voltage, total AC Current, power and power factor in real-time

5   Results and Discussion

The group performed system testing in two different environments: Laboratory and Household. The test scenario is as follows:

5.1   Test Results at the Laboratory

A. Scenario

- First, connect and measure Node 1 of a 5 W led bulb.
- Next, connect and measure Node 2 of a 5 W led bulb and 85 W laptop charger.
- Each measurement was made five times, 30 min each time, the average value obtained.
- The distance from the node to the main station is increased gradually with each test (15 m, 20 m, 25 m, 30 m and 35 m).

B. Desired Results

- Measure the voltage of the laboratory.
- First, measuring the lamp's current and displaying it on the LCD on Node 1, the Main station receives the signal and sends it to the software and the ThingSpeak server.
- Next, connecting and measuring the current of 3 devices: 2 led bulbs and laptop charger at the same time. The Main station automatically identifies new devices connected to the system, collects data from Node 2, and sends all information from the nodes to the software and the ThingSpeak server.

C. Test Results

Table 3. Test results in the laboratory

No.	Voltage (V)	Node 1	Node 2	
		Bulk current (A)	Bulk current (A)	Laptop charger current (A)
1	221	0.1	0.106	0.381
2	220	0.106	0.106	0.372
3	223	0.1	0.1	0.367
4	222	0.106	0.106	0.374
5	220	0.106	0.106	0.374

5.2 Test Results at a Household

A. Scenario

- Measurements of high-power appliances, air conditioners, hair dryers on Node 1 and washing machines, refrigerators on Node 2.
- Each measurement was made five times, 2 h each time, the average value obtained.
- The distance from the node to the main station is increased gradually with each test (20 m, 30 m, 40 m, 50 m and 60 m).

B. Desired Results

- Measure that household power consumption.
- Measure the current of devices with high power and stable operation. On the Main station, receiving signals from the Nodes, sending parameters to computer software and the Internet.

C. Test Results

Table 4. Household test results

No.	Voltage (V)	Node 1		Node 2	
		Refrigerators current (A)	Washing machines current (A)	Hair dryers current (A)	Air conditioners current (A)
1	219	2.81	5.63	3.12	4.78
2	220	2.84	5.57	3.12	4.75
3	220	2.79	5.63	3.07	4.78
4	218	2.81	5.59	3.12	4.69
5	221	2.81	5.63	3.14	4.81

5.3 Testing and Calibration

We performed tests with standard equipment to calibrate the SPDM system. Test equipment is U1212A Handheld Clamp Meter, 3 ½ Digit. Each test session is conducted for 7 h for the system to run continuously. Error-values in Table 5 are collected every 10 min, taking the average values in Tables 3 and 4.

Table 5. Comparison of system voltage measurement results with U1212A Handheld Clamp Meter, 3 ½ Digit

No.	Results measured by Smart PDM (V)	Results measured by U1212A (V)	Error	Image
1	215	217	0.92%	
2	216	214	0.93%	
3	215	218	1.38%	
4	217	215	0.92%	
5	217	216	0.46%	
6	221	219	0.91%	
7	220	223	1.35%	*Test results on Arduino Terminal*

The measurement error is within 0.46% to 2%. The average error of the AC voltage test is 1.00%, described in Table 6.

Table 6. Comparison of system current measurement results with U1212A Handheld Clamp Meter, 3 ½ Digit

No.	Device	Results measured by Smart PDM (A)	Results measured by U1212A (A)	Error	Image
1	LED bulk	0.106	0.11	3.77%	
2	Laptop charger	0.37	0.36	2.78%	
3	Hair dryers current	3.12	3.22	3.21%	
4	Fan	0.18	0.21	1.17%	LED bulk current measurement
5	Refrigerators	2.81	2.75	2.18%	
6	Washing machines	5.63	5.71	1.01%	
7	Air conditioners current	4.78	4.92	2.93%	Laptop charger current measurement

The measurement error is in the range of 1.01% to 3.77%. The average error of the AC current test is 2.44%.

5.4 Conclusion and Future Scope

In this paper, we have presented the results of the research to design the electric data measurement system capable of accurately measuring current parameters, voltage, power consumption, power factor with accuracy to 96%. The system is built according to the wireless sensor network model, in which multiple child nodes communicate with the main station via RF transmission. The system can be expanded up to 3125 nodes, each supporting eight current sensors with the ability to identify new nodes connected to the network automatically. SmartPDM -1.0 provides features such as offline data storage once a minute communicates with power management software on PC/Smartphone and sends data to Web Server. Mechanism of checking and detecting data errors on RF transmission automatically helps limit system errors.

In the near future, our focus will be to design SmartPDM v2 model, focusing on two issues: improving security using 128/256-Bit AES Encryption via LoRa Communication and automatic adjusting the power function to improve overall performance.

References

1. Patil, B., Limkar, M.: Machine to machine communication based electricity monitoring and billing system. Int. J. Electr. Electron. Eng. Res. (IJEEER) (2016). ISSN (P)
2. Team, B.I.: Behaviour Change and Energy Use. Cabinet Office, London (2011)
3. Rashid, M.T.: Design and implementation of smart electrical power meter system. Iraqi J. Electr. Electron. Eng. 10(1), 1–14 (2014)
4. Nagesh, D.R., Krishna, J.V., Tulasiram, S.S.: A real-time architecture for smart energy management. In: 2010 Innovative Smart Grid Technologies (ISGT), pp. 1–4. IEEE, January 2010
5. Temneanu, M., Ardeleanu, A.S.: Hardware and software architecture of a smart meter based on electrical signature analysis. In: 2013 8th International Symposium on Advanced Topics in Electrical Engineering (ATEE), pp. 1–6. IEEE, May 2013
6. Vani, G., Reddy, V.U.: Application of smart energy meter in Indian energy context. IOSR J. JEEE 10(3), 07–13 (2015)
7. Park, S., Choi, M.I., Kang, B., Park, S.: Design and implementation of smart energy management system for reducing power consumption using ZigBee wireless communication module. Procedia Comput. Sci. 19, 662–668 (2013)
8. McNally, C.: Arduino based wireless power meter. A Design Project Report Presented to the Engineering Division of the Graduate School of Cornell University (2010)
9. Srividyadevi, P., Pusphalatha, D.V., Sharma, P.M.: Measurement of power and energy using Arduino. Res. J. Eng. Sci. (2013). ISSN 2278, 9472
10. David, N., Anozie, F.N., Ebuka, F.O., Nzenweaku, S.A.: Design of an arduino based wireless power meter. Int. J. Sci. Eng. Res. 7(9), 446–449 (2016)
11. Khan, N., Naseer, Y., Alam, I., Abbas, T., Iqbal, Y.: Wireless controlled smart digital energy meter and theft control using GSM with GUI. In: 2018 International Conference on Computing, Mathematics and Engineering Technologies (iCoMET), pp. 1–6. IEEE, March 2018
12. Kulkarni, S., Myers, E., Lipták, S., Divan, D.: A novel approach to implement low-cost AMI functionality using delay-tolerant communication. In: 2019 IEEE Power & Energy Society Innovative Smart Grid Technologies Conference (ISGT), pp. 1–5. IEEE, February 2019
13. Lichtensteiger, B., Bjelajac, B., Müller, C., Wietfeld, C.: RF mesh systems for smart metering: system architecture and performance. In: 2010 First IEEE International Conference on Smart Grid Communications, pp. 379–384. IEEE, October 2010
14. Lin, H.Y., Tzeng, W.G., Shen, S.T., Lin, B.S.P.: A practical smart metering system supporting privacy preserving billing and load monitoring. In: Bao, F., Samarati, P., Zhou, J. (eds.) ACNS. LNCS, vol. 7341, pp. 544–560. Springer, Heidelberg (2012). https://doi.org/10.1007/978-3-642-31284-7_32

15. Zhou, L., Xu, F.Y., Ma, Y.N.: Impact of smart metering on energy efficiency. In: 2010 International Conference on Machine Learning and Cybernetics, vol. 6, pp. 3213–3218. IEEE, July 2010
16. Kuzlu, M., Pipattanasompom, M., Rahman, S.: A comprehensive review of smart grid related standards and protocols. In: 2017 5th International Istanbul Smart Grid and Cities Congress and Fair (ICSG), pp. 12–16. IEEE, April 2017
17. Perumal, S., Rajendiran, S., Souprayen, S.: Efficient network security architecture for heterogeneous smart meter environment. In: Karrupusamy, P., Chen, J., Shi, Y. (eds.) ICSCN 2019. LNDECT, vol. 39, pp. 469–477. Springer, Cham (2020). https://doi.org/10.1007/978-3-030-34515-0_49
18. McLaughlin, S., Podkuiko, D., McDaniel, P.: Energy theft in the advanced metering infrastructure. In: Rome, E., Bloomfield, R. (eds.) CRITIS 2009. LNCS, vol. 6027, pp. 176–187. Springer, Heidelberg (2010). https://doi.org/10.1007/978-3-642-14379-3_15
19. O'Flynn, C.P.: Message denial and alteration on IEEE 802.15. 4 low-power radio networks. In: 2011 4th IFIP International Conference on New Technologies, Mobility and Security, pp. 1–5. IEEE, February 2011
20. Van de Kaa, G., Fens, T., Rezaei, J., Kaynak, D., Hatun, Z., Tsilimeni-Archangelidi, A.: Realizing smart meter connectivity: analyzing the competing technologies Power line communication, mobile telephony, and radio frequency using the best worst method. Renew. Sustain. Energy Rev. **103**, 320–327 (2019)
21. Chan, J., Ip, R., Cheng, K.W., Chan, K.S.: Advanced metering infrastructure deployment and challenges. In: 2019 IEEE PES GTD Grand International Conference and Exposition Asia (GTD Asia), pp. 435–439. IEEE, March 2019
22. Rathee, D., Ahuja, K., Nayyar, A.: Sustainable future IoT services with touch-enabled handheld devices. Security and Privacy of Electronic Healthcare Records: Concepts, Paradigms and Solutions, 131 (2019)
23. Krishnamurthi, R., Nayyar, A., Solanki, A.: Innovation opportunities through Internet of Things (IoT) for smart cities. In: Green and Smart Technologies for Smart Cities, pp. 261–292. CRC Press (2019)
24. Mahapatra, B., Nayyar, A.: Home energy management system (HEMS): concept, architecture, infrastructure, challenges and energy management schemes. Energy Syst. 1–27 (2019)
25. Puri, V., Nayyar, A., Le, D.N.: Handbook of Ardunio: Technical and Practice. Scholars Press (2017)
26. Nayyar, A., Puri, V.: A review of Arduino board's, Lilypad's & Arduino shields. In: 2016 3rd International Conference on Computing for Sustainable Global Development (INDIACom), pp. 1485–1492. IEEE, March 2016
27. Nayyar, A.: An encyclopedia coverage of compiler's, programmer's & simulator's for 8051, PIC, AVR, ARM, Arduino embedded technologies. Int. J. Reconfig. Embed. Syst. **5**(1) (2016)
28. Puri, V., Nayyar, A.: Real time smart home automation based on PIC microcontroller, Bluetooth and Android technology. In: 2016 3rd International Conference on Computing for Sustainable Global Development (INDIACom), pp. 1478–1484. IEEE, March 2016
29. Tanwar, S., Tyagi, S., Kumar, S.: The role of internet of things and smart grid for the development of a smart city. In: Hu, Y.-C., Tiwari, S., Mishra, K.K., Trivedi, M.C. (eds.) Intelligent Communication and Computational Technologies. LNNS, vol. 19, pp. 23–33. Springer, Singapore (2018). https://doi.org/10.1007/978-981-10-5523-2_3
30. Saleem, Y., Crespi, N., Rehmani, M.H., Copeland, R.: Internet of things-aided smart grid: technologies, architectures, applications, prototypes, and future research directions. IEEE Access **7**, 62962–63003 (2019)
31. Ghorbanian, M., Dolatabadi, S.H., Masjedi, M., Siano, P.: Communication in smart grids: a comprehensive review on the existing and future communication and information infrastructures. IEEE Syst. J. **13**(4), 4001–4014 (2019)

32. Bodkhe, U., Mehta, D., Tanwar, S., Bhattacharya, P., Singh, P.K., Hong, W.C.: A survey on decentralized consensus mechanisms for cyber physical systems. IEEE Access **8**, 54371–54401 (2020)
33. Kumari, A., Tanwar, S., Tyagi, S., Kumar, N., Obaidat, M.S., Rodrigues, J.J.: Fog computing for smart grid systems in the 5G environment: challenges and solutions. IEEE Wirel. Commun. **26**(3), 47–53 (2019)
34. Aazam, M., Harras, K.A., Zeadally, S.: Fog computing for 5G tactile industrial Internet of Things: QoE-aware resource allocation model. IEEE Trans. Industr. Inf. **15**(5), 3085–3092 (2019)
35. Rehmani, M.H., Davy, A., Jennings, B., Assi, C.: Software defined networks-based smart grid communication: a comprehensive survey. IEEE Commun. Surv. Tutor. **21**(3), 2637–2670 (2019)
36. Kabalci, Y.: A survey on smart metering and smart grid communication. Renew. Sustain. Energy Rev. **57**, 302–318 (2016)

GSM Based Remote Distribution Transformer Condition Monitoring System

Wilson Kepa, Ashish Kr. Luhach[(⊠)], Moses Kavi, Joseph Fisher, and Ravindra Luhach

Department of Electrical and Communication Engineering, The PNG University of Technology, Lae, Papua New Guinea
ashish.kumar@pnguot.ac.pg

Abstract. The main motive of this thesis research pertains to design and implement a remote machine to human (M2H) and human to machine (H2M) communication system that provides remote distribution transformer condition monitoring (DTCM) system using Global System for Mobile Communications (GSM). DTCM will mainly monitor four distribution transformer operational parameters namely voltage unbalance, load current, oil temperature and winding temperature for oil cooled/insulated distribution transformers. The proposed system is a remote mobile embedded system (M2H) that integrates a GSM/GPRS module, interfaced with an Arduino microcontroller board, and sensor packages. It will be installed at the distribution transformer site monitoring the dynamic changes of the above mentioned parameters.

Keywords: GSM/GPRS · Arduino · Microcontroller · SMS · Distribution transformer

1 Introduction

Transformers are the important static electrical equipment in power system network that facilitates transmission and distribution of electricity. There are power transformers (PTs) and distribution transformers (DTs). PTs are used in the transmission network for step-up and step-down of higher voltages while DTs are used in distribution networks that step-down high voltage which distributes power to low voltage end users. Operation of DTs under rated condition guarantees a reliable operation with extended long life. However, their life is significantly reduced if they are subjected to critical conditions like overloading, imbalances in phase voltages, rise in oil and winding temperatures and decrease in oil level for oil cooled DTs. These are some of the major causes of failures in DTs which results in catastrophic failures many times when remain unnoticed. To address these reliability issues, remote condition monitoring of operational parameters of a large number of DTs over a wide area in power electric systems remains a challenge. Transformer downtime in absence of any condition monitoring can be as high as 20% of its life span. This can be reduced to less than 2% when proper condition monitoring techniques are adopted [1].

In recent years, many power utilities are adopting energy efficient, low-cost and reliable DT condition monitoring methods. A survey in [1] has mentioned some of the

© Springer Nature Singapore Pte Ltd. 2021
A. K. Luhach et al. (Eds.): ICAICR 2020, CCIS 1394, pp. 59–68, 2021.
https://doi.org/10.1007/978-981-16-3653-0_5

current industrial practices in DT condition monitoring which are: (i) online monitoring by using supervisory control and data acquisition system (SCADA), (ii) sweep frequency response analysis (SFRA), (iii) network condition based monitoring (NetCBM), (v) Zigbee and Adruino board, and (vi) Global System of Mobile Communication (GSM) and General Packet Radio Services (GPRS) systems. Of such methods, GSM based remote distribution transformer condition monitoring is employed in this study because of some reasonable advantages. GSM technology is chosen to be more user friendly and able to monitor individual DTs remotely where other methods like commonly used SCADA is expensive and localized. In real time, using GSM based remote condition monitoring of DT operational parameters helps to detect incipient faults and notify field engineers in the form of alert text SMS. The abnormal condition notified is vital for decision making and assessment which facilitate to keep downtime and maintenance cost low, to increase overall equipment life and to aid maintain system reliability.

In this study, nine parameters are monitored which includes 3-phase currents and voltages at the secondary of the DT, oil temperature, winding temperature, and oil level for oil cooled DTs using current sensors, voltage sensors, oil temperature sensor, winding temperature sensor and oil level ultrasonic sensor respectively. The Arduino Mega2560 is a microcontroller board based on the ATmega2560 controller which is the heart of the system designed where it scans the sensors and communicates with a GSM/GPRS SIM808 module that sends an alert SMS when an abnormal condition in any of the monitored parameters is detected. In parallel, the microcontroller is able to facilitate communication via a 16×2 LCD screen for visual display, trigger a buzzer alarm, indicate a RGB LED, switching a cooling fan and finally switch on and off the monitored phase with the help of a 5 V four channel relay.

In current practices, DTs are monitored manually where a field engineer periodically visits the transformer site for routine condition check, perform maintenance and even to check whether the transformer is online or tripped out. Remote DT condition monitoring methods like SCADA is very expensive and thus it is unable to cover a wide range of DTs of an electricity network and also network cables are messy and may leave the entire monitoring system offline when broken or faulty. Importantly, transformer failure would cause power outages, fatal accidents, environmental hazards, and high cost for maintenance and reduced life span. In spite of the arguments in GSM based DT condition monitoring, it provides real time detection and condition monitoring and notification through alert SMS over the wide area network coverage.

2 Literature Review

There are many researches being done in particular for condition monitoring of DT utilizing the GSM/GPRS technology. DT condition monitoring in [2] was designed and implemented that monitors parameter like oil level, oil temperature, output voltage range and status of power availability via SMS alert through GSM modem to the authorized persons whenever the parameters exceeds the predefined allowable limits. A review in [3] presents a design and implementation of a mobile embedded system that monitors and records the operation of a transformer like over voltage, over current, three-phase voltage and current, fall of oil level and total power of transformer. The embedded system consists of an Arduino Uno microcontroller board and a GSM modem and sensor packages where all parameters monitored where displayed on a 16×2 LCD screen. In [4] a GSM based monitoring of distribution transformer was presented where it solves and eradicate problems uncounted using local protection techniques such as fuses and circuit breakers. The research designs a microcontroller based transformer health monitoring with real-time data logging capabilities. The rise in voltage and current which linearly increases the transformer temperature is monitored and displayed on a 16×2 LCD screen and sends an alert SMS to the control room and to the Technical Service Manager, informing them of the parameters. A survey on different technologies used in the monitoring of DTs in power systems was documented in [1] where GSM based monitoring is considered the cost effective and provides reliable monitoring via alert SMS for vast range of remote DTs in a power system network. A more related research in [5] presents a design of a DT monitoring system using GSM. This research was aimed at designing a monitoring system for the DT by installing different sensors that monitor the level of transformer oil, temperature range and a magnetic sensor that monitors the transformer when it trips and gets out of service. With thorough review of all these related literatures, in this thesis, an embedded system is designed that monitors nine parameters namely three-phase voltages, three-phase currents, oil temperature, winding temperature, and oil level for oil cooled DTs. Consequently, output functions like a 16×2 LCD display, RGB-LED indicator, buzzer alarm, and relay enabled cooling fan and on/off functions of the monitored phases and subsequently an alert SMS will be sent to the field engineer when a critical conditions are notified.

3   Research Design

In order to implement the proposed DTCMS, a design approach is necessarily followed based on the design block diagram shown in Fig. 1.

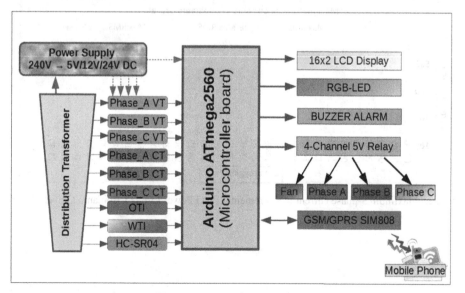

Fig. 1. DTCMS block diagram.

The algorithm flowchart was developed and programmed in Arduino IDE embedded C/C++ programming language. The DT operational parameters signals measured from the nine sensors are feed into the analog input pins of the Arduino ATmega2560 microcontroller board. The sensors require 12/24 V DC supply except for the HC–SR04 ultrasonic level sensor which is powered from the microcontroller. A reliable power supply is needed, where in case the mains supply if off, the backup should be powered for reliable monitoring. Based on the conditions of the sensors, the output functions are activated that includes sending alert SMS, LCD display, RGB-LED indicator, buzzer alarm and relay enabled phase isolation and cooling fans.

4   Case Study: PNG Power Ltd.

The utility PNG Power Ltd. is a state owned monopoly electricity company owned by the government of the Independent State of Papua New Guinea. A case study is presented from distribution transformer filed data provided by this utility where it indicated over-loading and voltage fluctuations. The case study was aimed at identifying the possibility of failures related to parameters monitored.

4.1   Distribution Transformer Current Measurement

The field data of two distribution transformers data measured are analyzed using Piv-otChart in Excel and presented in Fig. 2 and Fig. 3 respectively. The Fig. 2 shows the loading of transformer (*Tx-Boinamo Gravel*) and Fig. 3 for Tx ANZ Bank, Lae having a maximum rated load RMS current of 700 A measured for two days using power quality analyzer.

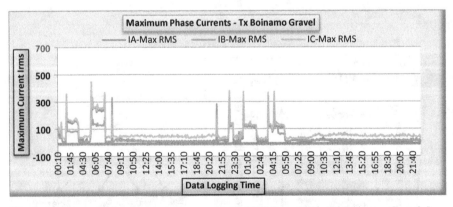

Fig. 2. Maximum 3-phase current measurement – PNG Power Ltd., Tx Boinamo Gravel, Lae.

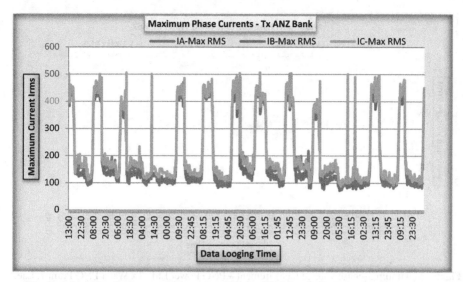

Fig. 3. Maximum 3-phase current measurement – PNG Power Ltd., Tx ANZ Bank, Lae.

4.2 Distribution Transformer Voltage Measurement

The voltage measurements are presented in Fig. 4 and Fig. 5 respectively. The Fig. 4 shows the voltage measurement of transformer (*Tx-Boinamo Gravel*) and Fig. 5 Tx Water, PNG Pump7, Lae for having a maximum rated load RMS current of 700 A measured for two days using power quality analyzer.

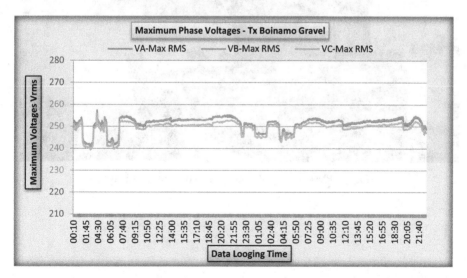

Fig. 4. Maximum 3-phase voltage measurement – PNG Power Ltd., Tx Boinamo Gravel, Lae

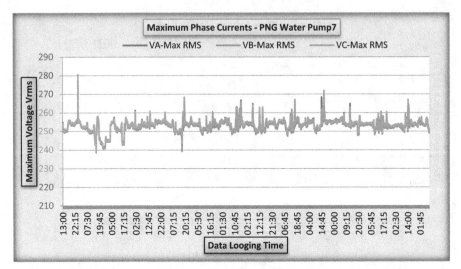

Fig. 5. Maximum 3-phase voltage measurement – PNG Power Ltd., Tx Water PNG Pump7, Lae.

5 Hardware Simulation

5.1 Hardware Simulation with LCD Display

See Figs. 6, 7, 8, 9 and 10.

Fig. 6. Phase A normal loading condition: LCD display

Fig. 7. Phase A normal voltage condition: LCD display

Fig. 8. Oil temperature normal conditions: LCD display

Fig. 9. Winding temperature critical condition: LCD display

Fig. 10. Oil level low conditions: LCD display

5.2 Hardware Simulation with GSM SIM808 Alert SMS

See Fig. 11.

Fig. 11. GSM SIM808 alert SMS simulations

6 Conclusion

The proposed system is a remote mobile embedded system (M2H) that integrates a GSM/GPRS module, interfaced with an Arduino microcontroller board, and sensor packages. It will be installed at the distribution transformer site monitoring the dynamic changes of the above mentioned parameters. The M2H will send an SMS alert message to the field staff mobile phone (H2M) when parameters measured reaches an abnormal condition contrast to ratings from the transformer manufacture. The received alert SMS will inform incipient faults that have potential to permanently damage the transformer and also provide early indication of a developing fault. Thus the proposed system minimizes faults and keeps downtime and maintenance cost low, while increasing overall equipment life and maintains system reliability.

References

1. Shifana, K.P.: A survey on different technologies used in the monitoring of distribution transformers in power system. IJEDR **6**(1), 175–179 (2018)
2. Bansod, P.M., Rojatkar, D.V.: Transformer parameter monitoring and controlling. Int. J. Trend Sci. Res. Dev. **1**(6), 812–814 (2017)
3. Pawar, R.R., Wagh, P.A., Deosarkar, S.: A review on health condition monitoring of distribution transformer **4** (2017). ISSN (Print): 2393-8374
4. Okeke, R.O., Ehikhamenle, M.: The GSM based monitoring of distribution transformer. Int. J. Sci. Eng. Investig. **6**(61), 89–96 (2017)
5. Ahmed, M.E.E., Abdelsalam, D.A.B.: Design of a distribution transformer monitoring system using global system mobile technology. Sudan University of Science and Technology (2017)
6. McKinlay, R.D., Mazidi, M.A., Mazidi, J.G.: The 8051 Microcontroller and Embedded Systems Using Assembly and C, 2nd edn. Pearson, New Jersey (2006)
7. 4 Channel 5V Relay Module. http://wiki.sunfounder.cc/index.php?title=4_Channel_5V_Relay_Module
8. HandsOn Technology: User guide - 4 channel 5V optical isolated relay module. Occup. Heal. Saf. **74**(2), 24 (2015)
9. Shea, J.J.: Power transformers-principles and applications [book review]. IEEE Electr. Insul. Mag. **19**(5), 75 (2003)

Networks

Performance Analysis and Classification of Node Capture Attack Models in WSN

Rohit Bathla[1]([⊠]) and Priyanka Ahlawat[2]

[1] Department of Computer Engineering, National Institute of Technology, Kurukshetra,
Yamunanagar, India
rohit_61900109@nitkkr.ac.in
[2] Department of Computer Engineering, National Institute of Technology, Kurukshetra,
Kurukshetra, India
priyankaahlawat@nitkkr.ac.in

Abstract. Wireless sensor networks (WSN) is a network grid of several self organizing, free, low prices, low control, and functional sensor nodes. The application
of these networks in military systems, battlefields, environmental monitoring,
smart buildings, and health care exposing the sensor nodes to a variety of physical security attacks. The node capturing attack is the most significant attack. In
this attack, the adversary physically catches nodes and extracts the confidential
data from the memory of nodes. Thus, analysis of adversary behavior becomes
very important in designing different defensive mechanisms for WSNs. The paper
presents an exhaustive survey on several node capture attack models in the sensor
network. The simulation results compare their performance such in energy cost,
attacking rounds, and traffic compromise.

Keywords: Node capture attacks · Security · Wireless sensor network ·
Adversary

1 Introduction

With technological advancements in wireless sensor network (WSN), several operations
like catastrophic and support monitoring, can be quickly deployed to WSN. The sensor
nodes are strongly distributed inside some sensor area inside WSN. Thus the distribution
of sensor nodes can communicate wirelessly to a central gateway, which provides a
connection to the world of an internet network where we can receive, process, analyze,
and display your measured data.

The nodes inside WSN are autonomous, but the network still suffers from essential
challenges: coverage, quality of service, security, and scalability. Security is one of the
significant concerns to be discussed in WSNs. Sensor networks are incredibly unsafe for
node capture attacks. The adversary obtaining keys and private data by physically catches
the node. It is a comprehensive attack; that's why this attack has low efficiency, and the
cost and time to find an adequate quantity of nodes for destroying the complete network
are very high. Due to hostile environments, it is very tough for completely recharge and

© Springer Nature Singapore Pte Ltd. 2021
A. K. Luhach et al. (Eds.): ICAICR 2020, CCIS 1394, pp. 71–82, 2021.
https://doi.org/10.1007/978-981-16-3653-0_6

totally replace battery. The critical and necessary task is to maintain energy efficiency while transferring of data through these sensor nodes.

Due to the hostile nature of, environments, the security of networks is a significant concern as these are sensitive to attacks. By the unsupervised nature of WSN, information can be accessed by communicating and senses that the sensor nodes and credential information from the node's memory can be easily stolen. We classified node capture attacks into two significant categories that are Active attack and Passive attack [1, 2]. Node Capture Attack acts as a compound or combined attack emerging from active, passive, and physical attacks by an attacker. It is a functionally and comprehensive attack inside which an attacker physically captures the nodes by selecting keys and secret messages. That are protected with producing efficient methods [3] to examine the advancement of the node capture attacks. Inside system node capturing is a significant difficulty, such as that attempts the consistency and security of nodes [4, 6]. Low efficiency and attacking methods are the earliest problems inside node capture attack techniques [7, 8]. An opponent's behavior is examined to express heuristic methodology to maximum compromised traffic in terms of high efficiency to attack [9, 10]. Hence that optimized modeling of node capturing attack increase attacking power [5]. Many research papers possess various methodologies to examining that attack behavior and introduce an absolute key management technique for functioning of WSN [11]. The arbitrary key pre-distribution system plays a significant rule in describing the node capture attack, and several researchers work in the direction of such a node attack [8].

2 Related Work

In this literature review, several researchers proposed different modeling techniques for vulnerability evaluation of node capture attacks. Attacker always wisely picks a sensor node to catch for eavesdropping data transmitting in the network. In [1], the problem of Key establishment in sensor networks using asymmetric key distribution within sensor nodes is discussed, so that adversary can physically compromise nodes. Some new mechanisms for each sensor node are presented for utilizing the random key distribution. Q-composite keys scheme along with multiple path reinforcement methods is used. A pair wise key scheme is distributed to increase the safety of the system. In [2], a distributed sensor and mobile networks that include nodes with low communication abilities. A key-management scheme is intended to serve both the operational and safety specifications. The probabilistic key distribution between the nodes uses simple protocols for key sharing and path establishing, re-keying, and key revocation.

In [3], is is mentioned that the Public-key and Diffie-Hellman schemes are used in public systems, are not fit for WSN. The paper proposed a randomly distributed key pre-distribution method and its improvements. Further knowledge of key deployment is not required; notifying that specific deployment knowledge may be available in many practical scenarios. In [5], the authors propose the node capture attack, in which the attacker effectively catches sensor nodes, thus removes some keys within the memory and destroy some security, confidentiality, reliability, and integrity of the WSN. However, this approach is limited with very low performance for attacking and a higher rate of resources expense. Further experiments are simulated to show and analyze the performance of MA with some another capturing attack in terms of number of rounds to attack, lower the execution timing, and improves attacking efficiency while conserving the cost.

In [6], a graph-based solution is used to model that attack on a randomly key pre-distribution method. Full graph is designed to concentrate on the relations among nodes to paths. Thus further, a matrix-based solution is used to evaluate the destructiveness. A *full graph attack* (FGA) simultaneously ensures the destructive value for every node reduces the attack and execution time. To increase the attacking efficiency of full graph attack, they introduced two optimized algorithms: (OGA) *optigraph* and (PCA) *path cover attack*. In [7], the paper shows the challenges for designing the energy-efficient node capture attack. It also shows that some techniques lack in concerning the minimum resource expenditure for model the attacking nature. From the researcher's point of view, a novel approach that transforms our requirements into a set cover that issue with a short Hamiltonian cycle that is NP-hard. They also produce the heuristic method called MREA. In [8], FiRAO-PG is presented that takes various objectives like: highest participation of node and keys, and smallest expenditure to determine optimized nodes using the technique of PSO optimization and GA.

In [9], a fruit fly optimization algorithm that depends on multiple objectives, that takes various objective functions like contribution of nodes, keys distribution, and smallest support expenses to find optimized nodes. For destroying the major area of the network with low cost and highest efficiency. In [10], by using the circuit mapping, they map the system traffic volume to the current flow within an electronic circuit and introduce a metric to explaining node vulnerability. In [11], the authors try to decrease the node capture influence by organizing an effective adversarial design. High node density, influence neighbor factor, and position of sink node exploit various vulnerabilities existing in the system. To improve the system protection toward node capture attack, they define hash chain length, including various rekey periods. In [12], a secure hybrid key distribution methods are described for node capture attacks in WSN. The robustness nature of q composite method within threshold resistance is described. It aims for securing the system against these attacks. A control based theoretic infrastructure is introduced for modeling physically node capture attack and present a clone node discovery and retraction of compromise sensor nodes [13]. With logically key graph with linearly controlling theory, we propose a dynamic nature model that always efficiently represents system performance under attack. In [14], authors developed models with multiple attackers inside a system, and express multiplayer game for display the non-cooperative nature within the system and the attackers side. They analyis two strategies: a time-invariant static point and a dynamically general point In [15], the authors examined the destructiveness of growing of node compromising ratio in WSN. They mainly concentrate on the potential of an epidemic breakout, where the whole system may drop victim of an attack. In [16], author enhance the resilience of WSN toward capturing attack, whereas keeping the versatility and low cost highlights of proposed schemes. In [17, 18], mainly focuses on the two crucial goals of WSN that are High reliable connectivity and security. For simultaneously achieving those two goals, the paper produced a key distributed scheme that depends upon hash chain and sensor memory of node.

3 Modeling in Wireless Network

3.1 Key Distribution Modelling

An absolute key is assigned to every sensor node ni $\in$ N. A key set represented by K represents Cryptographic keys. The interaction within nodes only takes place only if they lie in network range and share minimum one key that is common like Ki,j = Ki $\cap$ Kj _ = $\emptyset$.

3.2 Link-Based Modeling

Multiple links incorporate within routes and paths. A link is secure and reliable if it is encrypted with key Ki,j by which data can send transfer within nodes. The larger size of keys within nodes shows large security and guarantees high protection. Hence the safety of the link, is relatively directly dependent on the key size. We symbolize the set of links inside WSN by L, L = {La,|$Na \in$ N, $Nb \in$ N}.

3.3 Network-Based Modeling

Topological view of a network is represented as a digraph G = {N, L}, which is a network of N sensor nodes indisposed of using L links. Different protocols are used to route the transfer of information from within nodes. Routing protocols that are single-path and multiple-path are used to calculate impact of these node capture attacks in WSN.

3.4 Adversarial Based Modeling

The network is viewed as an attacker's viewpoint. The adversary is brilliant enough to discover the most unsafe nodes from the availability of information. The adversary knows the distribution of keys and routing used in the WSN. Source and destination nodes are meant to be secure with maximum security and protection, that's why the adversary cannot attack them. The adversary's main focus is to destroy the complete system by achieving objective like: resource cost, pool of keys, and total number of sensor nodes. To achieve the objective to reach optimal nodes that extract high vulnerability evaluation in WSN many algorithms are designed.

4 Classification of Node Capture Attack Models

4.1 Random Attack (RA)

In this, nodes are captured independently of each other without considering the network's topology. In every round, the adversary selects a node to be captured without considering any key management scheme. The possibility of multiple node capturing is neglected in this attack.

4.2 Maximum Key Attack (MKA)

In this kind of attack, nodes that have the maximum keys are to be captured in each round. That's why, even if the node does not belong to any route, it is likely to be captured if it has the more keys. Thus the attacker require to catch multiple nodes to destroy the complete system. A random key predistribution methodology is used for network distribution. So the running time to attack the system is very high.

4.3 Maximum Link Attack (MLA)

Inside this attack, in every round, sensor nodes having the highest number of links are compromised. In this, even if the node does not belong to any route, then it is likely to be captured. Hence the adversary require to catches a large number of nodes to destroy the complete system. The adversary require very large number of rounds to destroy the system. So the network topology is very important in this attack.

4.4 Dominating Node Attack (DNA)

In DNA, the adversary always need to catch some nodes that are in the dominating set of nodes with the maximum path compromise ratio and less capturing cost. The attacker aims to obtain that node step by step and follow the same procedure to compromise the network completely.

4.5 Maximum Traffic Attack (MTA)

Here, the fraction of the attacked traffic to the whole traffic is calculated in WSN, and nodes with the highest value of this ratio are captured in each round. The attack does not give any relation between paths and nodes. For that reason, total rounds of attacks is highest in this attack.

4.6 Greedy Node Capture Approximation Using Vulnerability Evaluation (GNAVE)

That leads susceptibility as the basic standards for capturing nodes. Nodes have the highest susceptibility, with the lowest capturing cost captured first. However, it considers only those nodes which belong to the path and ignore all the other nodes. Vulnerability evaluation is distributed in nature. The metrics calculated by this are not perfect. The energy cost and the attacking capability does not measure perfectly by using the vulnerability matrix. In terms of compromises traffic they give high attacking efficiency and the number of attacking rounds. The running time for attacking the system is not calculated.

4.7 Matrix Based Attack (MA)

In this method, a matrix driven methodology is used to increase the attacking efficiency by capturing the most vulnerable node with the least resource expenditure. A matrix is created, which shows the relationship between vertices and path. This is used to gain access over the complete network. The energy cost is least in this, and it causes maximum destruction. However, it does not consider attacking competency. This attack does not give any specific relation to energy cost and efficiency and only uses random key predistribution.

4.8 Full Graph Attack (FGA)

A full graph gives the relation between nodes to path and paths to keys. This attack considers that the captured node is the most vulnerable. It is a random node capture attack used to cause more destruction to the network. But it has huge overhead in terms of computation and does not work in dynamic networks.

4.9 Opti-Graph Attack (OGA)

These methods are used to enhance the effectiveness of FGA by decreasing the number of compromised nodes. However, these methods do not measure energy cost. This vulnerability evaluation modeling does not focus on any specific key distribution protocol.

4.10 Minimum Resource Expenditure Attack (MREA)

It calculates the total energy cost by the attacker. It causes maximum destruction with minimum resource expenditure. This type of attack only considers energy cost for vulnerability evaluation so that it does not provide the optimal node to destroy the network.

4.11 Path Covering Attack (PCA)

In PCA, the node list is implied which further reduces total nodes by the adversary that needs to record. Therefore, storage overhead in case of PCA is the smallest. PCA takes less energy and less time in destroying the whole network. But it has huge overhead in terms of computation and does not work in dynamic networks.

4.12 Generic Algorithm (GA)

The most generalize techniques is the Genetic Algorithm (GA) that provide the best optimal solution. GA is designed to produce optimal set of vertices from given vertices, which advances the optimized solution by evaluate the biological simulation. After initial distribution of the sensor nodes, this proposed scheme gives the minimum and the optimal locations of the sensor nodes that need further to be added. For evaluating the performance of genetic methodology several metrics are used, and distributed algorithm always optimize the system coverage in favor of the total coverage rate and the additional sensor nodes.

4.13 Fruit Fly Optimization Algorithm (FFOA)

That fruit fly optimization algorithm (FFOA) that is totally depends upon the multiple objectives attack algorithm which further has several objective functions like: least expenditure on resources, more node contribution, maximum key pool. But the limitation is further the robustness and safety of this optimization based techniques are not very clearly defined.

4.14 Finding Robust Assailant Optimization-Particle Swarm Optimization and Genetic Algorithm (FiRAO-PG (GA))

FiRAO-PG (finding robust assailant optimization-particle swarm optimization and genetic algorithm) are used for increasing the efficiency of attack in the WSN. FiRAO-PG include three objective functions that are higher key participation, minimum cost of resource expenditure and maximum participation of nodes for finding optimal nodes that gives best correlation of all three objectives and hence provide higher destructiveness inside system. Experiment result shows that FiRAO-PG gives a high rate of compromised volume of traffic, with comparing other matrix algorithm (Table 1).

Table 1. Comparision table of node capture attacks

Attack	RA	MKA	MLA	DNA
Description	In this, nodes are captured independently, without considering the network's topology	Nodes that have the long set of keys are to be captured in each round	For each round, nodes having the large set of links are compromised	In DNA, the attacker attack those sensor nodes that are in dominating set of nodes with the maximum path compromise ratio
Modeling	Vulnerable evaluation	Vulnerable evaluation	Vulnerable evaluation	Vulnerable evaluation
Mode of attack	Random mode of attack	Random mode attack	Random mode attack	Random mode of attack
Limitations	The adversary selects a node to be captured without considering any key management scheme The possibility of multiple node capturing	Even if the node does not belong to any route, it is likely to be captured if it contain a key set with maximum keys For destroying the network the attacker needs to capture large set of nodes Running time to attack the system is very high	Even if the node does not belong to any route, then it is likely to be captured For destroying the network the attacker needs to capture large set of nodes The adversary take high number of rounds for destroy the whole network	Even if the node does not belong to any path, it is likely to be captured if it is in the dominating set Not gives importance to the execution time It is suitable only for very short network
Type of node	Static	Static	Static	Static

(continued)

Table 1. (*continued*)

Attack	RA	MKA	MLA	DNA
Complexity	**O(1)**	**$O(n^2)$**	**$O(n^4)$**	**$O(n^2)$**
Attack	DNTA	MTA	GNAVE	MA
Description	In DNTA, the adversary captures those nodes in the dominating set with maximum path compromise ratio and less capturing cost. Then attack coefficient is calculating by considering the value of travelling cost	Here, the fraction of the attacked traffic to the whole traffic is calculated in WSN, and nodes with the highest value of this ratio are captured in each round	Nodes have the highest susceptibility, with the lowest capturing cost captured first and build a matrix of vulnerability using circuit theory	A matrix driven methodology is there to increase the attacking efficiency by capturing the most vulnerable node with the least resource expenditure
Modeling	Modeling Vulnerable evaluation	Modeling Vulnerable evaluation	Modeling Vulnerable evaluation	Modeling Vulnerable evaluation
Mode of attack	Random attack	Random attack	Distributed	Distributed
Limitations	Not gives importance to the execution time It is suitable only for very short network	Attack does not give any relation between paths and nodes. For that reason, The number of attacking rounds is highest in this attack	Does not focus on any key distribution protocol Does not account the running time to attack The energy cost and the attacking capability does not measure perfectly by using the vulnerability matrix	This attack does not give any specific relation to energy cost and efficiency and only uses random key predistribution
Type of node	Static	Static	Dynamic	Dynamic
Complexity	**$O(n^2)$**	**$O(n^2)$**	**$O(n^5)$**	**$O(n^2)$**
Attack	FGA	OGA	MREA	GA
Description	A full graph gives the relation between nodes to path and paths to keys. It is a random node capture attack used to cause more destruction to the network	These methods are used to enhance the effectiveness of FGA by decreasing the number of compromised nodes	It calculates the energy cost of the attacker. It causes maximum destruction with minimum resource expenditure. Modeling a heuristic approach using Hamiltonian cycle	Genetic algorithms (GA) gives a better established workplace for implementing AI tasks like as optimization, classification and learning. GA are known because of their remarkable general and versatility and apply for high variety of settings in WSN

(*continued*)

Table 1. (*continued*)

Attack	FGA	OGA	MREA	GA
Modeling	Vulnerability evaluation modeling	Vulnerability evaluation modeling	Vulnerability evaluation modeling	Vulnerability evaluation modeling
Mode of attack	Random attack	Random attack	Distributed	Distributed
Limitations	But it has huge overhead in terms of computation Does not work in dynamic networks	Do not measure energy cost Does not focus on any specific key distribution protocol	Attack does not gives importance to the relationship between cost matrix and attacking efficiency	It has huge overhead in terms of computation
Type of node	Static	Dynamic	Dynamic	Dynamic
Complexity	$O(n^2)$	$O(n^2)$	$O(n^2)$	$O(n^3)$
Attack	FFOA	PCA	FiRAO-PG	
Description	Fly Optimization Algorithm (FFOA) that is based on multiple objectives node capture attack algorithm which consists of several objectives: maximum node contribution, maximum key and least resource expenditure	In PCA, the node list is implied which reduces the number of nodes the attacker needs to record. Therefore, PCA has the smallest storage overhead PCA consume less time and less energy in compromising the network	An empirically designed multiple objectives node capture attack as an effective solution against the attacking efficiency of node capture attack. Finding robust assailant optimization-particle swarm optimization and genetic algorithm (FiRAO-PG)	
Modeling	Modeling Vulnerable evaluation	Modeling Vulnerable evaluation	Modeling Vulnerable evaluation	
Mode of attack	Distributed	Distributed	Distributed	
Limitations	The robustness and security of optimization techniques are not clearly defined	But it has huge overhead in terms of computation Does not work in dynamic networks	It is not controlling high mobility network	
Type of node	Dynamic	Dynamic	Dynamic	
Complexity	$O(n^2)$	$O(n^2)$	$O(n^2)$	

5 Simulations and Experiments

5.1 Fraction of Compromised Traffic

Here we analyzed compromise path with total number of paths in every round and their ratio gives value of compromised traffic. Along the x-axis, we have the number of nodes captured by the adversary whereas y-axis provides the insight of total compromised traffic. That further describes the accuracy of our attacking methods. After a few rounds, attacking paths get destroyed overall making the compromised traffic to one. Inside RA, randomly captures of nodes are taken by the adversary and thus resulting in an irregular rounds for various key sizes. Inside MKA, the nodes are captured to maximize key pool. Because of attacking property of the nodes even if they are not inside the path they get captured all in all increasing the total number of rounds as a whole. Inside MLA, the adversary capture nodes with maximum links. The number of rounds seems equal in our simulation results of MLA and MTA. Hence all these attacks like GNAVE, MTA, MKA, MLA and RA require more nodes to capture for destroying the confidentiality of the system. We observed that MA, FFOA and FiRAO-PG approach could destroy the system by the fewest attacking rounds in numbers compared with other attacking approaches. Inside our recommended strategy, we have included factors like dominating nodes, most node contribution, highest key contribution, crossover edges, and lowest cost of capturing to determine optimal node, which further enhances our node capture attack (Fig. 1).

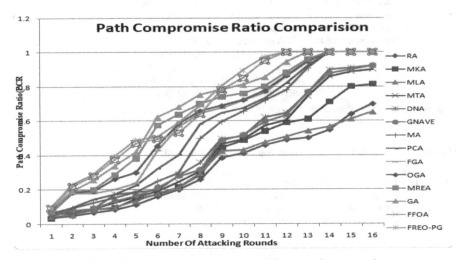

Fig. 1. Path comparision ratio under different routing protocols

5.2 Energy Cost

Cost of energy depends on the number of resources consumed to destroy the system traffic completely by the adversary. Total number of nodes captured directly affect the energy cost. The experiment here shows energy consumption of every algorithm. Each node applies (0–1) distribution while capturing a node hence with the increase in node capturing, energy consumption increases and vice-versa. Figure number shows the energy cost for node capture strategies. Among them, MA, FFOA, OGA and FiRAO-PG have very less energy cost as these strategies destroyed the system traffic by catching fewer nodes (Fig. 2).

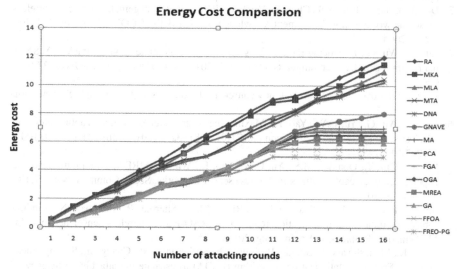

Fig. 2. Energy cost under different routing protocols

6 Conclusion and Future Work

We study various node capture attacks in this paper by the adversary to destroy the network's integrity, reliability, security, and confidentially. This paper studied these security models, using different strategies like Circuit theory, epidemic theory, key management, etc. Those methods signify either organized where the attacker begins from the common vulnerable link or scattered where the node is selected to capture randomly. Several key distribution strategies that are used by these methods are also studied. By studying the approaches to model those attacks, we can discover techniques to develop a robust system. The paper concludes that the enhanced node capture attack models outperform the basic attack models like MLA, MKA, and RA in practically all aspects. The reason for such improved performance as compared to other algorithms is its consideration to multiple objectives. In contrast, the simpler algorithms mostly work on a single objective, either capturing node with maximum key, maximum links, or minimum cost. While advanced attacks note of all these parameters and captures the node, which yields maximum damage in terms of links and keys with keeping minimum cost in mind due to its dynamic nature. The main problem with advanced or improved attacks is their time complexity concerning the number of nodes and paths. These algorithms take way longer than basic algorithms and can be improved further by inculcating dynamic behavior and consideration to the time taken.

References

1. Chan, H., Perrig, A., Song, D.: Random key predistribution schemes for sensor networks. In: 2003 Symposium on Security and Privacy, 2003, pp. 197–213. IEEE, May 2003
2. Eschenauer, L., Gligor, V.D.: A key-management scheme for distributed sensor networks. In: Proceedings of the 9th ACM Conference on Computer and Communications Security, pp. 41–47, November 2002
3. Du, W., Deng, J., Han, Y.S., Chen, S., Varshney, P.K.: A key management scheme for wireless sensor networks using deployment knowledge. In: IEEE INFOCOM 2004, vol. 1. IEEE, March 2004
4. Lin, C., Wu, G.: Enhancing the attacking efficiency of the node capture attack in WSN: a matrix approach. J. Supercomput. 66, 989–1007 (2013). https://doi.org/10.1007/s11227-013-0965-0
5. Ford, B.: An overview of hot-deck procedures. In: Incomplete Data in Sample Surveys, vol. 2 (1983)
6. Lin, C., Wu, G., Yu, C.W., Yao, L.: Maximizing destructiveness of node capture attack in wireless sensor networks. J. Supercomput. 71(8), 3181–3212 (2015). https://doi.org/10.1007/s11227-015-1435-7
7. Lin, C., Qiu, T., Obaidat, M.S., Yu, C.W., Yao, L., Wu, G.: MREA: a minimum resource expenditure node capture attack in wireless sensor networks. Secur. Commun. Netw. 9(18), 5502–5517 (2016)
8. Shukla, P.K., Goyal, S., Wadhvani, R., Rizvi, M.A., Sharma, P., Tantubay, N.: Finding robust assailant using optimization functions (FiRAO-PG) in wireless sensor network. In: Mathematical Problems in Engineering, 2015 (2015)
9. Bhatt, R., Maheshwary, P., Shukla, P., Shukla, P., Shrivastava, M., Changlani, S.: Implementation of Fruit Fly Optimization Algorithm (FFOA) to escalate the attacking efficiency of node capture attack in Wireless Sensor Networks (WSN). Comput. Commun. 149, 134–145 (2020)
10. Tague, P., Slater, D., Rogers, J., Poovendran, R.: Vulnerability of network traffic under node capture attacks using circuit theoretic analysis. In: IEEE INFOCOM 2008-The 27th Conference on Computer Communications, pp. 161–165. IEEE, April 2008
11. Ahlawat, P., Dave, M.: An attack model based highly secure key management scheme for wireless sensor networks. Procedia Comput. Sci. 125, 201–207 (2018)
12. Ahlawat, P., Dave, M.: An attack resistant key predistribution scheme for wireless sensor networks. J. King Saud Univ. Comput. Inf. Sci. 33, 268–280 (2021)
13. Bonaci, T., Bushnell, L., Poovendran, R.: Node capture attacks in wireless sensor networks: a system theoretic approach. In: 49th IEEE Conference on Decision and Control (CDC), pp. 6765–6772. IEEE, December 2010
14. Zhu, Q., Bushnell, L., Başar, T.: Game-theoretic analysis of node capture and cloning attack with multiple attackers in wireless sensor networks. In: 2012 IEEE 51st IEEE Conference on Decision and Control (CDC), pp. 3404–3411. IEEE, December 2012
15. De, P., Liu, Y., Das, S.K.: Modeling node compromise spread in wireless sensor networks using epidemic theory. In: 2006 International Symposium on a World of Wireless, Mobile and Multimedia Networks (WoWMoM 2006), 7 p. IEEE, June 2006
16. Ehdaie, M., Alexiou, N., Ahmadian, M., Aref, M.R., Papadimitratos, P.: Mitigating node capture attack in random key distribution schemes through key deletion. J. Commun. Eng. 6(2), 99–109 (2017)
17. Qin, T., Chen, H.: An enhanced scheme against node capture attack using hash-chain for wireless sensor networks. J. Inf. Technol. 11, 102–109 (2012)
18. Wang, Z., Zhou, C., Liu, Y.: Efficient hybrid detection of node replication attacks in mobile sensor networks. Mobile Inf. Syst. 2017 (2017)

An Efficient IoT Based Framework for Missed Call Messaging Services for Electricity Consumers

Kuldeep Sharma[✉], Arun Malik, and Isha

Department of Computer Science and Engineering, Lovely Professional University, Phagwara, Jalandhar, Punjab, India
{arun.17442,isha.17451}@lpu.co.in

Abstract. This paper is introducing the missed call messaging services to the consumers of the electricity. Nowadays, there are consumers who could not get their monthly bills in the form of physical papers, specially the consumers residing at the remote area/ far distinct from the utility offices. The consumers at remote area can pay their dues monthly very easily, but once the backlog is increased, the consumer becomes defaulters due to non-availability of huge amount in the form of backlog with heavy amount as delay payment charge/ penalty. So they are ready to pay the bills monthly, but due to non-awareness of their dues amount, they are not able to pay the bills. So for mitigating this issue, the missed call messaging service is proposed for the electricity consumers specially those who are not aware of the internet/ website/ smart phones etc. services. The consumers are not to bother about remembering their large number consumer id, the mobile number registered at utility office, is sufficient enough, they will be getting the messages about their pending dues at utility office after the consumer make a missed call on a specific number for getting the balance details. The missed call for No_Power_Supply complaint on the other number will lodge the no power supply complaint and a unique complaint number will be messaged to the consumer on their mobile phones (can be delivered on basic mobile phone as text message). The architecture is based on the open source solutions.

Keywords: Arduino/ESP32 SIM800L/REST API · IVR · VOIP · cURL · Energy · IoT

1 Introduction

Now a days, the urban area is so much advanced, the consumers are aware of the electricity website, android mobile applications etc. They are able to get the various information about their electricity bills due amount along with their due date and ultimately paying their bills online via any of the plenty of the services available within the prescribed period and even getting the benefits of paying the bills online before due dates with

K. Sharma—Research work carried out at Department of Computer Science and Engineering at Lovely Professional University, Punjab.

© Springer Nature Singapore Pte Ltd. 2021
A. K. Luhach et al. (Eds.): ICAICR 2020, CCIS 1394, pp. 83–100, 2021.
https://doi.org/10.1007/978-981-16-3653-0_7

some discounts on the same. On the other hand, the consumers of the rural area are not so much aware of the internet facilities, even they are not able to get their physical electricity bills in a few months in a year, sometimes, they misplace their physical bills in home and get forget and are not able to pay the bills in time. This pending behavior of the consumers make them defaulters and ultimately coverts to the non-paying consumers. For getting the duplicate bills, they even don't know their large size consumer id. So to mitigate the issue, the missed call messaging services from their registered mobile numbers (RMN) is proposed. By this, when any of the consumer places a missed call on a specific number, in return consumer if registered with utility billing engine, will get a short text message containing the consumer number with balance due amount and due date. A link for the latest pdf of the invoice/bill as a soft copy is also appended in the message, the consumer, if using the smart phone, can even download the latest electricity bill by pressing the link in the Message Text at the end of the message. If the consumer calls on the another specific number for No-Power Supply, then the consumer will be revert back with the complaint number of the No-Power-Supply to the specific consumer. By this, the consumers are not required to remember their consumer numbers. If the complaint is registered for the no-power- supply, and consumer once again calls on the same, then the consumer will be reverted back with the latest status of the complaint already registered against that consumer number, tagged with the mobile number (RMN) from which, the consumer is calling,. If the mobile no is not tagged with the consumer id in the utility database, then an SMS will be received with the message containing the link to tag the consumer id with the mobile number with one OTP for registering the same. The consumer can register the same via that SMS link.

The following two services proposed in this framework for the electricity consumers and may also be incorporated to ease the consumers who are not owning the android phones. As these services are mainly missed call/message based only. These two basic services are available on any of the mobile hand set with free of cost.

i.   Current Bill Due along with Due Date Message Receipt on Missed Call on any specific number - as the database of the consumers along with their mobile numbers is maintained, so the services may be initialled to get the billing details on the registered mobile number if consumer gives a missed call on the mobile no. provided by the utility.

ii. No Power Complaint should be registered at utility when a mobile registered consumer make a missed call on the specific number provided by the utility. A message to be delivered along with the complaint no. registered, so that the ease to be provided to the non-Android consumers.

iii. Purpose statement is to analyze the factors affecting the interruption in the continuous supply of electricity to the consumers and the unjustified AT & C Loss as far as revenue is considered. The interruption can be monitored after the analysis of the no power supply complaints of the specific DT for further maintenance of the same for the best quality services. Whereas the revenue enhancement can be done by the timely payment of dues amount to the consumers. The main factors affecting the commercial losses are ghost consumers, theft of the electricity and non-maintenance of the energy ledgers properly for a specific Distribution Transformer (DT) or even Feeder Level and GIS (Geographical Information System) of the feeders, DTs along with the consumers. The same may be analyzed based on the data gathered through these services, as explained in the following sections of this paper.

2 Review of Literature

The papers [12–14] inspired the idea for formulation of the architecture of this IoT based framework. 24 × 7 Qualitative Supply of Electricity and revenue collection are the main objective of the power distribution companies. There are two types of losses where electricity consumption is concerned. One is the Transmission loss, this is also termed as technical loss, and it is the loss incurred while supplying the electricity from one place to another. This loss can't be avoided. Another is commercial loss, arising in the power trading. The huge loss is occurred from the heavy debts, there are some regions in India, where the mentality of the consumers are not to pay the electricity invoices, most of these consumers states that due to non-availability of invoices, they are not able to pay the invoices, and due to long arrear, they are not able to pay the huge amount at a time, and even delay payment charges are also added with heavy amount. So the missed call services are introduced to such consumers to know their due amount on their mobile phones. without any long searching/surfing/or making a long talk on toll free number of customer care center, the initiative of no power supply complaint registration and the due amount with due date in the electricity sector is proposed in this paper by using the Open source Software. Now a days, a few consumers are not able to pay their electricity due amount due to non-receipt of their electricity bills or loss of the same. This case is especially in the rural area where the people are not aware of the online facilities/internet/website/ Android Applications/smart phones. It is very easy to such consumers to give a missed call with no any financial burden involved. Free of cost, the consumers can get the duplicate bill on their mobile phones in the form of text with due amount and due date. Such facilities can enhance the quality of services by analyzing the no-power-complaints accumulated via this facility for further decision making/policy drafting (Fig. 1).

Pre-requisites for this framework is discussed in detail as follows:-

Arduino ESP32. This is the Microcontroller which is the heart of the IoT based device. It will control and monitor the various components attached and will establish coordination among components by integration. This module is to be used for communication for the IoT device via Wi-Fi, Bluetooth. It has 34 GPIO Pins and each pin has multiple functionalities which can be configured using specific registers. This board supports I2C communication also. In the energy sector, IoT applications embedded the functionality of Wi-Fi include energy metering and building energy management [7–11].

GSM SIM800L Module. This is the module to be used for communication of the IoT with the cloud/DC through open internet via GSM Technology. SIM is inserted in the SIM slot provided with the GSM Module for the Cellular connectivity. This module will provide the missed call information and messages reading.

IIC OLED 1036. Display used in the IoT based device for various indications/messages/errors/dashboard presentations which also supports i2c Communication.

Arduino IDE. The Arduino IDE is used for programming the hardware ESP32 to integrate the SIM800L and functionality of APIs of Middleware.

Middleware. The middleware is the hardware server composed of the CPU 4Core with RAM 4 BG and internal disk Storage of about 100 GB.

The following are the Open Source Software used for this solution.

Linux (Cent OS). Linux Cent OS is the open source operating software, it is UNIX based OS.

Apache Web Server. The httpd apache web server is the open source web server. Author of [4] paper however reviews performance of the web servers specifically the Apache and Nginx Web Servers. The biggest players in the web server business, Apache and IIS, have had the field to themselves for a long time apache handles less requests per second at high concurrency memory usage Increases with increase in requests handles 350–390 requests per second. ith single worker, it can handle 7367 requests per second CPU utilization increases with workload [4].

PHP. PHP is the server side open source language, it is most commonly in use open source language. The web server side language has its features of auto connectivity with the open source database like MySQL. PHP- It is a server-side scripting language designed for web development. PHP commands can be embedded directly into an HTML source document rather than calling an external file to process data. PHP will work with virtually all database software, including local hosts as well online database tools [1].

MYSQL. MySQL is the open source most in use data base. This database can store huge data. The processing of the database is also much optimized. MySQL is the world's second most widely used open source relational database management system (RDBMS). This language is used for creating the database which is used for storing the details of each user. It has many in-built commands which helps in manipulation of data and manage the database [2].

Asterisk. This is the open source PBX/ VOIP software. This is the open source framework for the communication applications. This can be used for the missed call service notification generation. The other alternatives for this may be IVR/or the cloud telephony services. Which can provide the SMS API (the response API for the missed call containing specially the mobile number of the consumer).

Node.js. This is an open source java script runtime environment which can run outside a browser. It has cross-platform compatibility, so it can be run on various operating systems. It is standard extension for the existing JavaScript code. [5] Series of Node.js framework which are being used nowadays are React, Vue, Angular, Ember, Backbone.js [15].

REST API. It stands for Representational state Transfer Application Programming Interface. It is the best way of communicating between the various heterogeneous severs as well as with the clients. The API requests the source with some parameters and gets back the response from the source in the form of the data. In Web services that are based on open standards and protocols as SOAP/XML-RPC/REST.

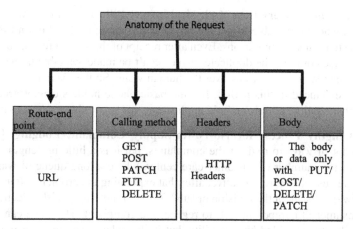

Fig. 1. Anatomy of the request

In paper [3] the author explains the role of RESTful or REST (Representational State Transfer) web APIs (Application Programming Interface). A collaborative big data analytics platform for big data as a service may enhance the applicability of the Big Data as services. Application/Program Developers can collaborate/communicate/interact with each other via various soap/wsdl/REST Web APIs on the platform by sharing its value i.e. stored data, procedures/steps/methods or algorithms, and services (REST API). [3].

Curl. This is the command line utility called cURL. Most of the APIs are called via the cURL in the php on Linux platform. However the uCurl is the in-built command for the Linux also. [6].

JSON. It is JavaScript Object Notation. It is very common data format for communication in the APIs. The sending as well as response in the API. One API can has request as JSON in the parameters and can have the response also in the JSON format.

Research Gap. Due to lock down imposed due to corona covid 19 pandemic, the human visits to the utility offices for the duplicate bills if not served is not possible, and also for lodging the complains for the no-power-supply, became the constrains. The urban consumers are using the internet and android mobile applications on their smart phones for these services which already provided by the energy supply utilities. But the rural consumers, due to lack of the internet usage, and lack of the knowledge of the android applications and smart phones usages, the consumers are not able to get updated information of their latest invoices of electricity consumption to be paid. Also due to lengthy process of lodging the complaint on the toll free number provided for these services, they could not get the benefits of these already developed features, the long consumer id remembering and a complicated processes in some cases, is also the constraint in these services.

Problem Formulation. The study formulated the following broad problems especially for the rural area consumers.

Occasionally Non Delivery/Loss of Physical Invoice Bill. There are a few consumers at rural area who are not able to get the physical invoice of energy bill on time occasionally due to numerous of reasons. Even after receipt of the same a few have lost their physical invoice copy. So the duplicate invoice can't be made available in the physical form due to pandemic restrictions over the human visits. So the eVersion of the all the services are enhanced in this period. But the basic phone holders cannot access such internet/website/online portals/android applications for smart phones/devices etc.

Complex/Lengthy Process for No-Power-Supply Complaint Lodging. However there are a lot of ways to register the complaints, but it is a little bit lengthy process over the toll free number of customer care center, where a long queue of waiting for talking to the customer care executive, after that explaining the problem, after that providing a few details about the division or subdivision of the supply of the electricity and a large consumer id number, at last, to register the complaint. The same can be done over the web sites provided by the utility, but it also takes some login or register the consumer, then fill a few details online on a web page and then raising the complaint. As no-power-supply, might not have access to these services due to no power supply at their premises.

Remembering of Long Consumer Id. The consumer Id is generally 8 to 16 or even 20 character long. So it is very difficult to remember the consumer id of the electricity connection.

Wrong Bill Generation on Door Lock Readings. The human meter readers are approaching to any door locked premises, then they either enter wrong readings or bills are not prepared and automatically the bills are not served on the actual consumption of the electricity. The consumer might get the average bill on the base of the past consumptions as the tariff of the concerned utility might be. But there should be some mechanism to send the readings by SMS and same can be incorporated in the bill generations if the premises is marked locked.

Proposal of Missed Call Messaging Service. To resolve the above problems the missed call messaging services framework is proposed. The mobile number tagged with the consumer id will automatically get the consumer id from the proposed system. By doing this, the long number remembering issue is resolved, the missed call can provide the bills due amount along with the due date with the soft copy of the same as a link of pdf. Hence the duplicate bill or the real-time outstanding bill of the energy consumption can be made available on just in a second only a missed call away. The no-power-supply complaint is also proposed by this framework to avoid the lengthy process of lodging the online/customer care center on call services.

3 Components of the Model

The following are the components composing the framework of missed call messaging service for enhancing the functionality of existing traditional legacy electronic no-power-supply complaint and issue of the duplicate energy bills.
The framework is broadly broken down in the following major parts:-

The Front-End Device. This machine is composed of Arduino Uno Microcontroller, GSM SIM800L, IIC OLED 1306 and Arduino IDE for Programming the hardware.

The Middleware Server. Hardware compute infrastructure of 4 core with 8 GB RAM with 100 GB storage with Linux Cent OS, Apache Web Server/Node.js, PHP, MySQL and Asterisk VOIP/IVR/cloud telephony service as optional.

Local Area Network/WifiZone. Ethernet connection or WiFi Connection for the connectivity between different parts.
    Access to utility billing engine for both customer care services as well as consumer database. Network access as per requirement, may require internet access if any database is hosted as services on the cloud storage as the case may be.

Connectors/Adaptors Connectors/Adaptors are API, cURL in-built utility of Linux, JSON, SOAP, XML-RPC, WSDL and REST.

The Back-End Data Storage. Depending upon the implementation of various schemes and selection of different bidders with different technologies, the utilities may have the heterogeneous database storage of various databases like ORACLE/MS SQL Server/Sybase/IBM DB2/Mongo dB/MySQL/PostgreSQL etc. used widely as Consumer Master Database, Metering/MDAS Database, Billing Database, Collection Database, Customer Care Services Database, SMS Gateways, Online Payments and ERP.

4 Block Diagram of Missed Call Messaging Service

The Fig. 2 explains the framework of the missed call messaging service, in this framework the utility billing engine has two different databases, of consumer database and the customer care service database. The consumer database contains all the information of the consumer of the electricity and their energy consumption details like electric meter readings i.e. metering, billing (generation of the invoices against the electricity consumptions over a period of time) and collection data (Revenue collection via different mode of payment of the invoices like Cash collection counters/online websites/smart mobile phone applications etc.). Based on the billing logics as per the tariffs, the consumers due amount (Real-time current outstanding amount against the consumer id) and due dates can be easily extracted with the REST API. In our case, the SIM800L, the GSM Module is attached with the Arduino ESP32 microcontroller. One prepaid SIM of available telecommunication operator is inserted into the SIM800L. The SIM is already activated and present in the ready to use stage. The ESP32, the microcontroller keep on checking the status of the SIM800L. Whenever it gets any call landing on the module, it scans the Wi-Fi availability and establishes the connection with the WiFiZone for the various network services. Here microcontroller is disconnecting the call and consumes an API of the middleware, with the secret key/tokens to keep the security as main concern. The API consumed at middleware, then further checks the mobile number and from the consumer database, it collects the consumer Ids from the consumer database. If there are more than one consumer electricity connections tagged then the balance of the both the consumer id are processed separately, and two different messages are generated. So there is scope of multiple connections tagging over one single RMN to avail such facilities. The API gets the Consumer number along with some other parameters like tokens for authentications, in the JSON format and returns the response in the form of the JSON format containing the various parameters along with payment due amount and due date, these two parameters are concatenated in the message along with the link of the current latest invoice pdf. This sums content is again formulated in the JSON format and passed to the API of SMS gateway servers. By this, the SMS is delivered to the consumer with invoice details. The requests and their corresponding logs are captured at the Linux OS (Cent os) in the MySQL database. The PHP language is used for the processing of the data.

The REST API are also built in the PHP, curl is the utility used in the PHP to talk with the utility billing engine for customer invoices as well as for the complaints lodging. The missed call information can be captured via API of the asterisk VOIP/IVR or the cloud telephony services as per the case of incorporation of such infrastructure. This API provides the destination and originator for the missed call, as per the destination the invoice details or no-power-supply triggers can be fired as per the case. Node.js/apache web server's works for the web services. The apache web servers runs the PHP REST API whenever called through curl. All these software are free and open source, can be utilized at anywhere. The hardware's used for the IoT devices are easily available and can be programmed via Arduino IDE. Arduino is the Open Source Electronic platform based upon easy-to-ease hardware's.

5   Algorithm/Working of IoT Based Device

Algorithm. Missed Call services for non-Android phone consumers:-
The following are the steps for the processing of the missed call services.

1.   First of all the consumer calls on the missed call number provided by the utility.
2.   The Device is designed with the Arduino Uno with GSM SIM800L module, SIM is inserted in the module with a specific mobile number. The device is keep watching for any incoming call on the device, the call is disconnected and the mobile number is passed to the API developed at the Middleware in the PHP, with the parameters as Mobile number i.e. originator of the call, the destination of the call, and the date and time of the call with a token to access the API for authentication purpose.
3.   The REEST API at middleware, is triggered. The mobile number with the date and time stamp is entered in the MySQL Database at middleware.

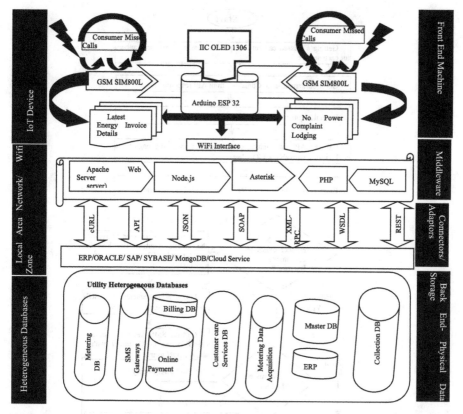

Fig. 2. IoT based framework of missed call messaging services for electricity consumers

4. The API provided by the IoT device designed (or missed call services via Asterisk VOIP/IVR or the cloud telephony service if not using IoT Device), will consume the REST API built on the framework. The JSON format will be passing the token number along with other parameters to the API, the response will return the JSON data. The data will provide the mobile number of the consumer.

5. The mobile number will be searched from the consumer data base via the REST API provided at the utility end to search the consumer id based on the mobile number.

6. After getting the consumer id, the utility billing engine will be queried on the consumer id, to retrieve the current payment due amount and due date along with a link of latest invoice details pdf.

7. If the destination number is for no-power-supply system, then the utility billing engine will be requested to lodge a complaint of type no-power-supply against the consumer id retrieved.

8. After that, accordingly the SMS will be drafted for the invoice details or the complaint number as the case may be, then the message API will be called to deliver the SMS to the consumer id tagged mobile number.

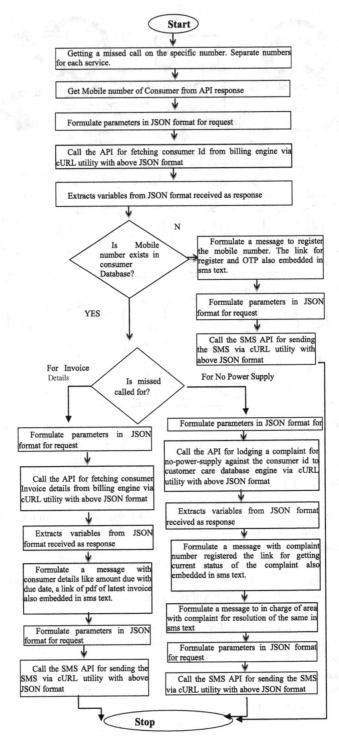

Fig. 3. Flow chart of missed call services for invoice details and no-power-supply complaints

9. In case the mobile number does not have any consumer id, then the SMS will be sent to mobile number with registration link with OTP for registration of the same at utility web portal.

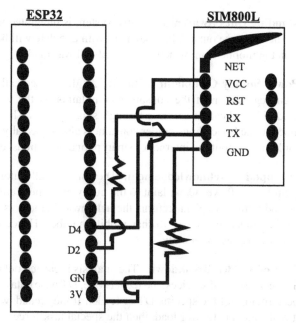

Fig. 4. Schematic diagram of IoT device

10. Figure 4 above is the schematic diagram of the IoT Device used to server the missed call services, the 3V3 Pin of the ESP32 is connected to the VCC Pin of the SIM800L. the GND pin is connected to the GND Pin of the SIM800L, if the power supply is served by the external device, then the registers at the GND must be used, otherwise the module SIM800L may get destroyed in case of any variation in the voltages more then or less the recommended voltages. (Average 3.7 V). As the SIM800L is the raw chip, it does not contain the voltage controller mechanisms. While connecting the Power supply, Always connect the GND part over the SIM800L, after that connect VCC. Same while disconnecting the connections of power supply online, if GND is not connected and VCC is remained connected, then the device my get destroyed, if the current is not as per the requirements, the SIM800L may get turned to deep shutdown mode. The Leds blinking on the Module can indicate the functioning and status of the SIM800L.

6 Advantages

Restriction of Human Movement. As of now due to covid19 corona pandemic, the restrictions on the movement of the human being is enforced due to lock down. This proposal can reduce the movement of human being to utility offices for the purpose of duplicate bill collection in case of non-receipt of the physical invoice of energy charges, and lodging of the no-power complaints. Now the proposed model can meet the both the requirements on the missed call services only.

Real-time Outstanding Dues Awareness. As the system is integrated with the utility billing engine, so the real time outstanding payment with due date will be sent as SMS to the consumer on the mobile from which the missed call was made.

Real-time No Power Supply Complaint Instantly. As the missed call service is not requiring any login/registration of the consumer complaints on the website through internet of the android application services through smart phone. The benefit of the service are extended to the basic phone holder consumers also, especially who are at the rural area and don't know about the internet or smart phone operations. etc.

Automatically Complaint Acknowledgement. The missed call automatically triggers the lodging of the No-Power-Complaint to the utility customer care services. The API integrated to lodge the complaint returns the acknowledgement as the complaint number made to the consumer tagged to that mobile number. Hence the complaint acknowledgement is server automatically.

Real-time Analysis of Sudden Breakdown. The analysis is carried out on the basis of data collected via the missed call services, the feeder wise, DT wise data can be analyzed to monitor the performance of the specific DT or feeder. If the breakdown of a specific DT is noticed at real-time due to over load, then the special task force can perform the vigilance tasks to identify the reason of sudden load increment, it might be due to theft by the unknown consumer on the specific DT. By this, various analysis on the data can be performed on real-time.

Can Trigger for Smart Meters Prepaid/Postpaid. This can also trigger the consumers smart meter activities, like after the recharge of the smart meter, if the reconnection is not done in time, then the missed call service for No-Power can trigger the smart meter billing solution to trigger the event of the recharge of the smart meter to reconnect the consumer. By this, if due to any communication issue, if the reconnection of the electricity connection of the smart meter is not carried out automatically due to numerous of reasons, then the missed call service can trigger that event also. By this, automatically reconnection can be benefit from this framework.

Automatically Tagging of Mobile Numbers of the Consumers. In both the services, if the mobile number is not tagged with the consumer number then the link of the webpage to register the mobile number as web self service is provided to the consumer's mobile number as SMS along with the OTP to be entered to correctly tag the mobile number with proper authentication. The process of tagging is also available on the link provided. The page is self-explanatory for the registration of the mobile number.

Automatically Call to Consumers by Customer Care Center. Analysis can be carried out on the patterns of the missed calls received from the specific consumers, the missed call received from a consumer for balance inquiry frequently and no any payment received indicates that the consumer might be facing the issue while paying the outstanding dues. Or there might be any online transaction which might not be completed due to numerous of reasons like network issue while performing the online transactions. So after analyzing such consumers, the customer care may be automatically prompted the list of such consumers. The customer care executives, automatically gets the list of mobile numbers with such cases, which can enhance the revenue collections.

7   Results and Discussion

An IoT Base Device is designed with Arduino UNO microcontroller as heart of the device. There is GSM SIM8000L module is connected to get the mobile number from which the missed call is made. The number is captured by the Arduino and an API developed at Middleware is consumed with the parameters with originator, destination and date and time of call. The API at Middleware is then filtering the type of missed call and sends the final SMS containing the information of invoice details in case of balance due, and complaint number in case of No-Power-Supply missed call. The consumers not tagged are also motivated to register the same to get instant alerts and easy services from the utility.

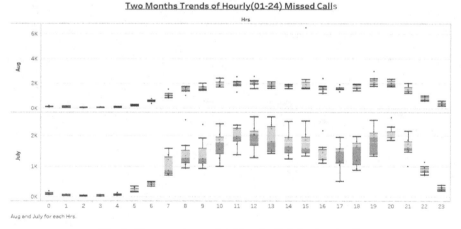

Fig. 5. Two months trends of hourly (0–24) missed calls

The data is received in the MySQL Database at the middleware server. This data is further analyzed and the following points revealed.

The analysis is performed in the both the types of the missed calls i.e. Payment/Invoice due as well as No-Power-Supply complaints.

Two Months Trends of Hourly (0–24) Missed Calls. The Fig. 5 shows the hourly trends from 00 h to 2359 h of a day. In the month of July 2020 and Aug 2020, the number of missed calls on the time duration from morning 5:00 to 10:00 makes a sharp slope. The peak missed calls are continued till 21:00 h. And then slope is downed till 23:00 h. The missed call from 23:00 h to next day 04:00 h are very negligible, as per the trends/patterns shown in the picture. The four quadrants Q1, Q2, Q3, and Q4 of a specific hour are also broken down in the four parts for easy analysis of the same. The micro analysis may be performed over this chart.

Two Months Trends of Weekly hour wise Missed Calls. Figure 6 shows the two months i.e. July 2020 and Aug. 2020 data of trends of weekly day wise, hour wise missed calls analysis. The pattern is found of the same type. The pattern falls down on the Sunday as being holiday, otherwise the other week days, the patters looks constant slope over the graph. The graph showed the sudden fluctuation over the graph, and was analyzed at micro level and found that a particular mobile keep on sending the missed calls, and made the system as a game, the same was dealt severely and the limit of maximum daily missed all applied to overcome such unnecessary interruptions. If a few number keep on calling in such pattern, can perform the DDOS (Dedicated denial of Service) attack on the system. So the database is also tuned in such a way at middleware, to tackle such requests and make them permanent barred if such occurrence of events are recurring in nature.

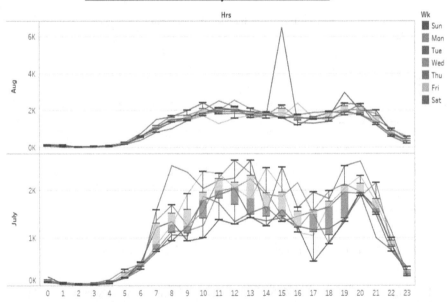

Fig. 6. Two months trends of weekly hour wise missed calls

Figure 7 shows the simple cured graph of the latest two months data i.e. July 2020 and Aug. 2020. Hourly consolidated Trends of two months Missed Calls as the broad view can be analyzed by this figure. The bell shape curve shows the pattern at daily, weekly and monthly pattern based on the hour's basis from 00:00 to 23:59 during each day. From this analysis the following initiatives should be taken by the power utilities especially for the Rural Consumers who are not able to take benefits of the online/Internet/Website/smart phone services.

Initiative for Self-mobile Registration with SMS. The Pull SMS facility also works, as soon as any SMS is received, the API from the middleware is consumed with parameters of Message and mobile number. The keywords at message are further analyzed and Registration through SMS by the consumers is facilitated. A consumer can register with this facility only by sending ACT consumer id to the specific mobile number which is used in the SIM800L module. The API at the middleware will perform the further actions at the next layer. The basic triggering is done via SIM800L with the high level parameters i.e. mobile number and the SMS contents.

Initiative for Self-meter-Reading with SMS. The Pull SMS facility also works, as soon as any SMS is received, the API from the middleware is consumed with parameters of Message and mobile number. The keywords at message are further analyzed and a consumer can send the Readings with the keywords Energy xxxxx KWH. Then the readings can be used by the utility for verification of the readings taken by the human meter reader. The quality of the meter reading can be enhanced by this initiative. If any consumer is reporting the readings via this SMS facility, and gets the invoice based on the wrong readings entered by the Meter Reader (Human Representative of the Utility office) in the two consecutive invoices/then necessary penalty over that meter reader may be incorporated to bring the quality in the meter reading services. This facility can also promote the self-assessment among the electricity consumers.

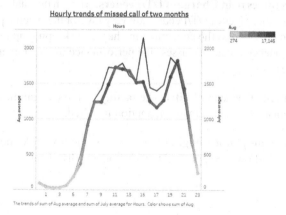

Fig. 7. Hourly consolidated trends of two months missed calls

If the premises of the consumers is locked while the human meter reader is approaching to the consumers premises, then he marks the place as door lock or guesses the readings automatically, if the consumer is aware of this facility, he can use this facility to perform the meter reading by self. And in case the readings are not marked, or wrongly marked, the correct readings by the consumer can be analyzed with the past and the bill can be generated on actual instead of average consumption of electricity.

Initiative for Self-meter-Reading with SMS. The Pull SMS facility also works, as soon as any SMS is received, the API from the middleware is consumed with parameters of Message and mobile number. The keywords at message are further analyzed and a consumer can send the Readings with the keywords Energy xxxxx KWH. Then the readings can be used by the utility for verification of the readings taken by the human meter reader. The quality of the meter reading can be enhanced by this initiative. If any consumer is reporting the readings via this SMS facility, and gets the invoice based on the wrong readings entered by the Meter Reader (Human Representative of the Utility office) in the two consecutive invoices/then necessary penalty over that meter reader may be incorporated to bring the quality in the meter reading services. This facility can also promote the self-assessment among the electricity consumers.

If the premises of the consumers is locked while the human meter reader is approaching to the consumers premises, then he marks the place as door lock or guesses the readings automatically, if the consumer is aware of this facility , he can use this facility to perform the meter reading by self. And in case the readings are not marked, or wrongly marked, the correct readings by the consumer can be analyzed with the past and the bill can be generated on actual instead of average consumption of electricity.

Initiative for Auto Maintenance of DT/Feeder. If the missed calls from the specific DT are in the more repetitive in nature, then the maintenance of the DT should be scheduled for the precautions, and maintaining the better quality of the supply of the electricity to the consumers.

Initiative for Incentives to in Charge of DT/Feeders. If from the analysis, if it is found that the break down messages of DT/Feeders are very low for the specific period, then the incentives may be provided to the concerned in charge for keeping up the good morale of the employees. Hence it can also assess the performance of the Human Resources of the Power Utilities.

24 × 7 Real-time Invoice Availability. The facility of missed call messaging service is 24 × 7 automatically, no any human interaction involved.

24 × 7 Real-time Complaint Lodging Facility. The facility of Automatically Complaints lodging of No-Power-Supply is 24 × 7 automatically, no any human interaction involved.

8   Conclusion

This paper focuses on the automatically call lodging for No Power Supply on the missed call services on a particular virtual mobile number. The missed call service is also playing a vital role in the revenue collection in the electricity supply system. The consumer can get the real time outstanding bill due along with due date. The consumer can timely pay the bill without any delay payment penalty even on no receipt of the physical energy consumption bill. The framework is designed with the help of the open source software/utilities. Ultimately the missed call service benefits to both consumer as well as power utilities. For consumer, the real time complaint of No Power supply, the framework will automatically inform the utility to take preventive steps if the multiple complaints received from the same location instantly, the cause may be of covering full area, may be due to sudden load over a particular DT or Feeder, the theft of the heavy electricity may be identified on the particular DT. A summarized SMS is also sent to particular in charge of DT of the power utility staff. The necessary detections of the causes may be analyzed at real-time.

9 Future Work

Further accumulated data/information collected from missed call services for invoices as well as for NO-Power-Supply related on distributed file system, can be analyzed on near to real-time by using big data analytics to formulate any decision making/policy drafting.

References

1. Mittal1, V.: A new approach to E-learning (E-Web Class). Int. J. Eng. Comput. Sci. **6**, 21323–21327 (2017)
2. Prokofyeva, N.: Analysis and practical application of PHP frameworks in development of web information systems. Procedia Comput. Sci. **104**, 51–56 (2017)
3. Park, K.: Web-based Collaborative Big Data Analytics on Big Data as a Service Platform, pp. 564–567. ICACT, PyeongChan (2015)
4. Kunda, D., Chihana, S., Sinyinda, M.: Web server performance of apache and Nginx: a systematic literature review. Comput. Eng. Intell. Syst. **8** (2017). ISSN: 2222-1719
5. Wikipedia, Node.js. https://en.wikipedia.org/wiki/Node.js. Accessed 12 Sep 2020
6. Hagay.   https://www.smashingmagazine.com/2017/04/secure-web-app-http-headers/ Accessed 12 Sep 2020
7. Martínez-Cruz, E.C.: "Manufacturing low-cost wifi-based electric energy meter". In: Proceedings of the 2014 IEEE Central America and Panama Convention (CONCAPAN), Panama City, Panama, 12–14 November 2014, pp. 1–6 (2020). Energies 13, 494 23 of 27
8. Karthika, A., Valli, K.R., Srinidhi, R., Vasanth, K.: Automation of energy meter and building a network using IoT. In: Proceedings of the 2019 5th International Conference on Advanced Computing Communication Systems (ICACCS), Coimbatore, India, 15–16 March 2019, pp. 339–341 (2019)
9. Rodriguez-Diaz, E., Vasquez, J.C., Guerrero, J.M.: Intelligent DC: homes in future sustainable energy systems: when efficiency and intelligence work together. IEEE Consum. Electron. Mag. **5**, 74–80 (2016)
10. Lee, Y., Hsiao, W., Huang, C., Chou, S.T.: An integrated cloud-based smart home management system with community hierarchy. IEEE Trans. Consum. Electron. **62**, 1–9 (2016)
11. Lee, T., Jeon, S., Kang, D., Park, L.W., Park, S.: Design and implementation of intelligent HVAC system based on IoT and big data platform. In: Proceedings of the 2017 IEEE International Conference on Consumer Electronics (ICCE), Las Vegas, NV, USA, 8–10 January 2017, pp. 398–399 (2017)

12. Batra, I., Luhach, A.K., Pathak, N.: Research and analysis of lightweight cryptographic solutions for internet of things. In: Proceedings of the Second International Conference on Information and Communication Technology for Competitive Strategies, pp. 1–5 (March 2016)

13. Pramanik, A., Luhach, A.K., Batra, I., Singh, U.: A systematic survey on congestion mechanisms of CoAP based Internet of things. In: Singh, D., Raman, B., Luhach, A.K., Lingras, P. (eds.) Advanced Informatics for Computing Research. CCIS, vol. 712, pp. 306–317. Springer, Singapore (2017). https://doi.org/10.1007/978-981-10-5780-9_28

14. Sai, K.B.K., Subbareddy, S.R., Luhach, A.K.: IOT based air quality monitoring system using MQ135 and MQ7 with machine learning analysis. Scalable Comput. Pract. Exp. **20**(4), 599–606 (2019)

15. Martin, S.: JavaScript. https://www.freecodecamp.org/news/complete-guide-for-front-end-developers-javascript-frameworks-2019/. Accessed 12 Sep 2020

A Divide and Conquer Based Data Aggregation Technique for WBANs

Roopali[1](✉) and Rakesh Kumar[2]

[1] Department of Informatics, Computer Science and Engineering, NITTTR,
Chandigarh, India
[2] Department of Computer Science and Engineering, Central University of Haryana,
Mahendargarh, India

Abstract. WBANs monitor health data in an on demand and timely
fashion and require effective communication of data from source to sink.
In today's tough times with pandemic taking its toll all over the globe,
personalized data from smart wearable devices is empowering medical
fraternity to make health care decisions with new insights. The latest
wearable devices are capable of monitoring detailed physiological parameters, therefore promoting diagnosing patients from afar. The data transmission using wearable or implanted sensor nodes consume more energy
and minimize network lifetime. Various solutions have been proposed
by researchers to address issues such as interference, energy consumption, body movement, network lifetime, propagation delay and quality
of services. However, issues still prevail in WBANs. In this paper, we
have proposed a data aggregation technique using divide and conquer
method which increases effectiveness of ubiquitous health care systems.
The proposed data aggregation technique efficiently communicates data
to the sink node, optimizes residual energy of sensor nodes, packet delivery ration, average delay and longevity of networks. The proposed technique reduces the number of packets to be transmitted by 28–29% and
enhances network lifetime by 63% as compared to the other state-of-the-
art techniques.

Keywords: Data aggregation · Energy optimization · Network
lifetime · Sensor analyst systems · WBANs · Ubiquitous healthcare

1 Introduction

With the increasing usage of wearable devices for vital sign monitoring, assisted
living and IoT, there is an increasing demand for the foolproof adoption of
WBANs by the society. WBANs must have efficient transmission from source
to sink and monitoring health data in real time [1]. Technological advancements
in health care allow the use of cloud computing, fog computing, Internet of
things and tele-health care technologies to transmit data between patients and
medical fraternity. Thus, WBANs have the capability to integrate healthcare
and information technology and revolutionize the way people utilize ubiquitous
healthcare applications [2].

© Springer Nature Singapore Pte Ltd. 2021
A. K. Luhach et al. (Eds.): ICAICR 2020, CCIS 1394, pp. 101–110, 2021.
https://doi.org/10.1007/978-981-16-3653-0_8

The smart wearable devices are available in diverse regions of the world due to their exceptionally advanced technological features. The sensors embedded in these devices are capable for activity detection and health monitoring [3,4]. Thus, helps in early detection of diseases and effective treatment which ultimately improves the quality of life. Wearable devices can monitor the physiological parameters unobtrusively using inbuilt sensors such as accelerometers, gyroscopes and magnetometers. To recognize daily activities, video based approaches capture images. Ambient devices monitor the interaction between humans and their environments that include sound, pressure, temperature and other sensors. Inbuilt sensors of smart phones have also attracted enormous researchers for human activity recognition [5]. Therefore, WBANs are capable of ubiquitously monitoring the patient and the data can be transmitted to the mHealth server with the help of various communicational technologies. The stored data can be analysed for early detection of abnormal conditions, frequent trends and non-occurring behavior [6–8]. However, many issues such as energy harvesting [9], path routing [10], data aggregation [11] and efficient routing [12,13] still prevail in WBANs.

In this paper, we propose an efficient data aggregation approach for in-door hospital scenario that uses an aggregator node to perform aggregation before its transmission to the sink node. The process of data aggregation depletes small amount of energy of the nodes as compared to conventional data forwarding mechanisms. Also, it avoids data redundancy and yields efficient and longer network life. In the proposed scheme, aggregation minimizes energy consumption or energy of the nodes will drain. Therefore, a sensor node with high residual energy, is selected as cluster head which receives continuous data and transmits to the nearest aggregator node. Aggregator node will perform the aggregation depending upon the variance in the data packets received at different time stamps. Aggregator node in turn sends the data to the sink node. This optimizes network energy and lifetime. The proposed technique is competent in optimizing transmission cost, energy consumption, network lifetime, packet delivery ratio and average delay. The simulation results show that the proposed technique is better in terms of the aforementioned parameters to aggregate the data as compared mto M-PEERPDCT [14] and EHDA [15].

This paper is organized as follows. Section 2 discusses the related work. Section 3 explicates the proposed data aggregation algorithm. Section 4 analyzes the complexity of the proposed algorithm and compares it with existing techniques. Finally, Sect. 5 concludes the paper with directions for future research.

2   Related Work

One of the major issue with WBANs is of data aggregation from heterogeneous sources received at different time stamps that can directly impact the network performance. In [16], a review of data fusion techniques is presented along with five major levels for data processing before aggregation can be performed. The most important contribution of this survey is that it provided the application scenarios where the various data fusion techniques could be applied. In [17,18], authors explicate the importance of data aggregation and discuss various data aggregation based routing protocols. In [19], various data aggregation issues in wireless sensor networks such as delay, redundancy, accuracy, energy consumption and traffic load have been discussed. Network lifetime is directly related to the amount of data aggregation performed at different levels in the network. In [15], authors propose secure data aggregation algorithm that makes use of fog computing service. It allows the nearest aggregator node to send encrypted data embedded in its own data to the next node until it reaches the fog server. The data is reduced in size which reduces the energy consumption. In [14], authors aggregate the data based on criticality and priority of the data which helps in eliminating redundant data packets. Also, forwarding only critical data reduces energy consumption. In [20], multiple classifier systems have been discussed focusing on human health monitoring and activity detection. The authors have focused on multimodal data fusion where data is collected form variety of sensors such as accelerometers, gyroscopes, magnetometer, heart rate, pressure and wearable camera. The different feature in time domain, frequency domain and wavelet transform are extracted from data that help in human activity classification and monitoring using machine learning approaches. Also, the authors have focused on different machine learning approaches which can be used in multiple classifier systems. Also, the authors have pointed out the existing research challenges such as security, privacy and use of deep learning techniques.

Thus, some of the gaps found in literature are as follows:

- Data fusion tend to reduce the data transmission cost. However, only fixed sized data can be fused.
- Most of the data transmission techniques focus on successful reception of data at the sink. However, packet length and overhead signals are ignored [21].
- Most of the data transmission techniques focus on data communication of sensors and the aggregator node. However, do not consider inter-sensor communication [22,23].

3   Data Aggregation

The proposed scheme uses divide and conquer approach for aggregating data. Thus, optimizing energy exhaustion and network lifetime in WBANs. It reduces data redundancy from the received data packets by exploiting temporal correlation amongst data before performing aggregation. Thus, decreasing number of transmissions from source to sink. Also, Fig. 1 shows flow of information from sensor node to the aggregator node in the network.

Sensor nodes sense data continuously and one packet of data is picked in one time slot t. The data packet is d_s^t where t denotes the time stamp when data is collected and s denotes the sensor id ($d_1^1, d_1^2, d_1^3....d_1^n$ denotes data from sensor id 1 at different time stamps). The information flows from cluster member to cluster head and from cluster head to nearest fixed node. Data received at fixed node is D_s^{ch} which represents data collected from cluster head (ch) and sensor

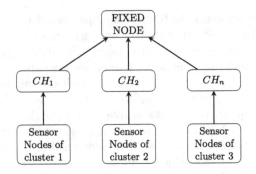

Fig. 1. Flow of information

node (s). It is necessary to discard duplicate or redundant measures of data accumulated at fixed node before forwarding it to the sink. If the data received from D_s^{ch} at different time stamps is similar then the difference is calculated as in Eq. 1 where δ is assumed to be an application specific threshold. Thus, if the $Diff$ is less than δ then they are supposed to be identical and should be aggregated. The data is combined in one data packet and is then forwarded to sink. If the data is dissimilar then it is not merged and forwarded as it is received at the fixed node. The whole process is explicated in Algorithm 1.

$$Diff(d_1^1, d_1^2) = \begin{cases} 1, & \text{if } |d_1^1 - d_1^2| \leq \delta \\ 0, & \text{otherwise} \end{cases} \tag{1}$$

$$Var_i = \frac{(d_i - \mu_i)^2}{l} \tag{2}$$

Algorithm 1. Data Reduction

Input: Collective data packets received at FN_i from various CHs
Output: Unit Data Packets

1: **if** $(n > i)$ **then**
2:    $M \leftarrow (i + n)/2$;
3: **end if**
4: Data Reduction (D_{si}^{CHi}, M);
5: Data Reduction $(M+1, D_{si}^{CHn})$;
6: $N \leftarrow$ data packets received at FN_i
7: **for** each data packet in N **do**
8:    Aggregate$(N_1, N_2, ..., N_\rho)$;
9: **end for**

After the clustered data packets from different cluster heads are received at the fixed node, the data packets are divided into two sub data packets. The division process is continued until a single data packet is extracted. Now, we can calculate the variance of each data packet using Eq. 2. The difference of variance of two data packets received from same cluster head and sensor is calculated using Eq. 1. If the two single data packets have large difference in their calculated variance then the data packets are received from two different sensors and should not be aggregated otherwise they will be aggregated as explained in Algorithm 2.

Algorithm 2. Data Aggregate

Input: Data packets received from sensor node s_i at CH_i at timestamp (TS_i)
Output: Aggregated Data Packet

1: $count \leftarrow 0$;
2: $N \leftarrow$ data packets received at FN_i
3: **for** each data packet in N **do**
4:     Calculate variance, $Var_i = \dfrac{(d_i - \mu_i)^2}{l}$ given in equation 2
5:     Calculate difference in variance for two packets d_i and d_j from same source given by equation 1
6:     **if** $Diff == 1$ **then**
7:         $D \leftarrow$ Combine (d_i, d_j)
8:         $count + +$;
9:     **else**
10:         Packets contain different information
11:     **end if**
12: **end for**
13: return count;
14: return D;

---

4   Implementation and Observations

The proposed protocol for data aggregation is simulated in Matlab. It involves n sensors that sense data continuously and are clustered. The cluster head then sends data to the fixed node which performs aggregation depending upon the information received at different time stamps from same sensor node. We have considered various parameters like total data aggregation at various thresholds (application specific), number of packets aggregated, energy consumption, communication cost, average delay, packet delivery ratio and network lifetime in comparison with existing techniques OCER [24], EERP [14] and EHDA [15]. The simulation results show that the proposed technique has outperformed existing techniques. Simulation assumptions are as follows:

- Random distribution of sensor nodes in the area.
- Aggregator node and sink node are fixed.
- Aggregator node is powerful node and performs aggregation.

- Homogeneous sensor nodes are used.
- Only cluster heads can communicate with aggregator node.
- Only aggregator node can communicate with sink node.
- Sensor nodes cannot be recharged.
- It is assumed that fixed nodes do not shred their energy soon and completely.

4.1 Performance Evaluation w.r.t. Number of Packets

It deals with removing redundant data packets from the network. This reduces the number of packet transmissions, energy consumption of the sensor nodes and network congestion. We have compared the total aggregation of the protocols w.r.t a particular threshold as shown in Fig. 2a. Also, we have compared data aggregation w.r.t the total number of packets aggregated as shown in Fig. 2b.

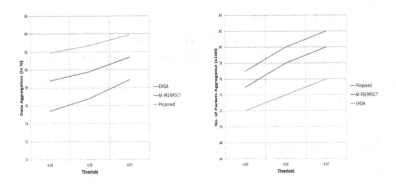

(a) Total Data Aggregated (in %)   (b) Total No. of Packets Aggregated

Fig. 2. Total aggregation

4.2 Performance Evaluation w.r.t. Energy Consumption

As lesser number of packets are transmitted, data communication phase requires less work which saves the energy of the sensor nodes in return. More the residual energy, network prevails for a longer time. We have compared the overall energy consumption of the protocols w.r.t a particular threshold as shown in Fig. 3a. Also, we have calculated communication cost w.r.t the total number of packets aggregated as shown in Fig. 3b.

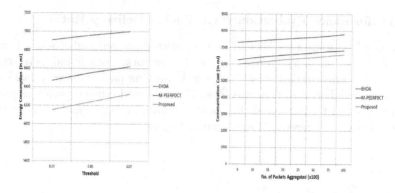

(a) Overall Energy Consumption   (b) Communication Cost

Fig. 3. Energy consumption

4.3   Performance Evaluation w.r.t. Average Delay

Due to less data loss and data aggregation, the proposed protocol has minimum average delay. The data from source reaches the CH which forwards it to the fixed node and then it finally reaches the sink node. We have compared the average delay of the protocols w.r.t a particular threshold as shown in Fig. 4a and w.r.t the number of packets aggregated as shown in Fig. 4b.

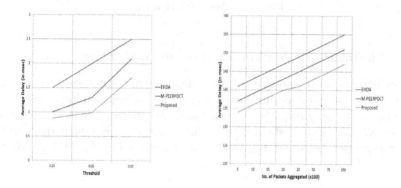

(a) Average Delay w.r.t Threshold   (b) Average Delay vs No. of Packets
                                         Aggregated

Fig. 4. Average delay

4.4   Performance Evaluation w.r.t. Packet Delivery Ratio

As the number of data packets to be transmitted are reduced, packet delivery ratio improves due to less congestion on the network. Data is indirectly transmitted from source to sink which helps in improving packet delivery ratio as it reduces the number of re-transmissions. The proposed scheme evaluates packet delivery ratio w.r.t a particular threshold as shown in Fig. 5a and w.r.t the total number of packets aggregated as shown in Fig. 5b.

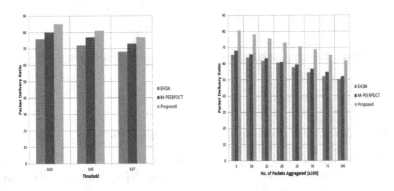

(a) Packet Delivery Ratio w.r.t Threshold   (b) Packet Delivery Ratio vs No. of Packets Aggregated

Fig. 5. Packet delivery ratio

4.5   Performance Evaluation w.r.t. Network Lifetime

Network lifetime is the measure of length of the life of the network, i.e., the time period till the last node dies in the network. Data aggregation improves lifetime of network as number of packet transmissions and the energy consumption are reduced. We have evaluated the network lifetime w.r.t a particular threshold for data aggregation as shown in Fig. 6a w.r.t the total number of packets aggregated as shown in Fig. 6b.

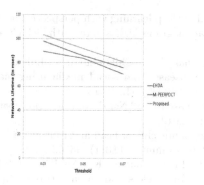
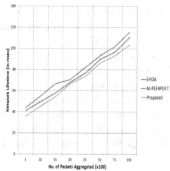

(a) Network Lifetime w.r.t Threshold   (b) Network Lifetime vs No. of Packets Aggregated

Fig. 6. Network lifetime

5   Coclusion and Future Scope

In this paper, we have proposed an efficient data aggregation technique for cost effective transmission of data from source to sink. The proposed technique uses divide and conquer approach for aggregating the data at intermediary node. The simulation results illustrate that the proposed scheme could achieve up to 28–29% of reduction in total number of packets to be transmitted. Also, energy is saved up to 63% and helps to improve the network lifetime of the WBANs. Thus, helps in improving the overall performance of the WBANs.

Further, the usefulness of soft computing techniques can be exploited for data aggregation. Also, the proposed scheme can consider security and privacy of the health data.

References

1. Pillai, R.R., Lohani, R.B.: Abnormality detection and energy conservation in wireless body area networks using hidden markov models: a review. In: 2020 International Conference on Communication and Signal Processing (ICCSP), pp. 0935–0939 (2020)
2. Punj, R., Kumar, R.: Technological aspects of WBANs for health monitoring: a comprehensive review. Wireless Netw. **25**(3), 1–33 (2018)
3. Cao, H., Leung, V., Chow, C., Chan, H.: Enabling technologies for wireless body area networks: a survey and outlook. IEEE Commun. Mag. **47**(12), 84–93 (2009)
4. Tobón, D.P., Falk, T.H., Maier, M.: Context awareness in wbans: a survey on medical and non-medical applications. IEEE Wireless Commun. **20**(4), 30–37 (2013)
5. Wu, H.-T., Tsai, C.-W.: A home security system for seniors based on the beacon technology. Concurr. Comput. Pract. Exp. **30**(15), 4496 (2018)
6. Nanglia, P., et al.: Detection and analysis of lung cancer using radiomic approach. In: Smart Computational Strategies: Theoretical and Practical Aspects, pp. 13–24 (2019)

7. Kumar, A., Mukherjee, S., Luhach, A.K.: Deep learning with perspective modeling for early detection of malignancy in mammograms. J. Discrete Math. Sci. Cryptogr. **22**(4), 627–643 (2019)
8. Pradeepa, S., Manjula, K., Vimal, S., Khan, M.S., Chilamkurti, N., Luhach, A.K.: DRFS: detecting risk factor of stroke disease from social media using machine learning techniques. Neural Process. Lett. (2020). (In Press)
9. Boumaiz, M., et al.: Energy harvesting based WBANs: Eh optimization methods. Procedia Comput. Sci. **151**, 1040–1045 (2019)
10. Roopali, Kumar, R.: Energy efficient dynamic cluster head and routing path selection strategy for WBANs. Wireless Pers. Commun. **113**(1), 33–58 (2020)
11. Yuan, X., Ma, Z., Li, W., Wang, H., Li, C., Zhang, K.: An IEEE 802.15. 6-based mac frame aggregation approach for wireless body area networks. In: 2019 11th International Conference on Wireless Communications and Signal Processing (WCSP), pp. 1–6 (2019)
12. Qureshi, K.N., Din, S., Jeon, G., Piccialli, F.: Link quality and energy utilization based preferable next hop selection routing for wireless body area networks. Comput. Commun. **149**, 382–392 (2020)
13. Raj, A.S., Chinnadurai, M.: Energy efficient routing algorithm in wireless body area networks for smart wearable patches. Comput. Commun. **153**, 85–94 (2020)
14. Navya, V., Deepalakshmi, P.: Energy efficient routing for critical physiological parameters in wireless body area networks under mobile emergency scenarios. Comput. Electr. Eng. **72**, 512–525 (2018)
15. Ullah, A., Said, G., Sher, M., Ning, H.: Fog-assisted secure healthcare data aggregation scheme in IoT-enabled WSN. Peer-to-Peer Netw. Appl. **13**(1), 163–174 (2019)
16. Castanedo, F.: A review of data fusion techniques. Sci. World J. **2013**(2013), 1–19 (2013)
17. Yadav, S., Yadav, R.S.: A review on energy efficient protocols in wireless sensor networks. Wireless Netw. **22**(1), 335–350 (2016)
18. Dhand, G., Tyagi, S.: Data aggregation techniques in WSN: survey. Procedia Comput. Sci. **92**, 378–384 (2016)
19. Sirsikar, S., Anavatti, S.: Issues of data aggregation methods in wireless sensor network: a survey. Procedia Comput. Sci. **49**, 194–201 (2015)
20. Nweke, H.F., Teh, Y.W., Mujtaba, G., Al-Garadi, M.A.: Data fusion and multiple classifier systems for human activity detection and health monitoring: review and open research directions. Inform. Fusion **46**, 147–170 (2019)
21. Misra, S., Chatterjee, S.: Social choice considerations in cloud-assisted WBAN architecture for post-disaster healthcare: data aggregation and channelization. Inform. Sci. **284**, 95–117 (2014)
22. Medjahed, H., Istrate, D., Boudy, J., Dorizzi, B.: Human activities of daily living recognition using fuzzy logic for elderly home monitoring. In: Proceedings of IEEE International Conference on Fuzzy Systems (FUZZ-IEEE), pp. 2001–2006 (2009)
23. Medjahed, H., Istrate, D., Boudy, J., Baldinger, J.L., Dorizzi, B.: A pervasive multi-sensor data fusion for smart home healthcare monitoring. In: Proceedings of IEEE International Conference on Fuzzy Systems (FUZZ), pp. 1466–1473 (2011)
24. Kaur, N., Singh, S.: Optimized cost effective and energy efficient routing protocol for wireless body area networks. Adhoc Netw. **61**, 65–84 (2017)

Open Research Challenges and Blockchain Based Security Solution for 5G Enabled IoT

Neha Gupta[1](✉), Sachin Sharma[1], Pradeep Kumar Juneja[1], and Umang Garg[2]

[1] Department of Computer Science and Engineering, Graphic Era Deemed to be University, Dehradun, India

[2] Department of Computer Science and Engineering, Graphic Era Hill University, Dehradun, India

Abstract. Internet of things (IoT) is an emanate automation in this competitive and innovative world. The emerging growth of IoT devices required high-speed Internet affinity, high data transmission, and low emission, etc. There are several limitations to existing communication technologies such as limited bandwidth, reduced network coverage, and scalability. Thus, IoT with an existing network is less capable to meet the above requirements. Therefore, there is a requirement for next-generation wireless communication 5G network to fulfil all these demands. This article presents an overview of 5G and IoT, as well as the integration of both technologies called 5G-enabled IoT, with their emerging technologies. Although, 5G enabled IoT is a powerful and prominent technology, it suffers from various technological challenges and compatibility issues. So, this paper also reveals the open challenges in 5G, IoT, and 5G enabled IoT. To address the security issue in 5G-IoT, it provides a solution using blockchain technology.

Keywords: IoT · 5G · 5G enabled IoT · Block chain · MIMO · Millimetre wave

1 Introduction

There are three independent technologies 5G, IoT, and Blockchain that can be integrated to get the best results in the real-time environment [12]. Internet of things (IoT) is prominent automation in today's world that touches on almost every aspect of human life. It is a popular technology that aims to transform the world with trigonous smart devices with offline connectivity. With the huge increase in various mobile devices and communications between them, there is an increase in demand in providing high connectivity, high data rates, high power efficiency, low latency, service quality, low interference, and other communication requirements (shown in Fig. 1). To meet these needs, the modern LTE (4G) mobile network may not be adequate. However, the emerging 5G mobile network can be tested as a Key enabler device that can meet these challenges of IoT technology. Besides, it can also be used to meet high communication requirements in IoT [8].

Therefore, 5G is a technology that supports the enhanced mobile broadband communication (eMBB), ultra-reliable low latency communication (URLLC), and massive machine-type communication (mMTC) endlessly and improves the overall IoT network

© Springer Nature Singapore Pte Ltd. 2021
A. K. Luhach et al. (Eds.): ICAICR 2020, CCIS 1394, pp. 111–120, 2021.
https://doi.org/10.1007/978-981-16-3653-0_9

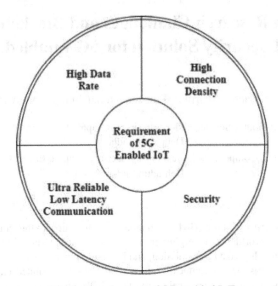

Fig. 1. Requirement of 5G enabled IoT.

performance. Although the integration of 5G with IoT provides powerful features. However, it still has several challenges and issues that are required to be discussed for the improvement and data management in the existing systems. There are several challenges [9] in 5G-IoT. These are the management of Radio resources, wavelength, good spectrum distribution, security and privacy issues, service quality requirements (QoS), etc. Since security or privacy is one of the most open issues in 5G-enabled IoT, this can be partially addressed by consolidating blockchain technology with IoT and 5G core network [12]. Blockchain is a technology in which data blocks are linked to antecedent block chain addresses and are much more secure than traditional server-client settings. Key features of blockchain technology include spatial distribution, point-to-point connectivity, improved security, agile contract, compliance, and dispersed documentation [5].

The main motivation of this research is to introduce the IoT and 5G with their functional technology and open issues. It also provides the integration of 5G-IoT with blockchain to secure device connectivity. Some important contributions can be discussed as follows:

- To present the open challenges and issues in 5G and IoT emerging technologies.
- To provide in-depth details about 5G enabled IoT with its open issues and challenges.
- To propose a countermeasure technique to deal with the security issues in IoT with 5G network using Blockchain.

The organization of the article is as follows: The qualitative information with an emphasis on 5G and IoT including their open-ended issues in Sect. 2. Section 3 provides a comprehensive overview of integrated technology (5G-enabled IoT) that allows technology and open problems and challenges. Finally, Sect. 4 focuses on the consolidation of blockchain technology in 5G enabled IoT.

2   Open Challenges in 5G and IoT

This section covers qualitative knowledge on 5G and IoT systems including enabling technology and their open research challenges.

2.1 IoT Emerging Technologies and Challenges

The main idea behind IoT is to collect information, process, and act accordingly. The adoption of IoT devices in several areas is growing steadily and is expected to hit approx. 100 billion devices by 2025 [15]. Although, IoT has covered almost every aspect of human life such as automation, retail, health, agriculture, and remote monitoring, etc. However, there are many open issues and challenges such as heterogeneity, collaboration, security and privacy, power issues, and problems due to big data sets [8]. This section highlights the emerging technologies and open issues in IoT. The IoT system can be summarized into four main domains like the application

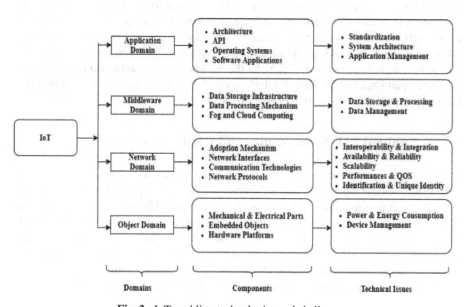

Fig. 2. IoT enabling technologies and challenges.

Domain, middleware domain, network domain, and object domain as shown in Fig. 2. The object domain comprises mechanical and electrical parts, embedded objects, and platforms for hardware components. The major issues along with these components are power and energy consumption, and device management. The network domain can build up using adoption mechanisms, interfaces, communication topologies, and protocols. There are some technological challenges with the network domain like interoperability and integration, availability, performance, and identification. After the transmission of data through the network, the data is stored at the third party storage module, called cloud component or middleware domain. This domain consists of data storage infrastructure and a data processing module. The major issues with this module are the security of stored data, and its management. The end-user of the IoT application can interact with the system using some android application or website, known as the application domain. This domain comprises API, operating system, and software applications. The lack of standard framework, architecture, and application management are some major issues with the application domain [8].

2.2 5G Emerging Technologies and Challenges

The wireless communication industry is putting great efforts into boosting system performance [10]. Therefore, the current spectrum needs to be used efficiently and more spectrum resources are needed to achieve power at the network level to serve more users with higher data levels [4]. Here, we describe some enabling technologies that will alter and explain the future generations of telecommunication standards and also discuss open research issues related to these technologies. To enhance the conduct of the whole system, there are several technologies that will be essential for future wireless standards.

These can enhance the capacity, coverage, or energy efficiency of the system. There are several challenges such as heterogeneous networks, device-to-device communication Software defined networking, Massive MIMO, Security and privacy, etc. as shown in Fig. 3. Although these technologies make the 5G system more agile and reliable, there are some open issues like inter-cell interference, device discovery, and link setting that need to be tested to get the full 5G capabilities.

3 5G Enabled IoT Technologies and Challenges

IoT network requires high connectivity, extended battery life, services that tolerate delays, narrowband operation, heterogeneous connectivity, Speed, Privacy, and reliability [6]. These requirements are met by next-generation 5G wireless communication that can provide high bandwidth, large battery life, antenna technology for narrowband, flexible time-frequency multiplexing, high MIMO, etc [1]. There are several researchers and a larger number of telecommunications industries involved in the employment of 5G in IoT considering the open-challenges and issues. This section contributes an in-depth discussion of the Key components in 5G-IoT and their open challenges [2].

3.1 Network Function Virtualization (NFV)

To enable the virtualization for the integral network function, NFV can decouple the hardware and focus on the generic cloud server [16], which can simplify the implementation of 5G-enabled IoT. The main aim of NFV is to provide flexible and scalable

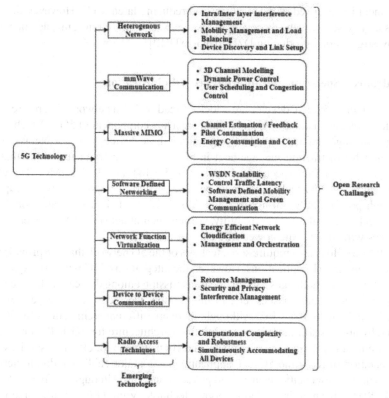

Fig. 3. 5G enabling technologies and issues.

5G IoT applications that can customize the subnetwork and build a programmable network for 5G-IoT applications [3]. The real-time processing can be achieved by using NFV that will provide capabilities for 5G IoT applications by optimizing the data speed, Bandwidth, and scope of logically carved networks to meet application requirements [2].

3.2 Heterogeneous Network (HetNet)

There is an essential requirement of a technology that can provide a novel communication process in 5G-IoT, this is known as Heterogeneous Networks (Het-Net) [3]. The concurrent operations with macro, Pico, femto, and microcells are known as HetNet. The HetNet facilitates 5G-IoT to accommodate on-demand hauling of data rate in a network.

3.3 Device to Device Communication

D2D transmission is a technique that enables the communication of two devices without an intermediate node or base station (BS). This technology provides the facility to use a licensed spectrum in 5G IoT which will improve the quality of service (QoS) by enhancement in the speed of data transfer and reducing latency [1]. However, different open issues like security, the discovery of resources, and interference management need to be investigated on introducing D2D to 5G-IoT [12].

3.4 Advanced Spectrum and Interference Administration

A large number of 5G IoT devices are widely spread within a network. Therefore, spectrum allocation and distraction management are a key component of 5G IoT technology to ensure coverage and traffic load balance among these devices [16]. HetNet is a bright clarification for distraction management in 5G IoT. An important technique that can be used to achieve high spectrum efficiency in 5G IoT is called MIMO. Therefore, some advanced MIMO techniques have been suggested to improve network capacity with a high-power number of horns in BS. Moreover, 5G IoT incorporates some optimization techniques like convex usability, artificial neural networks (ANNs), etc. These approaches will enhance the power efficiency of the system.

The future of IoT must require some features of the 5G network that can provide real-time processing in IoT applications. However, the integration of 5G with IoT expanded a new set of research challenges for reliable transmission among devices such as security, privacy, and management issues, etc. In this section, we focus on some key research challenges in the field of 5G-IoT. Although, there are different architectures for 5G-IoT proposed by authors still there is no well-defined architecture for 5G-IoT. Hence, there is a requirement to separate the user plane, and control plane for effective services. The implementation of real-time 5G-IoT applications is a major challenge due to network management, heterogeneity, security, and privacy concerns. Although, Software-defined network (SDN), is an eminent and emerging technology in 5G IoT. Still, some issues need to be covered in SDN such as

(a) Separation of two different planes in SDN (Control and data plane).
(b) Security is another important issue for SDN implementation.

The complementary technique for SDN is NFV that is highly recommended for 5G IoT [7]. Several challenges need to be addressed in 5G-IoT with respect to NFV like Virtualized network functions (VNFs) management and Security and privacy etc. Device connectivity is expected to provide high power 5G-IoT. In device design, power efficiency and appearance are two main challenges. In addition to these challenges, there are other issues such as Multi-vendor interaction, Improper use of Radio Spectrum, Excessive Signing, Hardware distribution resources, less power, and low cost [17]. Spectrum management is an important problem for 5G-enabled IoT [18]. We can explain this issue related to the core technologies of 5G, full-duplex (FD), and cognitive radio (CR). Although, FD can increase network capacity, however, strong distraction is an important problem with this technology. The CR technology will solve the problem of spectrum deficiency through dynamic spectrum management. Power management is a critical issue in the 5G-IoT network. The dramatic increase in IoT devices requires better battery performance due to the un-certainty of battery discharge. There is a requirement of new security techniques at the device and network level in 5G IoT to handle complex applications such as smart city, entertainment, etc. [16]. For the diverse 5G IoT systems, the designers should consider software intrusion for global and local intrusions.

4 Suggested Security Solution

As 5G is able to connect heterogeneous devices and deploying in all smart devices across the world due to some factors such as reduced latency, improved network capacity, and high speed. Although, 5G enabled IoT can set a new path to the distinct sectors such as technological healthcare, connected city, or many more. However, there are some challenges like the number of access points, low through-put, congestion, or security issues due to excessive human traffic. With the help of a secure and distributed ledger, some secure services can be provided. The blockchain integration with IoT enabled 5G can offer massive communication without security breach and develop trust factor among business and people.

4.1 Blockchain Technique

A series of blocks that are interlinked using cryptographic hash functions is known as Blockchain. Each block can have the hash function of the last block with transaction details and timestamp as shown in Fig. 4. Generally, it contains a set of distributed databases of records that can handle all the transactions efficiently and permanently. A blockchain can manage a p2p structure for inter-node transmission and can verify new blocks [19].

4.2 Proposed Solution

In the proposed scenario, there are three levels of 5G enabled IoT such as IoT sensing devices, 5G core networks, and IoT applications as shown in Fig. 5. At the very first level, IoT devices may be able to sense the data from the open environment and share it to the nearby gateway like a router, access point, or the base station. Each IoT device has a blockchain account that can join the blockchain network to commit the transactions. A resource-constrained IoT device can be treated as a lightweight node which keeps a hash key for validation purpose. It may solve the issue of unmanageable data volume and bloat of blockchain. IoT devices can interact with each other with the help of D2D (device to device) communication or through IoT gateways. Core 5G networks are a middleware between the IoT devices and its applications. It can define three services provided by International Telecommunication Union (ITU) which mainly focuses on enhanced Mobile Broadband (eMBB), massive Machine Type Communication (mMTC), and Ultra-Reliable and Low Latency Communication (URLLC). These technologies can be supported by 5G with some parameters such as ultra-low round trip latency (1 ms), high scalability (n connected smart devices), and high data rate (10 Gbps), etc. There is a major challenge with the 5G enabled IoT network is security and privacy which can be exploited by the vulnerability present in the 5G network or at the IoT devices. The proposed scenario can provide two benefits such as i) Generate a highly secure network using blockchain and ii) provides on-demand services for smart

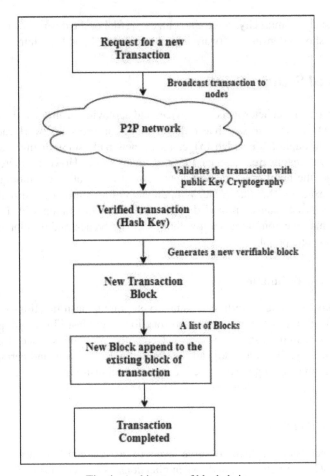

Fig. 4. Architecture of blockchain.

IoT applications. The third level of the proposed scenario is smart IoT applications that provide a direct interface to the end-users. The inclusion of blockchain services ensures its security and privacy in the applied domains which were started in the year 2008 as a virtual cryptocurrency by Satoshi Nakamoto. It can be defined as a public, distributed ledger-based peer-to-peer network [14]. To include the services of blockchain, here we discuss some basic properties and components of a block as follows: Data Blocks: Blockchain is a linear structure of blocks with a linking of another block which can be generated from the previous block. A block may have n number of transactions with a linking of the previous block through a hash key.

Each transaction may contain some basic information about the transaction such as user id, metadata, timestamp, and user signature [20]. A block can combine two or more transaction details and make a block header. A block header has the following information.

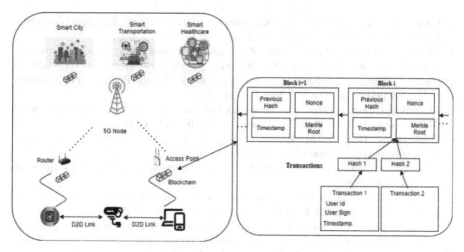

Fig. 5. 5G enabled IoT with blockchain.

i.   Previous hash for the validation,
ii.   Timestamp define the time at which block is generated,
iii. Merkle root refers to the root which stores a group of transaction in each block, and
iv.   Nonce (number only use once) refers to a number which can be added to hash value or encrypt the block below a target level.

5 Conclusion

IoT has gained lots of popularity in a short time period. 5G is one of the key innovations required to enhance the IoT network's performance and provides real-time results. This article presents an overview of IoT and 5G networks including their emerging technologies and challenges. Moreover, the requirements, features, and open challenges have been discussed for 5G enabled IoT. Although, 5G enabled IoT has various key challenges like resource management, security, and interoperability, etc. However, security is one of the prominent issues which need to be resolved. Here, the consolidation of blockchain technology with 5G enable IoT has been proposed which can resolve the security issue. This solution can be implemented or simulated using some open source tools or real-time hardware for better results in the future.

References

1. Agiwal, M., Saxena, N., Roy, A.: Towards connected living: 5G enabled internet of things (IoT). IETE Tech. Rev. **36**(2), 190–202 (2019)
2. Rizwan, A., Malviya, A.K., Kaur, M.J., Mishra. V.P.: Comprehensive survey of key technologies enabling 5G-IoT. In: Proceedings of 2nd International Conference on Advanced Computing and Software Engineering (ICACSE) (2019)
3. Sahar, A., Muzammil, M.B., Jamil, A., Abbas, S.M., Iqbal, U., Touseef. P.: Survey on cache schemes in heterogeneous networks using 5g internet of things. In: Proceedings of the 3rd International Conference on Future Networks and Distributed Systems, pp. 1–8 (2019)

4. Cengiz, K., Aydemir, M.: Next-generation infrastructure and technology issues in 5G systems. J. Commun. Softw. Syst. **14**(1), 33–39 (2018)
5. Abdulla, C., Salah, K., Lima, C., Ray, P.P., Sheltami. T.: Blockchain for 5G: opportunities and challenges. In: 2019 IEEE Globecom Workshops (GC Wkshps), pp. 1–6. IEEE (2019)
6. Chettri, L., Bera, R.: A comprehensive survey on internet of things (IoT) toward 5G wireless systems. IEEE Internet Things J. **7**(1), 16–32 (2019)
7. Woon Hau, C., Fan, Z., Haines. R.: Emerging technologies and research challenges for 5G wireless networks. IEEE Wireless Commun. **21**(2), 106–112 (2014)
8. Čolaković, A., Hadžialić, M.: Internet of things (IoT): a review of enabling technologies, challenges, and open research issues. Comput. Netw. **144**, 17–39 (2018)
9. Waleed, F., et al.: Internet of things (IoT) in 5G wireless communications. IEEE Access **4**, 10310–10314 (2016)
10. Ghosh, A., Maeder, A., Baker, M., Chandramouli, D.: 5G evolution: A view on 5G cellular technology beyond 3GPP release 15. IEEE Access **7**, 127639–127651 (2019)
11. Gupta, N.: Sharma, S., Juneja, P.K., Garg, U.: SDNFV 5G-IoT: a framework for the next generation 5G enabled IoT. In: 2020 International Conference on Advances in Computing, Communication & Materials (ICACCM), pp. 289–294. IEEE (2020)
12. Haris, R.M., Al-Maadeed, S.: Integrating blockchain technology in 5G enabled IoT: a review. In: 2020 IEEE International Conference on Informatics, IoT, and Enabling Technologies (ICIoT), pp. 367–371. IEEE (2020)
13. Höyhtyä, M., Apilo, O., Lasanen, M.: Review of latest advances in 3GPP standardization: D2D communication in 5G systems and its energy consumption models. Future Internet **10**(1), 3 (2018)
14. Sharma, S., Ghanshala, K.K., Mohan. S.: Blockchain-based internet of vehicles (IoV): an efficient secure ad hoc vehicular networking architecture. In: 2019 IEEE 2nd 5G World Forum (5GWF), pp. 452–457. IEEE (2019)
15. Lee, I., Lee, K.: The internet of things (IoT): applications, investments, and challenges for enterprises. Bus. Horiz. **58**(4), 431–440 (2015)
16. Shancang, L., Xu, L.D., Zhao. S.: 5G Internet of things: a survey. J. Ind. Inf. Integ. **10**, 1–9 (2018)
17. Mehmood, Y., Haider, N., Imran, M., Timm-Giel, A., Guizani, M.: M2M communications in 5G: state-of-the-art architecture, recent advances, and research challenges. IEEE Commun. Mag. **55**(9), 194–201 (2017)
18. Sharma, S., Ghanshala, K.K., Mohan, S.: Advanced spectrum management for next-generation vehicular communication: an AI approach. In 2019 IEEE 10th Annual Information Technology, Electronics and Mobile Communication Conference (IEMCON), pp. 0632–0637. IEEE (2019)
19. Mistry, I., Tanwar, S., Tyagi, S., Kumar, N.: Blockchain for 5G-enabled IoT for industrial automation: a systematic review, solutions, and challenges. Mech. Syst. Signal Process. **135**, 106382 (2020)
20. Nguyen, D.C., Pathirana, P.N., Ding, M., Seneviratne, A.: Integration of blockchain and cloud of things: architecture, applications and challenges. IEEE Commun. Surv. Tutor. **22** (2020)

A Performance Discussion of Web Crawler Using Some Advanced Factors

Gaurav Chaudhary[✉] and Vijay Laxmi

Department of Computer Application, Guru Kashi University, Talwandi Sabo, Punjab, India
deanca@gku.ac.in

Abstract. Research is considering the error rate to enhance the accuracy and reducing space and time during web crawling considering advanced parameters such as TTL, frequency of web page visiting and spam reported by users. The proposed work is supposed to minimize the errors by filtering the urls on the bases of advance parameters. This would increase the accuracy during crawling. More over the time and storage space consumption would be reduced due to elimination of use less links. Accuracy in case of proposed work would be more than previous research because previous research did not considered the advanced parameter to filter the list of URL. The simulation that is representing the accuracy, error rate, time and storage comparison has been made using Matlab. Research is considering the frequency of visiting the page. Another parameter for the crawling is weight age of the page i.e. how much time page gets visited by the end users. The page which is most visited get high weight age. Moreover the research work would consider the TTL value of the page. TTL value shows what the expiry time of the page is. It is considering the pages that are having the less expiry time. The web crawling is capable to filter the web page list during searching considering visiting frequency, weight age and TTL value. The filter has also removed URLs that are reported as spam.

Keywords: Web crawling · Weight age · TTL value · Visiting frequency · Storage space · Error rate · Accuracy · Security

1 Introduction

A web crawler is a program which systematically navigates the internet indexing Web-Pages. Tradition web crawlers are suffering from several limitations they are ignoring following key points. Here frequency of visiting page represents most frequently visited web pages must be ranked in order to prioritize during web crawling. Life span of webpage considers the TTL. Time-to-live (TTL) is a value in an Internet Protocol (IP) packet that limits the lifespan. It is defining a date and time at which the content is stale in HTML page headers. There is need to introduce a mechanism of TTL during web crawling so that the pages that are not live should be filtered out. Time spent on web page shows the interest of user. The maximum time spent by user on web page should be considered during deciding the priority of web page for crawling. Some pages are highly

© Springer Nature Singapore Pte Ltd. 2021
A. K. Luhach et al. (Eds.): ICAICR 2020, CCIS 1394, pp. 121–140, 2021.
https://doi.org/10.1007/978-981-16-3653-0_10

insecure but they are considered in list during web crawling the pages that are unsecure must be filtered out. There is need to introduce a mechanism that could eliminate the unsecure pages from the list during web crawling. The most famous application of web crawling is Google's Search Engine. Below is a diagram of the internal workings of a typical web crawler.

Traditional web crawler performs following steps to achieve its goals.

1. Initialize frontier by getting seed URL
2. Dequeue URL from frontier
3. Fetch web page
4. Extract URLS and add to frontier for further dequeue URL from frontier
5. Store page to repository
6. if all linked pages not considerd then get next URL and goto step 2 otherwise stop (Fig. 1)

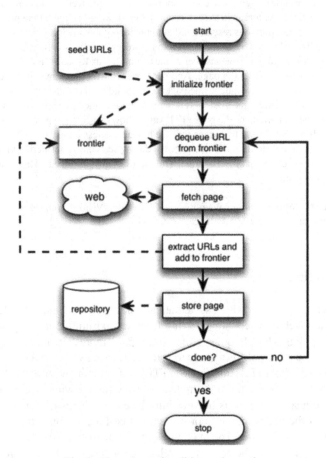

Fig. 1. Flow chart of tradition web crawler

2 Literature Review

In 2020, J. Xu et al. [1] The Application of Web Crawler in City Image Research. Grasping the city image accurately is always a challenge for city manager. They propose a distributed crawler architecture and collect city-related data based on the architecture. Subsequently, several example specific cities are crawled successfully.

In 2019, V. V. Mahale et al. [2] did research on advanced web crawler for deep web interface using binary vector page rank. Experimental results on a set of various domains depicts the agility & accuracy of our proposed crawler framework, which effectively retrieves deep-web interfaces from large-scale sites & attains higher collection rates as compare to the state of art crawlers.

In 2018, Y. Wang et al. [3] Research on LDA Model Algorithm of News-oriented Web Crawler. LDA model algorithm is used to classify keyword texts to reach the purpose of classifying different types of news.

In 2018, S. M. Nakashe et al. [4] Smart Approach to Crawl Web Interfaces Using a Two Stage Framework of Crawler. In present scenario, internet is very important part of our life.

In 2017, Z. Shi et al. [5] The Implementation of Crawling News Page Based on Incremental Web Crawler. This paper implements incremental Python web crawler, uses Scrapy crawler framework, crawls news web pages from mainstream web sites incrementally in real time, and deposits data in the database.

In 2016, M. Kumar et al. [6] Design of a mobile Web crawler for hidden Web. The World Wide Web (WWW) is a diverse source of information. The webpages in the hidden Web are not accessible by following hyperlinks and hence are not indexed by the search engine.

In 2015, N. Kumar et al. [7] Framework for Distributed Semantic Web Crawler. Relevant information retrieval from the www mainly depends on the technique and efficiency of a crawler. So crawlers must be capable enough to understand the text and context of a link which they are going to crawl.

In 2015, S. Sharma et al. [8] The anatomy of web crawlers. World Wide Web (www) is the gigantic and richest source of information. In this paper a survey of different architectures of web crawlers along with their comparisons has been carried out that takes into account various important features like scalability, manageability, page refresh policy, politeness policy etc.

In 2015, A. Gupta et al. [9] Focused web crawlers and its approaches. Rapid growth of WWW poses unpredictable challenges for the crawlers and search engines. In this work, They propose focused web crawler architecture to expose the underneath secrets of web crawling implementation.

In 2015, G. H. Agre et al. [10] Keyword focused web crawler. Users and uses of internet is growing tremendously these days which causing an extreme trouble and efforts at user side to get web pages searched which are as per concern and relevant to user's requirement.

In 2013, A. Aghamohammadi et al. [11] A novel defense mechanism against web crawlers intrusion. In this paper, a novel method to identify web crawlers is proposed to prevent unwanted crawler to access websites. This new method suggests Five-factor identification process to detect unwanted crawlers.

In 2012, K. S. Shetty et al. [12] Symbolic verification of web crawler functionality and its properties. The aim of this paper is to model check the crawling process and crawler properties using a symbolic model checker tool called NuSMV. The basic operation of a hypertext crawler and the crawler properties has been modeled in terms of CTL specification and it is observed that the system takes care of all the constraints by satisfying all the specifications.

In 2012, W. Ma et al. [13] Advanced deep web crawler based on Dom. Due to the fact that large amount of data today can only be stored in deep web. In view of the work done by others on deep web crawlers, it is extinct that no perfect, or even complete crawlers for deep web data has been made.

In 2012, W. Guo et al. [14] A web crawler detection algorithm based on web page member list.

The experiment shows that the new algorithm can detect the unknown crawlers and unfriendly crawlers who do not obey the Standard for Robot Exclusion.

In 2011, O. Jalilian et al. [15] A new fuzzy-based method to weigh the related concepts in semantic focused web crawlers. The results show that the proposed approach presents better precision rate compared with breadth-first and best-first search.

In 2011, F. Ahmadi-Abkenari et al. [16] A clickstream-based web page significance ranking metric for web crawlers. This paper proposes an analysis on clickstream data in order to discover the popularity of Web pages in crawl frontier through proposing the metric itself and presenting the experimental results on ranking the UTM Web pages based on the proposed discussed metric.

In 2010, M. S. Zhao et al. [17] An intelligent topic web crawler based on DTB. This paper proposes an intelligent topic Web crawler based on DTB. Experimental results show that the proposed Web crawler can fetch more topic relevant Web pages by crawling less Web space and in less time.

3   Problem Statement

However there have been several researches in field of web crawling but still there is need of updates. Many researches focused on frequency of visiting web page but ignored the weight age and TTL. Some research considered weight age but they are not considering security. The researchers that consider security are not considering the performance during web crawling. Proposed system is suppose to resolve the issue of web page filtering considering TTL and issue of ranking considering weight age, frequency of web page visiting.

4   Proposed Work

In proposed system the website URL is passed to intelligent crawling system where web crawler perform the web crawling and URL filter is checking for the TTL, weight age and frequency of web page visiting. List of URL is ranked as per weight age and frequency of page visiting. The TTL represent the status of page whether is it is available or not at the time of browsing. Then the accuracy, time consumption, storage and error rate are considered. These factors are considered from existing researches in web crawler.

The proposed work implementation provides the list of URL after filter that leads to high accuracy and less storage space, time and error. The proposed system is to suppose less error prone as compare to existing research. More over it will take lesser space and time.

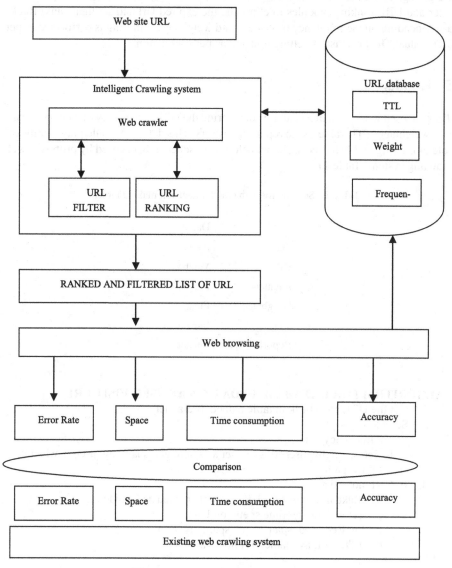

Fig. 2. Process flow of proposed work

The process flow of proposed work has been shown in Fig. 2. Proposed algorithm has considered the frequency of visiting the page. Another parameter for the crawling is weight age of the page represents the time page visited by users. Most visited page is getting high weight age so it is provided rank as per weight age. Proposed work has considered the TTL value of the page. TTL value shows the expiry time of the page to filter it. It is considering the pages that are having the less expiry time. The web crawling is capable to filter the web page list during searching considering visiting frequency, weight age and TTL value. The intelligent web crawling system is consisting of URL filter and URL ranking modules to eliminate the expired Url and set their rank. Ranks are depending on the frequency of visiting and weight age. Filtering is performed as per TTL value. The database is getting updated as per user action.

5   Results

The proposed work need the database considering the URL, Frequency of web base visiting, weightage, TTL value, spam reported by users. This database would play significant role in filtering. Table has been shown below with schema that is used by proposed web crawling system (Table 1).

Table 1. Schema for web crawler decision making table

Field	Data type
Sno	Integer
Url	Varchar
Frequency	Integer
Weightage	Float
TTL	Integer
Reported_spam	Integer

ALGORITHM FOR DATABASE UPDATION AS USER VISIT URL
1. Get the URL and check in table named as crawler
2. Set dataset as
    a. frequency = 1
    b. get_spam_by_user=0 is not set as spam, get_spam_by_user=1 when user set it as spam.
3. If URL not exist
    a. Make new entry for URL in table named as Crawler
    b. Set weightage=time spent on URL.
    c. Set Reported_spam = get_spam_by_user.
    d. TTL= 1 if available, 0 if not available.
Else
    e. Update frequency = Frequency +1
    f. Update weightage= weightage + time spent
    g. Update Reported_spam = Reported_spam + get_spam_by_user
    h. TTL= TTL + (1 if available , 0 if not available)
    End If
4. End.

Following dataset has been generated after implementing above algorithm (Table 2**)**

Table 2. URL dataset

S no	URL	Frequency	Weightage	TTL	Reported_spam
1	http://trdinfotech.com/page1	34	21	32	0
2	http://trdinfotech.com/page2	20	22	17	0
3	http://trdinfotech.com/page3	21	34	13	0
4	http://trdinfotech.com/page4	6	66	4	0
5	http://trdinfotech.com/page5	7	55	4	0
6	http://trdinfotech.com/page6	9	44	5	0
7	http://trdinfotech.com/page7	50	33	29	0
8	http://trdinfotech.com/page8	70	55	12	0
9	http://trdinfotech.com/page9	21	32	13	0
10	http://trdinfotech.com/page10	43	65	34	0
11	http://trdinfotech.com/page11	100	34	80	0
12	http://trdinfotech.com/page12	50	23	40	0
13	http://trdinfotech.com/page13	50	44	43	0
14	http://trdinfotech.com/page14	70	32	56	0
15	http://trdinfotech.com/page15	4	44	3	0
16	http://trdinfotech.com/page16	6	32	3	0
17	http://trdinfotech.com/page17	2	54	1	0
18	http://trdinfotech.com/page18	1	76	0	1
19	http://trdinfotech.com/page19	8	77	0	0
20	http://trdinfotech.com/page20	9	45	0	0
21	http://trdinfotech.com/page21	40	76	0	2
22	http://trdinfotech.com/page22	100	75	0	2
23	http://trdinfotech.com/page23	70	12	35	2

The line graph considering above listing is plotted below (Fig. 3)

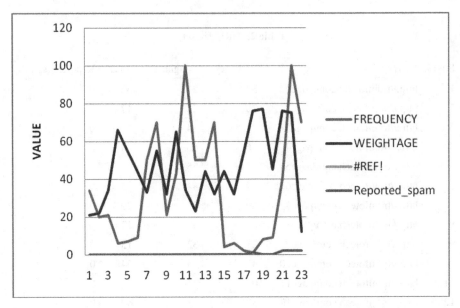

Fig. 3. Graphical representation of line chart for dataset of visited sites

SQL QUERY TO CHECK THE RANK CONSIDERING FREQUENCY ONLY
SELECT * FROM CRAWLER where REPORTED >= 1 ORDER BY FREQUENCY
DESC
See Table 3.

Table 3. Rank considering frequency

S no	URL	Frequency	Weightage	TTL
11	http://trdinfotech.com/page11	100	34	80
8	http://trdinfotech.com/page8	70	55	12
14	http://trdinfotech.com/page14	70	32	56
7	http://trdinfotech.com/page7	50	33	29
12	http://trdinfotech.com/page12	50	23	40
13	http://trdinfotech.com/page13	50	44	43
10	http://trdinfotech.com/page10	43	65	34
1	http://trdinfotech.com/page1	34	21	32
3	http://trdinfotech.com/page3	21	34	13

(continued)

Table 3. (*continued*)

S no	URL	Frequency	Weightage	TTL
9	http://trdinfotech.com/page9	21	32	13
2	http://trdinfotech.com/page2	20	22	17
6	http://trdinfotech.com/page6	9	44	5
20	http://trdinfotech.com/page20	9	45	0
19	http://trdinfotech.com/page19	8	77	0
5	http://trdinfotech.com/page5	7	55	4
4	http://trdinfotech.com/page4	6	66	4
16	http://trdinfotech.com/page16	6	32	3
15	http://trdinfotech.com/page15	4	44	3
17	http://trdinfotech.com/page17	2	54	1
18	http://trdinfotech.com/page18	1	76	0

Line diagram considering above chart (Fig. 4).

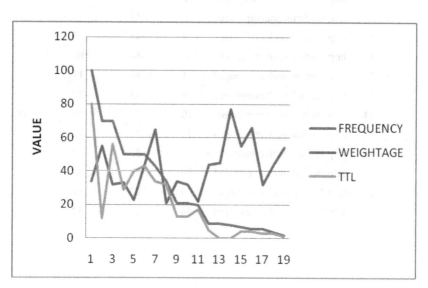

Fig. 4. Graphical representation of line chart for dataset of visited sites consider only frequency

SQL QUERY TO CHECK THE RANK CONSIDERING WEIGHTAGE ONLY
SELECT * FROM CRAWLER where REPORTED >= 1 ORDER BY WEIGHTAGE DESC
See Table 4 and Fig. 5.

Table 4. Rank considering weight age

S no	URL	Frequency	Weightage	TTL
19	http://trdinfotech.com/page19	8	77	0
18	http://trdinfotech.com/page18	1	76	0
22	http://trdinfotech.com/page22	100	75	0
4	http://trdinfotech.com/page4	6	66	4
10	http://trdinfotech.com/page10	43	65	34
8	http://trdinfotech.com/page8	70	55	12
5	http://trdinfotech.com/page5	7	55	4
17	http://trdinfotech.com/page17	2	54	1
20	http://trdinfotech.com/page20	9	45	0
13	http://trdinfotech.com/page13	50	44	43
6	http://trdinfotech.com/page6	9	44	5
15	http://trdinfotech.com/page15	4	44	3
11	http://trdinfotech.com/page11	100	34	80
3	http://trdinfotech.com/page3	21	34	13
7	http://trdinfotech.com/page7	50	33	29
14	http://trdinfotech.com/page14	70	32	56
9	http://trdinfotech.com/page9	21	32	13
16	http://trdinfotech.com/page16	6	32	3
12	http://trdinfotech.com/page12	50	23	40
2	http://trdinfotech.com/page2	20	22	17
1	http://trdinfotech.com/page1	34	21	32

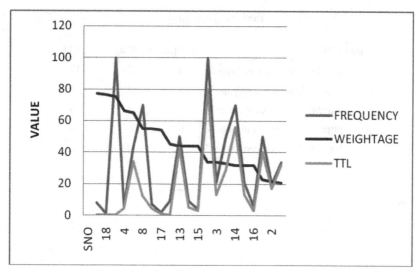

Fig. 5. Graphical representation of line chart for dataset of visited sites consider only Weightage

SQL QUERY TO CHECK THE RANK AND FILTERING DURING WEB CRAWLING

SELECT * FROM CRAWLER WHERE REPORTED >= 1 AND TTL > (FREQUENCY/2) ORDER BY FREQUENCY DESC, WEIGHTAGE DESC, TTL DESC
The list of url is represented after eliminating TTL with less than half of frequency and ranking as per frequency and weightage (Table 5 and Fig 6).

Table 5. Table after filter on basis spam reported and TTL frequency

S no	URL	Frequency	Weightage	TTL
11	http://trdinfotech.com/page11	100	34	80
14	http://trdinfotech.com/page14	70	32	56
13	http://trdinfotech.com/page13	50	44	43
7	http://trdinfotech.com/page7	50	33	29
12	http://trdinfotech.com/page12	50	23	40
10	http://trdinfotech.com/page10	43	65	34
1	http://trdinfotech.com/page1	34	21	32
3	http://trdinfotech.com/page3	21	34	13
9	http://trdinfotech.com/page9	21	32	13

(*continued*)

Table 5. (*continued*)

S no	URL	Frequency	Weightage	TTL
2	http://trdinfotech.com/page2	20	22	17
6	http://trdinfotech.com/page6	9	44	5
5	http://trdinfotech.com/page5	7	55	4
4	http://trdinfotech.com/page4	6	66	4
15	http://trdinfotech.com/page15	4	44	3

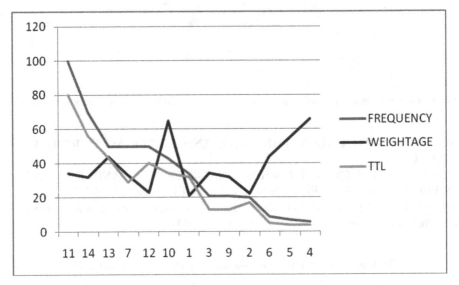

Fig. 6. Graphical representation as per proposed work considering all parameters

6   Comparison Chart

Following chart is representing the optimization, error, space consumption and time consumption in case of proposed work and previous work (Table 6).

Table 6. Comparison chart representing accuracy, error, space and time

	Previous	Proposed
Filtered data set	23 URLs	14 URLs
Data crawling time	557 ms	509 ms
Storage	997 Byte	605 Byte

Results are depending on the size of website and number user visits the web page. The accuracy, error, time and space are influenced by several factors such as time spent by users and number of visits by them. Moreover the positive and negative feedback is also influencing the results. Comparison between influencing factors for accuracy, error, space and time in previous and proposed work has been shown in following Table 7.

Table 7. Rank considering influencing factors of accuracy for proposed and previous work frequency

	Proposed work	Previous work
Accuracy	Proposed work filters the urls that are not safe and not visited by users frequently thus the accuracy is high. The result may vary site to site. The accuracy is influenced by number of pages and number of time the visitors have opened website. If the website is frequently visited by visitors and consisting feedbacks from users then crawler would be capable to produce more accurate results. In proposed work, Data set reproduced the efficient data with 14 urls. Hence it proves that data is more accurate than the previous work	The previous work has considered limited parameter. Thus the list of url crawled is consisting irrelevant data many times (here irrelevant data seems as the data which has less number of user hits in search engine). i.e. urls that are not of user interest are considered during crawling. In traditional Web crawler, we are considered 23 urls

Error Rate

As we know that accuracy and error rate is inversely proportional to each other. When accuracy of data get increased then error rate get decreased and vise versa (Tables 8 and 9).

Table 8. Represent influencing factors of error rate improvement for proposed and previous work

	Proposed work	Previous work
Error rate improvement	In proposed work, we have used some filters to make the crawler's data more relevant. Thus accuracy has been improved and the error rate get reduced. In proposed work, We can calculate the error rate improvement using the accuracy	In the previous work, many criteria are used like frequency, priority of the page etc. In traditional web crawler, all the links are updated as per the schedule run. Hence complete data set get crawled every time and possibility of error rate get high. In traditional work, we consider that error rate is X

Error Rate improvement Calculation:
Let Error Rate in Previous Work = X
ERROR_PREVIOUS=23-x=E1
ERROR_PROPOSED=14-x=E2
If
E1 : E2
23-X : 14-X
23-X> 14-X
E1>E2
This means error in case of previous work is more than error in proposed work
Space Occupied:

Table 9. Represent influencing factors of space occupied for proposed and previous work

	Proposed work	Previous work
Storage	The space consumption is less due to filter of url considering security, TTL, frequency of revisiting web pages. As per our data set, in proposed work space occupied is 605 byte	As no filtering has been performed the space consumption is high. As per our data set, in previous work space occupied is 997 byte

Graphical Representation
See Fig. 7.

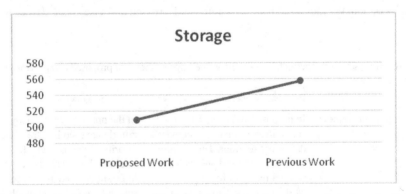

Fig. 7. Graphical representation of line chart for dataset of space occupied of crawler links

Time Consumption
See Table 10.

Table 10. Represent influencing factors of data crawled time of proposed and previous work

	Proposed work	Previous work
Data crawling time	On other hand the filtered list of URL takes comparatively less time. In Proposed Work, crawling time of the links is 509 ms	The huge list of URL that is not filtered, is shown that is taking lot of time. In previous Work, crawling time of the links is 557 ms

Graphical Representation
See Fig. 8.

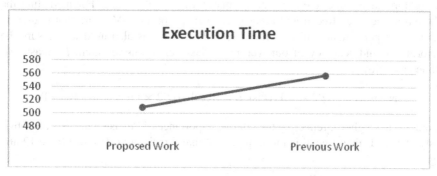

Fig. 8. Graphical representation of line chart for crawling time of the crawler links

Simulation Performance and Accuracy
The performance and accuracy of web page classifier is showing availability of considered crawler. Thus, it is important to check performance of web page classifier. Several classification tasks have been evaluated with the support of Precision, Recall, and F-Measure. Precision for text classifying is the fraction of documents assigned which is relevant to class. It is measuring how well it is going to rejecting or eliminating irrelevant webpage links. Recall is considered as ratio of relevant documents that have been assigned using classifier. Classifier is measuring how well it is doing at check relevant web pages. We assume that T is the set of relevant web pages in test dataset; U is the set of relevant web pages assigned by classifier (Table 11).

Precision = (|U ∩ T|/|U|)*100
Recall = (|U ∩ T|/|T|)*100
In research U = 23
T1 (Previous case) = 21
T2 (Proposed case) = 14

Table 11. Parameter chart

Parameters	Traditional work	Proposed work
U	23	23
T	21	14
Precision	2/23 = 0.08	9/23 = 0.39
Recall	2/21 = 1 = 0.09	9/14 = 0.64

The Recall and Precision play very important role in the performance and accuracy evaluation of classifier. However, they have certain defects; for example, when improving one performance value, the other performance value will decline. For mediating the relationship between Recall and Precision, Lewis proposes *F*-Measure that is used to evaluate the performance of classifier. Here, *F*-Measure is also used to measure the performance and accuracy of our web page classifier in this research. *F*-Measure is defined as follows:

$$\text{F-Measure} = ((\beta 2 + 1)\text{Precision} \times \text{Recall})/(\beta 2 \times \text{Precision} + \text{Recall})$$

where β is a weight for reflecting the relative importance of Precision and Recall. Obviously, if $\beta > 1$, then Recall is more important than Precision; if $0 < \beta$ (Table 12 and Fig. 9).

Table 12. F-measure chart

β	Previous	Proposed
1	0.0847	0.4847
2	0.0878	0.5673
3	0.0889	0.6014
4	0.0893	0.6167
5	0.0896	0.6246
6	0.0897	0.6291
7	0.0898	0.6319
8	0.0898	0.6337
9	0.0899	0.6350
10	0.0899	0.6360

Matlab script to simulate F measure

```
P1=0.08
P2=0.39
R1=0.09
R2=0.64
for b=1:10
   x[b]=b;
   F1[b]=(((b*b)+1)* P1 * R1)/(b*b*P1 + R1)
   F2[b]=(((b*b)+1)* P2 * R2)/(b*b*P2 + R2)
end

hold on

plot(x,F1,'r+-')

plot(x,F2,'b+-')

title('Comparison between traditional and proposed work')

ylabel('F measure');

xlabel('B')
```

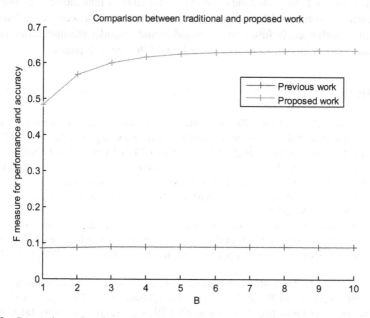

Fig. 9. Comparison of performance and accuracy between traditional and proposed work

The performance and accuracy of focused crawler can also reflect the availability of crawling directly. Perhaps most crucial evaluation of focused crawler is to measure rate at which relevant web pages are acquired and how effectively irrelevant web pages are filtered out from the crawler.

7 Conclusion

It has been concluded that proposed work has reduced the space and time consumption. Moreover the error rate has been reduced. The accuracy is comparatively high. Research has successfully count the frequency of visiting the page along with weight age of the page that represents the time page visited by users. This work has used TTL value. This value has helped to find expiry time of the page to filter it. Proposed system is found capable to filter web page list during searching considering visiting frequency, weight age and TTL value. The intelligent web crawling system has successfully performed URL filter and URL ranking modules and eliminated the expired Url and set their rank. The system is intelligent as the database is updated as per user action to store the TTL value, weight age and frequency of page visiting. The filter has also eliminated the urls that have been reported as span.

8 Future Scope

However proposed intelligent web crawling system is performing URL filter and URL ranking modules and eliminated the expired Url and set their rank along with integration of the security. It is observed that several web sites are acting as virus carrier and influence the system of web user. In future the proposal would consider the integration of more security and prioritization mechanism to rank and filter the web pages.

References

1. Xu, J., Duan, C., Du, L., Li, M.: The application of web crawler in city image research. In: 2020 IEEE 5th International Conference on Cloud Computing and Big Data Analytics, ICCCBDA 2020, pp. 270–274 (2020). https://doi.org/10.1109/ICCCBDA49378.2020.9095599
2. Mahale, V.V., Dhande, M.T., Pandit, A.V.: Advanced web crawler for deep web interface using binary vector page rank. In: Proceedings of the International Conference on I-SMAC (IoT Social, Mobile, Analytics and Cloud), I-SMAC 2018, pp. 500–503 (2019). https://doi.org/10.1109/I-SMAC.2018.8653765
3. Wang, Y., Hong, Z., Shi, M.: Research on LDA model algorithm of news-oriented web crawler. In: Proceedings of the 17th IEEE/ACIS International Conference on Computer and Information Science, ICIS 2018, pp. 748–753 (2018). https://doi.org/10.1109/ICIS.2018.8466502
4. Nakashe, S.M., Kolhe, K.R.: Smart approach to crawl web interfaces using a two stage framework of crawler. In: Proceedings of the 2018 4th International Conference on Computing Communication Control and Automation, ICCUBEA 2018, pp. 1–6 (2018). https://doi.org/10.1109/ICCUBEA.2018.8697592

5. Shi, Z., Shi, M., Lin, W.: The implementation of crawling news page based on incremental web crawler. In: Proceedings of the 4th International Conference on Applied Computing and Information Technology. 3rd International Conference on Computational Science/Intelligence and Applied Informatics. 1st International Conference on Big Data, Cloud Computing, Data Science & Engineering, ACIT-CSII-BCD 2016, pp. 348–351 (2017). https://doi.org/10.1109/ACIT-CSII-BCD.2016.073

6. Kumar, M., Bhatia, R.: Design of a mobile web crawler for hidden web. In: 2016 3rd International Conference on Recent Advances in Information Technology, RAIT 2016, pp. 186–190 (2016). https://doi.org/10.1109/RAIT.2016.7507899

7. Kumar, N., Singh, M.: Framework for distributed semantic web crawler. In: Proceedings of the 2015 International Conference on Computational Intelligence and Communication Networks, CICN 2015, pp. 1403–1407 (2016). https://doi.org/10.1109/CICN.2015.272

8. Sharma, S., Gupta, P.: The anatomy of web crawlers. In: International Conference on Computing, Communication & Automation, ICCCA 2015, pp. 849–853 (2015). https://doi.org/10.1109/CCAA.2015.7148493

9. Gupta, A., Anand, P.: Focused web crawlers and its approaches. In: 2015 1st International Conference on Futuristic Trends on Computational Analysis and Knowledge Management, ABLAZE 2015, pp. 619–622 (2015). https://doi.org/10.1109/ABLAZE.2015.7154936

10. Agre, G.H., Mahajan, N.V.: Keyword focused web crawler. In: 2nd International Conference on Electronics and Communication Systems, ICECS 2015, pp. 1089–1092 (2015). https://doi.org/10.1109/ECS.2015.7124749

11. Aghamohammadi, A., Eydgahi, A.: A novel defense mechanism against web crawlers intrusion. In: 2013 International Conference on Electronics, Computer and Computation, ICECCO 2013, pp. 269–272 (2013). https://doi.org/10.1109/ICECCO.2013.6718280

12. Shetty, K.S., Bhat, S., Singh, S.: Symbolic verification of web crawler functionality and its properties. In: 2012 International Conference on Computer Communication and Informatics, ICCCI 2012 (2012). https://doi.org/10.1109/ICCCI.2012.6158649

13. Ma, W., Chen, X., Shang, W.: Advanced deep web crawler based on Dom. In: Proceedings of the 2012 5th International Joint Conference on Computational Sciences and Optimization, CSO 2012, pp. 605–609 (2012). https://doi.org/10.1109/CSO.2012.138

14. Guo, W., Zhong, Y., Xie, J.: A web crawler detection algorithm based on web page member list. In: Proceedings of the 2012 4th International Conference on Intelligent Human-Machine Systems and Cybernetics, IHMSC 2012, vol. 1, pp. 189–192 (2012). https://doi.org/10.1109/IHMSC.2012.54

15. Jalilian, O., Khotanlou, H.: A new fuzzy-based method to weigh the related concepts in semantic focused web crawlers. In: ICCRD 2011 - 2011 3rd International Conference on Computer Research and Development, vol. 3, pp. 23–27 (2011). https://doi.org/10.1109/ICCRD.2011.5764237

16. Ahmadi-Abkenari, F., Selamat, A.: A clickstream-based web page significance ranking metric for web crawlers. In: 2011 5th Malaysian Conference in Software Engineering, MySEC 2011, no. 1, pp. 223–228 (2011). https://doi.org/10.1109/MySEC.2011.6140674

17. Zhao, M.S., Zhu, P., He, T.C.: An intelligent topic web crawler based on DTB. In: Proceedings of the 2010 International Conference on Web Information Systems and Mining, WISM 2010, vol. 1, no. 1, pp. 84–86 (2010). https://doi.org/10.1109/WISM.2010.155

18. Shekhar, S., Agrawal, R., Arya, K.V.: An architectural framework of a crawler for retrieving highly relevant web documents by filtering replicated web collections. In: ACE 2010 - 2010 International Conference on Advances in Computer Engineering, pp. 29–33 (2010). https://doi.org/10.1109/ACE.2010.64

19. Wang, H.C., Ruan, S.H., Tang, Q.J.: The implementation of a web crawler URL filter algorithm based on caching. In: 2nd International Workshop on Computer Science and Engineering, WCSE 2009, vol. 2, pp. 453–456 (2009). https://doi.org/10.1109/WCSE.2009.851

20. Xiang, P., Tian, K., Huang, Q.: A framework of deep web crawler. In: Proceedings of the 27th Chinese Control Conference, CCC, pp. 582–586 (2008). https://doi.org/10.1109/CHICC. 2008.4604881

21. Kaewmarin, V., Arch-Int, N., Arch-Int, S.: Semantic web service discovery and integration using service search crawler. In: 2008 International Conference on Computational Intelligence for Modelling Control & Automation, CIMCA 2008, pp. 884–888 (2008). https://doi.org/10. 1109/CIMCA.2008.78

22. Akilandeswari, J., Gopalan, N.P.: An architectural framework of a crawler for locating deep web repositories using learning multi-agent systems. In: Proceedings of the 3rd International Conference on Internet and Web Applications and Services, ICIW 2008, pp. 558–562 (2008). https://doi.org/10.1109/ICIW.2008.94

Internet of Things in Healthcare: A Review

Batyrkhan Omarov[1,2(✉)], Altynzer Baiganova[3], Saya Sapakova[4],
Zhanna Yessengaliyeva[5], Sapar Issayev[6], Saltanat Baitenova[1], and Bota Maxutova[1]

[1] Al-Farabi Kazakh National University, Almaty, Kazakhstan
[2] Khoja Akhmet Yassawi International Kazakh-Turkish University, Turkistan, Kazakhstan
[3] Aktobe Regional University named after K. Zhubanov, Aktobe, Kazakhstan
[4] International Information Technology University, Almaty, Kazakhstan
[5] L.N. Gumilyov, Eurasian National University, Astana, Kazakhstan
[6] Kazakh National Women's Teacher Training University, Almaty, Kazakhstan

Abstract. Currently, we are witnessing rapid changes in the modern socio-economic system through the introduction of various digital technologies. The healthcare sector is no exception, but on the contrary, digitalization of this industry leads to optimization of medical services, improvement of quality control and reduction of costs. In the article, the authors consider the problems and prospects of it in the healthcare industry in the world. In the context of modern digital transformation processes, the healthcare system is being modernized in the main areas that stimulate technological progress - the use of medical information systems, the introduction of Internet of medical things products, advanced big data Analytics and the practical application of expert medical systems. In conclusion, the main conclusions based on the results of reviews in the use of IoT in the health sector are given.

Keywords: Internet of things · Internet of medical things · IoT · IoMT · Information systems · Healthcare · Medicine

1 Introduction

The active introduction of information technologies in the health sector has led to a fundamental change in the quality of life of people. Currently, the problem of increasing health care costs around the world is becoming more acute. In this regard, it has become vital to use low-cost and effective health care solutions. All these conditions contributed to the development of a special type of health protection – mobile health (mHealth) [1–3].

The Internet of things (IoT) and large-volume data analysis are becoming increasingly popular for e-and mobile health services [4]. Along with the obvious advantages, there are also complex situations that require consistent, safe, flexible, and energy-efficient solutions.

Information technologies in medicine are faced with the task of creating new replicated monitoring solutions for personal diagnostics of a person's condition, which will allow a qualitative "leap" from an expensive reactive model of health care to a preventive

© Springer Nature Singapore Pte Ltd. 2021
A. K. Luhach et al. (Eds.): ICAICR 2020, CCIS 1394, pp. 141–150, 2021.
https://doi.org/10.1007/978-981-16-3653-0_11

model, thanks to which medical organizations and/or private practitioners will be able to predict changes in people's health and provide them with more effective care. The technological basis of these technologies should be sensors ("smart" sensors), fast-acting methods of data transmission (network information technologies, health management technologies) and influencing devices for monitoring the main vital functions of the body, as well as devices for visualizing the internal structure and parameters of human tissues and organs, small-sized sensors of physical and physiological parameters of a person [5]. This technological transition with mass implementation should help reduce health care costs and, at the same time, improve the quality of life of patients [6]. To solve these problems, it is necessary to develop new and/or improve existing technologies, which will be based on methods for non-contact diagnosis of a person's condition with a correction system in case of a detected deviation. For example, non-invasive monitoring of blood sugar levels with the order of administration of the required amount of insulin or glucose in cases of Hyper-or hypoglycemia, respectively. However, until the predicted mass introduction of fully functioning effective monitoring technologies that minimize the participation of medical personnel, medical applications of the Internet of things will be in demand for some time, providing a reduction in space-time communications between patients and medical personnel.

Any business project implemented in the target IoT segment requires an understanding of its key parameters, features, preferred economic models, user preferences, a special technological map and innovative processes of this particular segment. Figure 1 illustrates IoT market segments.

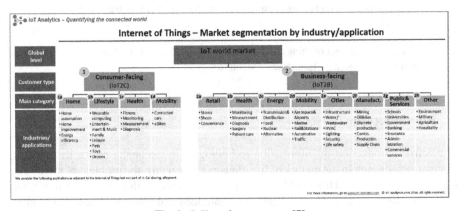

Fig. 1. IoT market segments [7]

In this review, we describe application of IoT in medicine. Figure 2 illustrates advantages of IoT in healthcare sector.

The demand for Internet of things (IoT) solutions in healthcare is growing as healthcare systems around the world seek to implement the latest tools, devices, and remote monitoring technologies that enable more effective disease tracking, early diagnosis, and treatment.

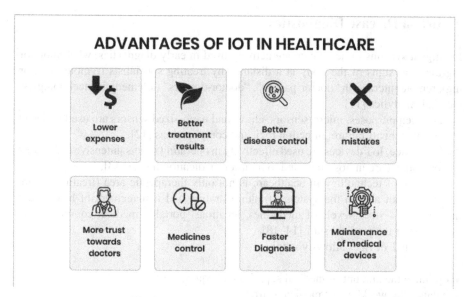

Fig. 2. Advantages of IoT in healthcare [8].

Shujaat Ali, founder and editor-in-chief of Medical Travel Market, predicts that over the next five years, the healthcare-related IoT market will more than double in size over the next five years, reaching more than us $ 135 billion (125 billion euros) [9]. Figure 3 demonstrates IoT market prediction in healthcare sector.

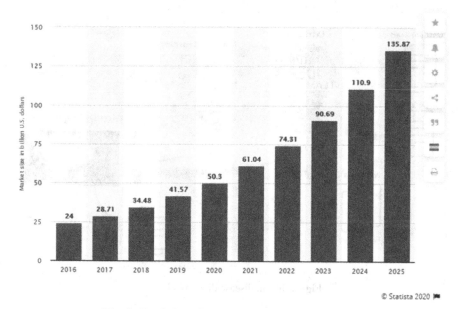

Fig. 3. Prediction of IoT in healthcare market size [10]

2 IoT in Disease Diagnostics

Intelligent systems in healthcare are actively used in early diagnostics, when monitoring the vital signs of the body at a distance by treating specialists (remote monitoring), remote interaction "doctor-patient", "doctor-doctors" (telemedicine technologies), medical Analytics [11].

For such purposes, micro-sensors, chips, and nano-sized sensors are used to detect, for example, heart failure, infection foci, and complications [12].

In practice, IoT devices are used effectively in operating rooms, intensive care wards, postoperative care in hospitals, and to monitor medication intake [13].

The use of technology in healthcare is not only therapeutic area (treatment, care, diagnosis), but also in the system of administration and management of health care, monitoring of stock levels of medicines, locations, portable medical equipment, the evaluation of the medical staff [14–18].

Using IoT devices allows you to:

- optimize the amount of medical supplies and equipment;
- balance the workload of medical staff;
- reduce the cost of treatment;
- improve the effectiveness of medical activities in the direction of diagnostics, monitoring, and obtaining qualified advice;
- increases the mobility of hospital employees and their productivity;
- faster processing of patient data;
- reduces the risk of error and miscalculation due to the human factor;

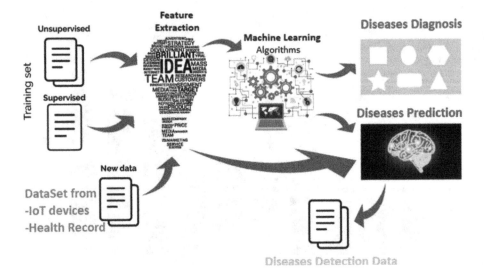

Fig. 4. IoT in disease diagnosis [19]

Figure 4 demonstrates diseases diagnosis and diseases prediction system structure that can be used in medicine. In this system, IoT devices collect data, and machine learning algorithms ensures intelligence by diagnosis or predict diseases.

3 IoT for Health Monitoring

One of the most obvious and popular applications of Internet of things technologies in healthcare has become remote health monitoring, or telemedicine. In some cases, patients do not need to visit emergency departments or their doctor. The work of medical professionals is usually performed by different devices in a compartment with different applications. Doctors use remote monitoring to draw more informed conclusions about patients' health. With the help of telemedicine reduces the cost of a patient on a hospital visit [20].

Internet of medical things helps to monitor the condition of equipment in wards, monitor the condition of serious patients using special sensors. For example, such devices can track and monitor the health of patients from the moment they arrive at the clinic, collect and update data about them, without involving Junior medical staff (which saves time and resources) [21].

According to the company's analysts, the greatest potential for IoT technologies now lies in monitoring the condition of patients both at a significant distance from the doctor and directly in the hospital. In the second place in the category of demand, the use of sensors for tracking the state of medical equipment is expected. Such devices should inform engineers about problems, so they can be quickly repaired and continue to treat patients with minimal downtime. In addition to monitoring, Ios devices will increasingly be used for administrative and management tasks. For example, they can be used for monitoring and accounting of medicines and equipment used, experts of Meticulous Research emphasize.

Smart sensors that are used in medical institutions are most often located in hospital beds. For example, SMI produces special sensors that prevent bedsores in severe patients. They measure the pressure on the mattress and help to distribute it correctly so that a person does not have ulcers. There are also devices that monitor your heart rate and breathing. They monitor patients' vital signs and alert hospital staff if critical changes occur [22].

And Florida Hospital Celebration Health uses special badges with sensors that track the movement of all people inside the clinic: both medical workers and patients. This allows you to optimize the work inside the premises: to place warehouses with medicines with maximum convenience, to make staff work schedules, to distribute patients to wards. Figure 5 illustrates example of health monitoring using internet of things.

4 IoT in Predictive Medicine

Technologies based on big data processing can bring modern medicine to a fundamentally new level. With the help of Autonomous monitoring of patient indicators, specialists will be able to prevent the appearance of diseases instead of fighting them after the fact [24]. Processed and structured data allow specialists to calculate the effectiveness of

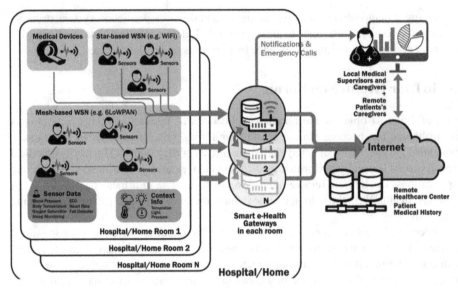

Fig. 5. IoT in health monitoring [23]

different stages of treatment, evaluate the interaction of drugs and reduce the likelihood of medical errors. For example, computer vision in symbiosis with machine learning is able to analyze medical images with a high degree of accuracy and draw the doctor's attention to areas with possible pathology [25].

Combining the capabilities of medical IoT sensors, which collect data, and machine learning, which accumulates and analyzes it in streaming mode, will help to ensure that the individual approach will become a ubiquitous phenomenon. Today, personalized medications are used mainly for the treatment of patients with cancer and autoimmune diseases, and most often we are talking about the selection of individual dosage of active substances [26]. A thorough change in the formula is a rarer phenomenon: medicines can be made according to a special prescription, but, in addition to serious monetary costs, you will need to pass a whole series of genetic and molecular tests. With permanent medical monitoring using sensors, there is no need to constantly take tests [27].

According to experts, the most revolutionary idea in the field of big data medicine will be the digital avatar technology-a copy of a physical object (an organ, medical equipment, and an entire hospital system), which at the same time retains all the functionality. Simply put, special sensors located on the human body (or inside it) transmit data about their anatomy, physiology, and genome to a third-party system [28] They accumulate in one place and are transformed into a virtual avatar, which is constantly updated, filled with new information and eventually becoming almost one hundred percent copy of the original.

5   IoT in Storage of Medicine

Installing temperature and humidity sensors in cold rooms and medicine storage cabinets allows you to remotely monitor conditions and quickly respond to deviations from the norm. The module integrated into the sensor transmits information over the IOT network using LoRaWAN technology [25]. The data is sent directly to the responsible employee for taking appropriate measures.

Sensors are wireless devices and can be installed almost anywhere, regardless of the location of the object (indoors or outdoors), without additional repairs. Devices are independent of stationary power sources, so data will come even if the refrigerator itself or the room where it is located is de-energized [29].

The solution is especially in demand for objects with a large number of storage locations distributed across the territory, where they have to be checked manually. This can include not only medical institutions, but also pharmacies, warehouses, and pharmaceutical companies.

6   Challenges

Internet of things in medicine and other medical technologies of the future can signifi-cantly improve the lives of millions of people, but for their widespread use to become possible, it will be necessary to solve the security problem. The neurostimulator sends electrical signals to certain areas of the brain, which helps to relieve the symptoms of Parkinson's disease, obsessive-compulsive disorder, major depressive disorders and other diseases. Modern neurostimulator implants are controlled remotely using special SOFTWARE on professional tablets of treating doctors. If the channel between the stimulator, the SOFTWARE, and the network is not secure, data can be intercepted: steal confidential information or cause the patient significant physical discomfort. Other groups of gadgets have similar vulnerabilities, such as insulin pumps synced with a smartphone.

A group of functional neurosurgery at the University of Oxford, led by Lori Pyecroft, found that doctors often use tablets that control implants for other purposes: they access the Internet through unsecured communication channels, install third-party programs and applications, and most devices have factory passwords. The Pycroft team even introduced a new term, brain jacking, to describe the consequences that a negligent attitude to security can lead to.

In addition to basic security, an ethical issue remains unresolved. By allowing appli-cations to access personal data, for example, the user cannot know exactly how their developer will use it later. Some experts believe that commercial companies may trans-fer patient data to third-party organizations to advertise certain medications and services, or share it with recruiters, banks, and insurers, leading to higher interest rates and job rejections. Apple, Google, and Microsoft claim to use them exclusively for collecting statistics and research when developing new IT products for health.

7   Discussion and Conclusion

IoT technologies in the field of medicine and healthcare have significant potential to improve the availability and quality of medical services. The presence of smartphones in the vast majority of urban residents is a material and technological Foundation for the start of mass implementation of medical applications that connect medical personnel and patients. In the future, an informatized healthcare system based on IoT will allow you to ergonomically combine information resources into a single space of analyzed data and effectively reduce space-time costs when implementing measures for the prevention and treatment of socially significant diseases. Due to the large number of applications that implement health services using IoT technologies, there are different requirements for storing and transmitting information. To implement a differentiated approach to managing e-health systems based on IoT, a hybrid architecture using foggy computing technologies is proposed. With the growing volume of information and the use of cloud services, cloud computing will play a key role in reducing latency, as well as improving the usability of medical IoT systems.

Among the factors contributing to the increase in medical IoT costs on a global scale, experts include the growing number of chronic diseases, the introduction of favorable initiatives by governments in various countries, and the evolution of artificial intelligence technologies.

The main barriers to market development are the weak efficiency of implementing IoT solutions, data privacy and security issues, as well as insufficient technical knowledge in the market as a whole.

The fastest growing segment Of the IOT market in the healthcare sector in ResearchAndMarkets is called systems and software that provide a high level of data security and visual research.

In terms of geographical growth, the Asia-Pacific region is leading due to the growing number of hospitals and surgical centers in this market [3].

The study says that the Internet of things in healthcare is used in tasks such as clinical work, workflow optimization, network visualization, telemedicine, drug management, and inpatient patient monitoring.

References

1. Nilsen, W., et al.: Advancing the science of mHealth. J. Health Commun. **17**(sup1), 5–10 (2012)
2. Omarov, B., et al.: Applying face recognition in video surveillance security systems. In: Mazzara, M., Bruel, J., Meyer, B., Petrenko, A. (eds.) Software Technology: Methods and Tools. LNCS, vol. 11771, pp. 271–280. Springer, Cham (2019). https://doi.org/10.1007/978-3-030-29852-4_22
3. World Health Organization: mHealth: New Horizons for Health Through Mobile Technologies. World Health Organization, Geneva (2011)
4. Fong, B., Fong, A.C.M., Li, C.K. Internet of things in smart ambulance and emergency medicine. In: Internet of Things A to Z: Technologies and Applications, pp. 475–506 (2018)
5. Cecil, J.: Internet of Things (IoT)-based cyber–physical frameworks for advanced manufacturing and medicine. In: Internet of Things and Data Analytics Handbook, pp. 545–561 (2017)
6. Wang, L., Li, K., Chen, X.: Design and implementation of remote medicine monitoring system based on internet of things. In: Proceedings of the 4th International Conference on Computer Science and Application Engineering, pp. 1–6, October 2020
7. https://iot-analytics.com/iot-market-segments-analysis/
8. https://www.mobileappdaily.com/what-can-iot-do-for-healthcare

9. https://www.7wdata.be/internet-of-things/iot-in-healthcare-8-examples-from-around-the-world/
10. https://medicaltravelmarket.com/
11. Dikovic, L.: Internet of things in healthcare as an innovative form of personalized medicine. In: Encyclopedia of Information Science and Technology, 5th edn., pp. 1933–1943. IGI Global.
12. Yu, L., Huang, F., Yang, Y., Tao, Q., Shen, T., Zhang, L.: Key technologies of traditional Chinese medicine traceability based on internet of things. In: Mao, R., Wang, H., Xie, X., Lu, Z. (eds.) 5th International Conference of Pioneering Computer Scientists, Engineers and Educators. CCIS, vol. 1059, pp. 545–555. Springer, Singapore (2019). https://doi.org/10.1007/978-981-15-0121-0_42
13. Ranjana, P., Alexander, E.: Health alert and medicine remainder using internet of things. In: 2018 IEEE International Conference on Computational Intelligence and Computing Research (ICCIC), pp. 1–4. IEEE, December 2018
14. Qin, J.: Application of internet of things technology in tradition Chinese medicine pharmacy of general hospital. Int. J. Trad. Chin. Med. **39**(11), 964–967 (2017)
15. Omarov, B., et al.: Indoor microclimate comfort level control in residential buildings. Far East J. Electr. Commun. **17**(6), 1345–1352 (2017)
16. AbdulGhaffar, A., Mostafa, S.M., Alsaleh, A., Sheltami, T., Shakshuki, E.M.: Internet of things based multiple disease monitoring and health improvement system. J. Ambient. Intell. Humaniz. Comput. **11**(3), 1021–1029 (2020)
17. Omarov, B., et al.: Fuzzy-PID based self-adjusted indoor temperature control for ensuring thermal comfort in sport complexes. J. Theor. Appl. Inf. Technol. **98**(11) (2020)
18. Omarov, B., et al.: Ensuring comfort microclimate for sportsmen in sport halls: comfort temperature case study. In: Hernes, M., Wojtkiewicz, K., Szczerbicki, E. (eds.) Advances in Computational Collective Intelligence. CCIS, vol. 1287, pp. 626–637. Springer, Cham (2020). https://doi.org/10.1007/978-3-030-63119-2_51
19. Raeesi Vanani, I., Amirhosseini, M.: IoT-based diseases prediction and diagnosis system for healthcare. In: Chakraborty, C., Banerjee, A., Kolekar, M.H., Garg, L., Chakraborty, B. (eds.) Internet of Things for Healthcare Technologies. SBD, vol. 73, pp. 21–48. Springer, Singapore (2021). https://doi.org/10.1007/978-981-15-4112-4_2
20. Tan, S.S.L., Goonawardene, N.: Internet health information seeking and the patient-physician relationship: a systematic review. J. Med. Internet Res. **19**(1), e9 (2017)
21. Hibbard, J.H.: Patient activation and the use of information to support informed health decisions. Patient Educ. Couns. **100**(1), 5–7 (2017)
22. Randazzo, V., Ferretti, J., Pasero, E.: A wearable smart device to monitor multiple vital parameters—VITAL ECG. Electronics **9**(2), 300 (2020)
23. Rahmani, A.M., et al.: Exploiting smart e-Health gateways at the edge of healthcare Internet-of-things: A fog computing approach. Future Gener. Comput. Syst. **78**, 641–658 (2018)
24. Gupta, P.K., Nawaz, M.H., Mishra, S.S., Parappa, K., Silla, A., Hanumegowda, R.: New age approaches to predictive healthcare using in silico drug design and internet of things (IoT). In: Ahad, M.A., Paiva, S., Zafar, S. (eds.) Sustainable and Energy Efficient Computing Paradigms for Society. EICC, pp. 127–151. Springer, Cham (2021). https://doi.org/10.1007/978-3-030-51070-1_8
25. Farahani, B., Firouzi, F., Chang, V., Badaroglu, M., Constant, N., Mankodiya, K.: Towards fog-driven IoT eHealth: promises and challenges of IoT in medicine and healthcare. Future Gener. Comput. Syst. **78**, 659–676 (2018)
26. Bhatia, M., Sood, S.K.: A comprehensive health assessment framework to facilitate IoT-assisted smart workouts: a predictive healthcare perspective. Comput. Ind. **92**, 50–66 (2017)
27. Abbas, S.: An innovative IoT service for medical diagnosis. Int. J. Electr. Comput. Eng. **10**, 2088–8708 (2020)

28. Zhang, P., Schmidt, D., White, J., Mulvaney, S.: Towards precision behavioral medicine with IoT: Iterative design and optimization of a self-management tool for type 1 diabetes. In: 2018 IEEE International Conference on Healthcare Informatics (ICHI), pp. 64–74. IEEE, June 2018

29. Gupta, K., Rakesh, N., Faujdar, N., Kumari, M., Kinger, P., Matam, R.: IoT based automation and solution for medical drug storage: smart drug store. In: 2018 8th International Conference on Cloud Computing, Data Science & Engineering (Confluence), pp. 497–502. IEEE, January 2018

Inter-Vehicular Communication for Intelligent Collision Avoidance Using Machine Learning: An Overview

Darshit Pandya[1]([⊠]) [iD] and Hiren Mer[2]

[1] Indus University, Ahmedabad, Gujarat, India
darshitpandya211@gmail.com
[2] Department of Computer Engineering, Indus University, Ahmedabad, Gujarat, India
hirenmer.ce@indusuni.ac.in

Abstract. Following the inconsistencies encountered on the Indian terrain, the concept of autonomous vehicles has practically vanished from the Indian market. One major cause for the failure of self-driven vehicles in India is the collision occurring due to some common factors including poor lane-markings, deficiency of sign-boards, and most importantly – violation of traffic-rules by human drivers. Apart from the lack of markings, the lack of traffic-sense in human drivers is a major threat to autonomous driving in India; as no machine is capable enough to respond to the fluctuating mindset of a human being. In order to combat this challenge, a novel approach is presented that relies on the inter-vehicular communication strategy for avoiding critical collisions on the Indian roads. A unique application of machine learning technology to collision avoidance is outlined within this work.

Keywords: Autonomous driving · Collision avoidance · Machine learning

1 Introduction

Over the past few years, the research on autonomous vehicles has been at the peak. Though the recent developments in machine intelligence have proven to be successful in the autonomous driving domain, the scenario has been on the contrary. In addition to the uncertainties present on the Indian terrain, the irregularities in human driving have significantly affected the implementation of autonomous vehicles in India. India has been ranked within the Top-20 countries for having "The Worst Drivers" [1]; the main cause being the unpredictable nature of Indian drivers.

It is quite obvious that the autonomous driving concept cannot be implemented whole at once in a country. Accordingly, the system needs to be robust enough to deal with any unforeseen reactions of human-drivers. To achieve this, it becomes necessary to provide real-time information about the human-driven vehicles to the autonomous system. This would help the machine to predict some of the upcoming actions of the human-driven vehicle and can act accordingly. Subsequently, if this goal is accomplished, the autonomous systems can be implemented in India effectively.

© Springer Nature Singapore Pte Ltd. 2021
A. K. Luhach et al. (Eds.): ICAICR 2020, CCIS 1394, pp. 151–159, 2021.
https://doi.org/10.1007/978-981-16-3653-0_12

A novel approach to autonomous driving (within the Indian terrain) based on inter-vehicular communication and machine learning is presented in this paper.

2   Motivation

2.1   The Economy

The automotive industry accounts for a whopping 7.1% of India's Gross Domestic Product [2]. It can be firmly quoted that the economy greatly relies on this sector. Accordingly, the Research & Development (R&D) in this industry could play a major role in India's growing economy. However, India ranks 6th in the world for automotive research. The reason for not being in the Top-5 is directly attributable to the fact that India lags in the research and development of next-gen autonomous driving.

2.2   The Lesson

The statistics concerning road accidents in India are seemingly daunting. According to a report by the Ministry of Road Transport & Highways (Government of India), about 449,000 accidents took place in the year 2019 which resulted in about 150,000 deaths and 451,000 injuries [3]. These numbers correspond to the situation where humans are on the driver seat and no autonomous vehicles exist. If the powerful human brains are unable to respond to unpredictable events, then the machines are far behind in the race. Imagine if the autonomous vehicles were allowed on the road, the figures would easily pass the 500,000 mark (for accidents). Accordingly, these numbers serve as a crucial lesson for the robustness of future autonomous driving research and implementation.

2.3   The Problem

A survey concerning the topic: "Reliability of Autonomous Vehicles in India" clearly indicated the core reason behind the failure of autonomous vehicles in India: lack of lane-marking & sign-boards. However, apart from the markings, one major aspect is the use of "Prediction" in the autonomous driving concept. These are based solely on the training dataset trends and cannot be generalized for every situation. Furthermore, these autonomous systems would have to deal with the actions of the "Unpredictable" human brain – the human-driver of another vehicle. For such scenarios, the autonomous system must be fed with data from other nearby vehicles. This notion put us on a path to develop an Inter-vehicular communication (IVC)-based robust system.

3   Background

The methods proposed herewith are designed considering the benefit of the accuracy of the Navigation with Indian Constellation (NavIC) over the Indian subcontinent [4]. The system functionality outlined within this paper is designed to work seamlessly with techniques mentioned in the Thesis of Darshit Pandya[1] at Indus University [5].

---

[1] The First-Author of this paper.

4 Conventional System

Over the past decade, Artificial Intelligence (AI) has started to take its spot in numerous applications ranging from a smartphone to space technology. Such a giant leap has opened-up paths for improving the currently existing methodologies. One such path is the introduction of autonomous vehicles in the automobile industry.

Though there have been major improvements and technology inclusions in driverless cars, Computer Vision (CV) has been the dominant technology in the domain for years. However, it majorly depends on the input from the cameras. This is one of the significant drawbacks of Computer Vision (CV) for a developing country like India due to the lack of road-markings and sign-boards. Also, apart from the markings, there exist the challenges arising due to the unpredictable actions performed by the human-drivers in the manual vehicles. Such challenges lead to the failure of autonomous systems over the Indian terrain and can result in loss of life.

5 Proposed System

The proposed system aims to improve the current autonomous driving systems by adding the functionality of Inter-Vehicular Communication (IVC) and Navigation with Indian Constellation (NavIC). Although, machine learning would continue to be a common asset for both. These functionalities are presented as an add-on to the conventional system and are not intended to function as a standalone system.

The system comprises of the following modifications to the current system:

5.1 Inter-Vehicular Communication (IVC)

The system works on the principle of Vehicle-to-Vehicle (V2V), the infrastructure of which is explained in the paper titled "Inter-vehicular Communication Systems, Protocols and Middleware" [6]. The overview of the infrastructure can be visualized via Fig. 1. This type of design structure is used to communicate the required vehicle-related metrics with nearby vehicles. The usage is discussed later in the chapter.

Fig. 1. V2V communication infrastructure (Source: iStock.com/metamorworks)

5.2 Navigation with Indian Constellation (NavIC)

The NavIC satellite system is an alternative to the Global Positioning System (GPS) which provides accurate positioning and timing information over the Indian subcontinent. The purpose of using NavIC (within the realm of this system) is to identify the vehicles for the information exchange. Furthermore, NavIC's timing information can be utilized for the synchronization of the systems running on numerous vehicles.

As the proposed system is designed with respect to the Indian terrain, NavIC data can be utilized instead of GPS. The connectivity and accuracy of NavIC have been outstanding over the Indian subcontinent. Furthermore, there are numerous rural areas in India where the GPS connectivity is limited. For such scenarios, the NavIC satellite system will prove to be useful as it is positioned to focus as well as cover the complete land-area of India.

5.3 Machine Learning

For the purpose of collision avoidance, machine learning technology is employed within each system. Online Supervised learning is used for the proposed system. This enables experience-based learning and significantly improves the accuracy of the predictions by learning from real-time data. The application of machine learning is discussed later in the chapter.

It is to be noted that for classification purpose, the Support Vector Machine (SVM) has been selected as it provided the maximum efficacy compared to other major techniques due to the linear nature of the training dataset. Moreover, instead of using a standard Support Vector Machine (SVM), the Online Support Vector Machine (Online-SVM) [7] has been used in order to respond to the dynamic nature of the terrain and also to promote experience-based learning for a more reliable system.

5.4 Sensors

With an aim to minimize manufacturing & computational cost of the Computer Vision (CV) technology, only Ultrasonic sensors have been utilized under this system.

6 Functioning Methodology

It is quite evident that the system works on the basis of V2V, NavIC, and Machine Learning. The working of the system is categorized into two phases as follows:

6.1 Phase-I: Training[2]

Firstly, a machine learning model, selected based on the requirement (Online-SVM [7]), is trained with real-world simulation data including the following headers:

---

[2] This is the initial step and is done only once, prior to the actual implementation.

- Readings of Ultrasonic sensors of nearby[3] vehicles (U_{50})
- Readings of Ultrasonic sensors of the current vehicle (U)
- Relative speed (compared to current vehicle) of nearby vehicles (S_{50})
- Speed of the current vehicle (S)
- Stopping Distance of the current vehicle (SD) [defined by Eq. 1]
- Stopping Distance of the nearest vehicle (SD_N)
- Label: Collision Detected (CD)/Collision Not-Detected (CND)

$$\text{Stopping Distance}(SD) = \text{Reaction Distance}(RD) + \text{Braking Distance}(BD) \quad (1)$$

The data used for training (including the output Label-CD/CND) has been collected considering a small-sized rover prototype under real-world conditions. This classification model, when used, would provide an output label – CD or CND, based on the data fed to the model[4,5].

6.2 Phase-II: Actual Implementation

The functioning of the system is based on the following algorithm (assuming the system is deployed across all the vehicles):

1. Get the Ultrasonic sensor readings (U) and the speed (S) of the current vehicle.
2. Get the Ultrasonic readings (U_{50}) of nearby (50 m) vehicles using V2V Network.
3. Get the speeds of the nearby (50 m) vehicles using V2V Communication protocol.
4. Calculate relative speed for each speed-data received (S_{50}).
5. Calculate Stopping Distance (SD) of current vehicle based on speed (S).
6. Calculate Stopping Distance (SD_N) of the nearest vehicle from the speeds received.
7. Feed U, S, U_{50}, S_{50}, SD, and SD_N to the machine learning model trained in Phase-I.
8. Get the output – CD/CND.
9. If output is CD: Transmit "Alert" to all nearby (50 m) vehicles using V2V network.
10. Follow Diversion Procedure[6].

This algorithm is followed by all the vehicles simultaneously. The nearby systems will calculate the same metrics as mentioned in the algorithm and the corresponding alert is transmitted. If a system receives as well as transmits an alert, it will strictly follow the Diversion Procedure mentioned in the thesis [5]. In case a system just receives an alert and does not transmit one, it will continue its normal operation without diversion. This is due to the fact that a collision can occur only if it is detected by both systems. Hence, the corresponding systems would act accordingly.

Here, it is to be noted that the "nearby vehicles" mentioned in the above-mentioned algorithm can be detected on the basis of the NavIC-coordinates of each vehicle. Accordingly, it can be said that NavIC is a critical component of the proposed system.

---

[3] Nearby indicates the vehicles in the vicinity of 50 m as per the NavIC-coordinates.

[4] Reaction Distance is the distance traveled by the vehicle before actual braking starts.

[5] Braking distance indicates the distance traveled after applying brakes, till halt/rest position.

[6] The procedure is mentioned in the thesis listed in the References Section [5].

7   System Workflow

An abstract-view of the system workflow is presented in Fig. 2 below.

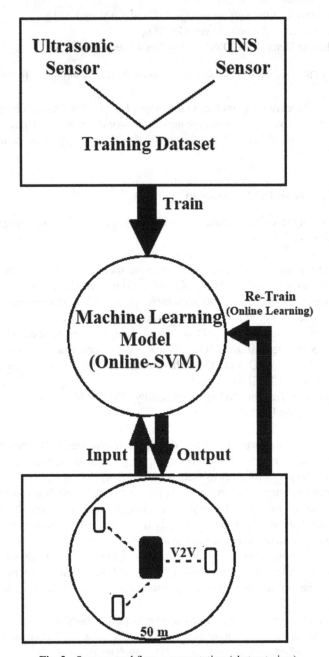

Fig. 2. System workflow representation (abstract view)

8 Performance Measure

The system proposed herewith is developed at the simulation-level only. The training data used has been generated using small-sized rover prototypes. Accordingly, the performance measure mentioned in Table 1 is solely based on simulation testing within a laboratory setting. Accordingly, it may not be 100% accurate for the actual implementation environment. The detailed pictorial representation of the type of test cases used is presented in Fig. 3 below.

Table 1. Performance of the proposed system

Environment/setting	Types of path[a]	#Test-case	Collision avoidance accuracy[b]
Crossroads	2L	15000	98.59%
Straight-roads	1L, 2L, 6L	35000	99.98%
Bridge/Slope	2L	25000	94.18%

[a]Types of Path include: Single-Lane (1L) / Double-Lane (2L)/Six-Lane (6L)
[b]Average accuracy of all Path-Types combined

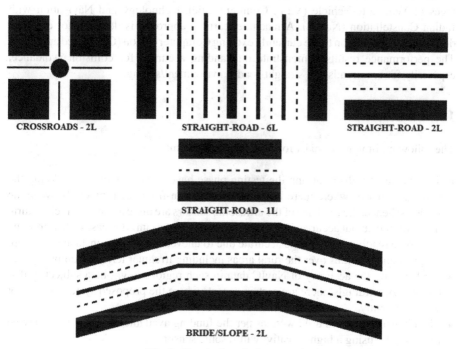

Fig. 3. Types of roads (test-cases)

9 Observations

The following points can be clearly observed based on the results mentioned in the above section of performance measurement:

- The Collision Avoidance Accuracy is quite high for straight-roads
- Although not explicitly listed, the accuracy on straight-roads decreased as the number of lanes increased (Refer Eq. 2 below)

$$\text{Accuracy}_{1L} > \text{Accuracy}_{2L} > \text{Accuracy}_{6L} \tag{2}$$

- The accuracy of the proposed system decreases for the bridges/slopes due to uneven altitude of the path which in-turn, affects the accuracy of the NavIC data. Subsequently, it affects the 50 m range mentioned in the algorithm.

10 Conclusion

A novel approach to collision avoidance in autonomous vehicles is presented. A unique collision detection/avoidance algorithm is outlined, which takes into account the advantages of Vehicle-to-Vehicle (V2V) Communication technology and Navigation with Indian Constellation (NavIC). A machine learning approach is detailed, for collision detection, as an addition to the currently existing Computer Vision (CV)-based approach. The performance results demonstrate outstanding accuracy for collision avoidance, especially for crossroads and straight-roads environment/setting.

11 Limitations

The following limitations exist for the proposed system:

- The test cases utilized during the testing phase have been designed considering the general scenarios where there is a clear (obstruction-free) environment between the vehicles; hence, the readings of the ultrasonic sensors are quite accurate which in-turn, improves the output accuracy. However, there may be certain edge cases wherein some ultrasonic readings may not be accurate due to uneven terrain. For instance, there are frequent uncertainties over the rural areas including irregular terrain (humps).
- Furthermore, the accuracy of NavIC data in such regions might be a subject of discussion. Accordingly, there are certain aspects where the proposed system might not work efficiently.
- The ultrasonic sensors used were as per the funding available. The accuracy may be increased by using a high-sensitivity ultrasonic sensor.
- The positioning data utilized for training and testing the rover prototype in the laboratory environment was not the actual NavIC data; the reason being the area of the laboratory is quite limited and concise. Accordingly, the position coordinates were fed using some pre-defined position values for the pre-designed paths.

- The combinations of the road-type and number of lanes considered within the testing phase are limited. Further combinations are yet to be tested.
- The testing performed has been conducted within the laboratory setting. Accordingly, the results may not perform equally well in the real-world conditions.

12 Future Work

The work proposed herewith has been tested in a simulation/laboratory environment[7]. There is a future scope to test the proposed algorithm in a real-world environment to get more precise results and to better understand the functionality of the system in extreme conditions. Furthermore, the types of path used for testing may be extended by including numerous variations to the simple test cases. Moreover, we are planning to present the detailed test results and observations in another publication, once the testing procedure is concluded for the real-world conditions and variations.

In addition, the system proposed within this paper has been trained with the data pertaining to the urban environment. Subsequently, for establishing a reliable system, we are working on gathering data surrounding the rural conditions.

Finally, a minor improvement can be made to the positioning data. Instead of using just NavIC, a combination of NavIC and Global Positioning System (GPS) may be used for better accuracy and performance of the proposed system [8]

Acknowledgements. We would like to extend our sincere thanks to the Department of Computer Engineering (The Department of Computer Engineering falls under the Indus Institute of Technology & Engineering (IITE) – Indus University, Ahmedabad (Gujarat, India 300015)), Indus University (Ahmedabad) for providing the required resources to perform the implementation and testing of the proposed notion.

References

1. The Travel. https://www.thetravel.com/ranked-by-country-car-drivers/
2. Make-In-India.   https://www.makeinindia.com/article/-/v/make-in-india-sector-survey-aut omobile
3. Ministry of Road Transport & Highways (MORTH) (Government of India). https://morth.nic. in/sites/default/files/RA_PDF_for_Uploading_Compressed.pdf
4. Indian Space Research Organisation.
5. Pandya, D.: NavIC-based automated optimal path selection & obstacle avoidance using machine learning. Technical report, ResearchGate (2020). https://doi.org/10.13140/RG.2.2. 28264.08961
6. Jawhar, I., Mohamed, N., Zhang, L.: Inter-vehicular communication systems, protocols and middleware. In: Fifth International Conference on Networking, Architecture, and Storage, pp. 282–287. IEEE Press, New York (2010). https://doi.org/10.1109/NAS.2010.49
7. Laskov, P., Gehl, C., Kruger, S., Muller, K.: Incremental support vector learning: analysis, implementation and applications. J. Mach. Learn. Res. **7**, 1909–1936 (2006)
8. Zaminpardaz, S., Teunissen, P.J.G., Nadarajah, N.: IRNSS/NavIC and GPS: a single- and dual-system L5 analysis. J. Geod. **91**(8), 915–931 (2017).

---

[7] Laboratory environment refers to the simulation environment within the labs at Indus University, Ahmedabad. The rover prototype mentioned has been developed as a miniature robotic toy.

Wireless Sensor Networks Source Location Privacy Preservation Mechanism

Syed Umar[1]([✉]), Misganu Tuse Abetu[1], Bodena Terfa Efa[1], Etana Fikadu Dinsa[2], and Parmanand Prabhat[3]

[1] Department of Computer Science, Wollega University, Nekemte, Ethiopia
[2] Department of Information Technology, Wollega University, Nekemte, Ethiopia
[3] Department of Computer Science and Engineering, Himalayan University, Itanagar, Arunachal Pradesh, India

Abstract. Computing and communication had already taken a gigantic step forward with the continuous improvements of the WSNs. In the meantime, security has not received similar consideration regarding compelling event turns. This paper discusses a hot safety research subject called WSN's source privacy problem and presents WSN PSLP privacy policy. In order to adapt to any of this enemy, nodes of apparition and fake sources that reflect the behaviour of the source are used to broaden the direction. The weight of each hub is then determined as a measure for the next candidate to choose from. In addition, two modes of transmission are designed to convey true bundles. The results of the redevelopment have shown as the proposed PSLP plot enhances the time for good without negotiating the use of vitality.

Keywords: Computing and communication · Wireless sensor networks · Fake source · Phantom node · Source location privacy

1 Introduction

Usually WSNs involve various sensors and conventions based on management such as authentication of information [1], event awareness [2] and hub loading [3]. WSNs include the following. These nodes are a microcomputer function and are dispersed under different conditions. There is a number of communication and data transmissions between nodes. In this regard, safeguarding security [4, 25] is essential. WSN's security encompasses many aspects, such as privacy of data [5] and privacy of location [6]. Data privacy could be guaranteed via encryption algorithms, but privacy cannot be guaranteed to be ridiculous. Data protection Due to the time similarity of data transmission between two nodes, the opponent may provide position information through analysis. From the point of view of the period, location privacy includes privacy of source location and privacy of the sink site. This article deals with the privacy of the source site, which in view of the source's significance is a research point in the area of protection. Several strategies can be applied to ensure privacy from sources, such as secure routing.

© Springer Nature Singapore Pte Ltd. 2021
A. K. Luhach et al. (Eds.): ICAICR 2020, CCIS 1394, pp. 160–168, 2021.
https://doi.org/10.1007/978-981-16-3653-0_13

In our simulations the proposed PSLP showed a superior performance in terms of increasing safety while balancing energy consumption than two other ongoing plans.

The major contributions of this paper as follows:

1) The proposed PSLP integrates both fantasy nodes and fake sources which improve the privacy of the source location.
2) An even more notable local adversary is taken into consideration that can use the Hidden Markov model to predict the status of the source.
3) The distance from the source to the sink which improves data location security, is used to structure two data transmission modes.

2   Existing Works

Since Ozturk initially proposed his ideasocial networks [7] etc. have been investigated in general.

The privacy of location covers the privacy of the source location and the privacy of the sink. In this paper, we focus on confidentiality in the source location. In order to ensure the privacy of source location, Manjula et al. used virtual sources [8]. A routing process for maximizing the safety time was proposed in its plan. By randomly adding nodes to the routing procedure in the not-hotspot areas, multiple routing routes have been established. The safety time was subsequently increased without affecting the life of the network.

In order to ensure privacy in the source location, **Matthew** and others proposed two algorithms which use fake sources [9]. Fake sources have been sent dynamically around the sink in the primary algorithm. The sink used floods to use false sources at that point. This algorithm will provide a strong privacy source at the cost of tremendous energy consumption. Another algorithm was introduced for this purpose, named the single hierarchical path routing algorithm. With the use of a coordinated random path, the source nodes were chosen as false sources that greatly reduced energy consumption. However, the source and sink's relative position have been connected with fake sources; sensor nodes can absorb energy in a particular region.

Jing et al. perceived an even more impressive opponent and suggested an algorithm for the enhancement of the privacy of the location [10]. A global opponent who uses a Bayesian assessment technique (MAP) has attempted to screen correspondence between study nodes. A dynamic framework developed at that point in order to reduce the probability of discovery for the adversary. The problem was finally changed into parameter adjustment.

Huang et al. concentrated on the usage rate of WSN energy while preserving source secrecy These branches were also later combined in a number of routing paths. However, it does not clearly characterize the amount of joined routing paths and the energy collected by the knots around the sink may not be precisely the energy cost through packet transmission.

A restricted randomwalk model was developed by **Chen et al.** in [11]. A next-hop candidate determination domain was generated in its mechanism based on the balance angle of neighbouring hubs and the danger distance that made a domain of choice look like a circle. The enlargement of each hub in the domain has now been computed by the ratio of counterbalanced angles to the whole balance angle of the present hub. The smaller the ratio, the more likely the next hop would be this hub. In this case, the equilibrium angle of the node has been set and weight is also likely not to change. The nodes which served as a next-hop applicant would consume a lot of energy. To guarantee the privacy of the source location, Chen et al. have used fantasy nodes and proposed a restricted flood algorithm [12].

3   Problem Definition

Although it inevitably threatens the safety of the observed destination by introducing the source hub position at WSN, the data privacy source hub assurance becomes a critical problem for understanding. However, since sensor nodes have limited computational capability, storage capacity, and power resources, the balance of safety and network performance is unavoidable.

Current study on privacy assurances at source hub locations is based mainly on cyclic entangling [13] and fantasy routing [6, 7, 12, 13]. The cyclical entrapment idea was presented by Ouyang et al. [11] as a special case for routing sham data sources. Multiple nodes act as sham data sources in cyclic entanglement and interconnect in a circle. The primary objective of cyclic trapping is to mistake the opponent for such circles during a hop-by - hop trace attack so that the attacker can not return to the real source hub. Whether this happens, at least one circle must be activated for the attacker to be contained, and the inside knowledge nodes, which act as the fake source of data, must periodically generate sham information, which causes a great deal of abnormal overhead communication, generate energy [19] and genuinely damage the network performance.

4   Network Model

Throughout this study the network model is specified on the traditional Panda-Hunter model e level decreases the chance of the opponent finding the source. We make the following assumptions in this way:

1) Randomly deployed sensor nodes. Each sensor hub remains unchanged after deployment. More and more every sensor node is homogeneous, meaning it has the same initial energy, the same computational ability and the same memory cache.
2) In the network there is only one sink. The sink remains within the network community, as in different schemes or conventions [12].
3) Every sensor hub has its own neighbour information. With an encryption algorithm, packets sent by each sensor hub are scrambled. This part, however, goes beyond the scope of this review.

5   Adversary Model

The adversary starts from the sink because of the potential value of the source and tries the best to identify the source location. The range of observation of the opponent is equal to the radius of the sensor hub, so that the adverse kind is a local opponent. The local opponent has a control range that must be equal or slightly larger than a typical hub communication range. Thus, the local opponent can only screen network parts. The adversary uses passive attacks to avoid being found by the network administrator, for example, eavesdropping and backtracking.

In this paper we think of an even more impressive opponent. We assume, apart from the passive attack, that by checking the header of each packet the opponent realizes the packet type. At that point, the opposing party may induce the probable condition of the source for some time using the Hidden Markov model (HMM), which is based on his observation. The purpose of HMM was to help the opponent identify the direction from the source from the influence of the HMM approximation relative to walking through the network. The HMM estimation will also allow the adversary to reduce the extent of source determination.

The competitor, though, knows the source status and not the source position. We assume that the adversary is more likely to locate the source from the approximate source condition if it has adequate knowledge about the network. The key objectives of our proposed PSLP are to manufacture legitimate packets and false packets in various transmitted states from various cookies which have drawn the opposition's attention and reduced the accuracy of the evaluation.

6 PSLP Implementation

A detailed representation of PSLP is provided in this segment. The beacon message is continuously transmitted either by sink to the sensor nodes during the initialization process. The hop count is recorded at the point where a hub receives the message, Every hub records the number of base hop. Each nude thus realizes its towards its neighbours. Although the would at some stage know the source status when the source is still elusive, our goal is to extend the possible locations of the source. The first stage is the determination of imaginary nodes. The next level is the determination of false sources. PSLP contains three steps: The figure shows a diagram of PSLP (Fig. 1).

As specified in the, opponent will to assess the status conduct target. the potential source increasingly. Fantasy nodes and fake sources fit our demands superbly. The capability of the excellent hub and the falsified source is close, but the importance of both is exceptional. The great hub refers to nodes of the source that simulate the power of the source. Even the false source refers to nodes simulating the skill of the source. The inaccurate source, though, is far from the source near the drain. The object of consolidating the fantasy centre and the false source is to diversify headings of the transmission. In non-HotSPot, the effect on network existence is little preferred, both fictional nodes and fictional outlets.

7 Phantom Nodes Determination

When we consider the ability of phantom nodes, the more the distance entre the phantom hub and the source is extended, the more the private life insurance system is grounded. The main reason is to coordinate the opponent from the actual source. In,

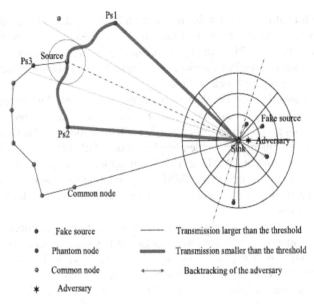

Fig. 1. Proposed implementation model

however, authors have shown that there is a probability that a phantom hub is $1-e-H/25$ within 20% of Hops. So we choose to use a guided random walk to select fantasy nodes. Packets are transmitted in a coordinated random fashion. Therefore, the phantom hub chosen is kept away from the source when coordinated random walking stops.

For further information, the source will send the packets via co-ordinated random walk to one of its neighbours in Hops. In its far neighbour's rundown, the neighbour sends the packets to a hub. the current hub becomes a fantasy hub, and forward packets sent from the source. During each transmission, the fantasy hub changes. Furthermore, the phantom hub has to remain outside the apparent area (hover). Because when the opponent returns to the obvious area, he immediately perceives the source. Furthermore, the There is also an assumed secure transition between the source and the fantasy centre. Noted the zeal and commitment of fantasy nodes are the difference.

8   Fake Sources Determination

Fake sources are mostly triggered around the sink as shown in the previous definition to increase headings of the packets from. The range of sending of a falsified source is defined by the angle of $\theta2$ in Fig. 2. The sink divides the network into several rings, especially. The rings are divided into n divisions at that point. Fake sources are chosen in the correct part of a route perpendicular to the route that connects the source with the sink for separating fake sources and the sources. The actual application controls the quantity of fake sources. The fake source system is generated at the time of initialization.

Each counterfeit source is best maintained in different sectors to ensure that the heading of each counterfeit package is unique. The opponent knows the source condition

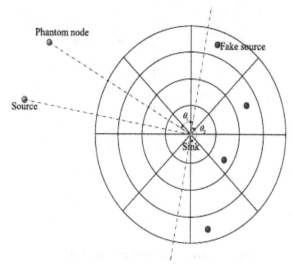

Fig. 2. Sink ring areas around it.

in a given moment, so that the source is found, he needs to analyse the packet stream. Thus, the privacy of source location is secured by using fake sources to improve the source location. For a fixed period, a hub acts as a fake source. Another fake source appears when the time period is exhausted. To reduce the use of energy from counterfeit sources, we assume that for a certain period of time, there is only one fake source.

Establishment of Routing from Source to Sink
The very first step is the propagation of phantom nodes and false sources from the original source to the sink. Whenever it happens the source sends a message to suggest the sink. After which, after getting the post, the sink chooses a false source. Since the source happens spontaneously, the source and sink are likely to have a slight gap. We thus place a threshold between source and sink in view of these factors (Fig. 3).

This indicates that the routing process from source to sink takes place in two cases. The key condition is that the hop count of the source and sink is greater than the point. The next example will be that the number of hops between sources and sinks is less than that of the edge. In particular, because as source sends packets originally to such a phantom hub, the primary contrasts are the choice of fantasy nodes and the transfer from the fantasy hub to the sink.

9 Performance Evaluation

We assess the performance of PSLP throughout this area. The average values of the experimental data are all the results given in this area The simulation assesses four measures: security time, energy use, network life and transmission time. In this field, four measures are assessed. We give the meaning of every measurement as a matter of first importance. The time of security is the difference between the source sending the primary

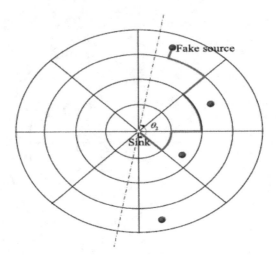

Fig. 3. Possible fake packets transmission

packet and the source location of the opponent. We use hop counts of backtracking by the adversary to speak more and more explicitly about the time of safety. The energy consumption refers to the average cost of energy per simulation run. Because the control packages take no energy, we ignore this part and concentrate mainly on energy use during transmission of packets.

The network's lifespan corresponds to the time gap between the network setup and the demise of the main core. The delay in delivery means the typical packet transmission and the time needed for simulation planning (Fig. 4).

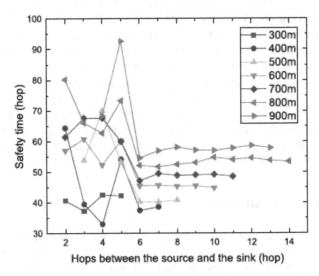

Fig. 4. Safety time versus different hops from the source to the sink.

The PSLP is contrasted to another two schemes, the SLP-E, the enhanced Source location Protection Protocol (SLP-E) [9] and the dynamic single path routing algorithm. DynamicSPR uses fake sources to safeguard the location of the source, while the SLP-E uses ghost nodes. Both are integrated into the PSLP. Consequently, developers select DynamicSPR and SLP-E for the comparing.

10 Conclusions

Over the last decade, the importance of safety in WSNs has grown. The subject of this paper is on source location protection, a security testing hotspot and a WSN Probabilistic Protection System (PSLP) recommendation. In this investigation, a groundbreaking opponent who uses HMM is considered. In order to adapt to this problem, the packet transmission headings are modified with fantasy hub in comparison with DynamicSPR and SLPE. Future exams will focus on securing the source location by reducing the probability of control by the opponent and ensuring secure communication between nodes.

References

1. Lu, H., Li, J.: Privacy-preserving authentication schemes for vehicular ad hoc networks: a survey. Wirel. Commun. Mobile Comput. 16(6), 643–655 (2016)
2. Han, G., Yang, X., Liu, L., Chan, S., Zhang, W.: A coverage-aware hierarchical charging algorithm in wireless rechargeable sensor networks. IEEE Netw. Mag (to be published)
3. Han, G., Guan, H., Wu, J., Chan, S., Shu, L., Zhang, W.: An uneven cluster-based mobile charging algorithm for wireless rechargeable sensor networks. IEEE Syst. J. (to be published)
4. Han, G., Wang, H., Jiang, J., Zhang, W., Chan, S.: CASLP: a confused arc-based source location privacy protection scheme in WSNs for IoT. IEEE Commun. Mag. 56(9), 42–47 (2018)
5. Lu, H., Li, J., Guizani, M.: Secure and efficient data transmission for cluster-based wireless sensor networks. IEEE Trans. Parallel Distrib. Syst. 25(3), 750–761 (Mar. 2014)
6. Han, G., Zhou, L., Wang, H., Zhang, W., Chan, S.: A source location protection protocol based on dynamic routing in WSNs for social internet of things. Future Gener. Comput. Syst. 82(5), 689–697 (2018)
7. Lu, H., Li, J., Kameda, H.: A secure routing protocol for cluster-based wireless sensor networks using ID-based digital signature. In: Proceedings of the IEEE Global Communications Conference, pp. 1–5, December 2010
8. Bradbury, M., Jhumka, A., Leeke, M.: Hybrid online protocols for source location privacy in wireless sensor networks. J. Parallel Distrib. Comput. 115, 67–81 (2018)
9. Chen, J., Lin, Z., Hu, Y., Wang, B.: Hiding the source based on limited flooding for sensor networks. Sensors 15(11), 29129–29148 (2015)
10. Han, G., Miao, X., Wang, H., Guizani, M., Zhang, W.: CPSLP: a cloud based scheme for protecting source-location privacy in wireless sensor networks using multi-sinks. IEEE Trans. Veh. Technol. 68(3), 2739–2750 (2019)
11. Bhatt, M., Sharma, S., Luhach, A.K., Prakash, A.: Nature inspired route optimization in vehicular adhoc network. In: 2016 5th International Conference on Reliability, Infocom Technologies and Optimization (Trends and Future Directions) (ICRITO), pp. 447–451. IEEE, September 2016

12. Kumar, S., Dhull, K., Arora, P., Luhach, A.K.: Performance of energy conservation models, generic, micaz and micamotes, using AODV routing protocol on a wireless sensor network. Scalable Comput. Pract. Exp. **20**(4), 631–639 (2019)
13. Singh, A.P., Luhach, A.K., Gao, X.Z., Kumar, S., Roy, D.S.: Evolution of wireless sensor network design from technology centric to user centric: an architectural perspective. Int. J. Distrib. Sens. Netw. **16**(8), 1550147720949138 (2020)
14. Maratha, P., Gupta, K., Luhach, A.K.: Improved fault-tolerant optimal route reconstruction approach for energy consumed areas in wireless sensor networks. IET Wirel. Sen. Syst. **10**(3), 112–116 (2019)

A Study on Secure Data Aggregation and Routing for Wireless Sensor Networks

Mahantesh Mathapati[✉], T. Senthil Kumaran, Kavita K. Patil, Sunita S. Patil, and H. N. Veena

ACS College of Engineering, Affiliated to Visveswaraya Technological University, Belagavi, India

Abstract. In the present scenario, deployment of large-scale sensor nodes in the heterogeneous environment is the challenging factor for the network designers. While designing future networking, there are several performance parameters (i.e., cost, energy, delay, bandwidth, transmission rate) involves securing the routing path as well as improves the network lifetime. In this regards data aggregation suitable approach which scales up the overall network lifetime as well as saves the cost and energy in the networking. In this study have to discuss the prior research study on both routing strategy as well as data aggregation mechanism and can be known that there is need to develop a network model that ensures the high level of security in data-aggregation for future WSNs. Also needs to present a optimize routing scheme for data transmission and aggregation for resisting any lethal attacks that significantly drains the energy of sensors. Finally, have discusses a research gap towards data aggregation with optimal routing strategy.

Keywords: Data-aggregation · Clustering · Routing algorithm · Security protocol · WSNs

1 Introduction

A wireless sensor network contains a number of small sensor devices that are arranged to collect and transmit the ambient data. The sensor devices are static and interact via wireless channels that have limited communication range, vulnerable and unreliable to environmental noises, wireless interferences and physical obstacles [1]. The primary reason behind the establishment of WSN is to offer cost-effective ambient information services. The sensor nodes are typically small, low cost with limited energy, communication; storage computation resources are capable of performing computation and communication tasks.

WSN is a kind of Ad-hoc network that deploys on the large area with multiple low-cost sensor nodes scattered over the area of interest. The key advantage of these networks can be deployed or implement anywhere without any particular communication infrastructure. These are potentially utilizing in many applications ranging from education to research, military to civil and healthcare applications. The collected data may be as simple as to measure the environmental parameters, e.g. nose, temperature, humidity,

A. K. Luhach et al. (Eds.): ICAICR 2020, CCIS 1394, pp. 169–185, 2021.
https://doi.org/10.1007/978-981-16-3653-0_14

etc., to as difficult as a multimedia file, wireless audio, video or visual sensor devices for many applications [2, 3].

Apart from memory limitations, the low-cost sensor devices have low computation capacity as well as communication capacity with limited energy. Hence, such resource-constrained sensors need high energized systems. based protocols [4]. Thus security routing protocols are the essential part of WSNs.

The typical architectural diagram of the secure routing model for WSN is given in the Fig. 1. Primary intention of deployment of WSNs is to sense and collect the data from certain instance for specific applications and transmit it in a secure way. There are several types of security protocols have been introduced [5]. Additionally, for the data transmission and the communication sensor needs a reliable route, during this some sensor devices act like a router and discovers a path over the network. Thus, routing is the essential factor in the WSNs. It has the privilege of interconnecting the sensors vie single/multihop links. The WSN routing includes the discovery of route, link establishment and routing management. The key goal of WSN routing is to send the data packet from source-node to cluster head. During packet transmission sensors would consume a high amount of network-resources like energy, if they require send particular sensed data to the sink node.

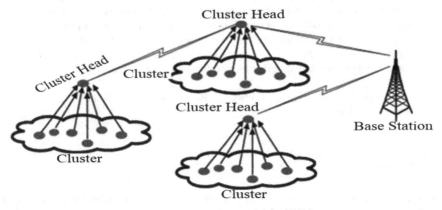

Fig. 1. Secure routing model for WSNs

There are several WSN routing mechanisms are exists. Example; a trust-based secure routing mechanism (TSSRM) for WSN improves the data security for the multihop routing system and effectively decreases the routing overhead in wireless sensor network [6], Nature inspired route optimization [7] achieves the efficient and reliable data transmission,. Once the cluster head deployed, EACO algorithm finds a reliable route to forward the information. In various WSN based real time applications, the user wants to access the real-time information from sensor node [8]. In this regard, before accessing the authenticity of the user needed to verify from a secure authentication method. Therefore, in [9] author designed a Lightweight authentication protocol for wireless sensor application without compromising of any other anonymity support. In [10], a Trust based X-layer approach provides the minimal defense against security attacks and also introduced the TruFiX protocol which uses the multiple parameters via interlayer information swap to reduce the effects of threats in a network.

However, data aggregation is the significant primitive in WSNs. It is about collection of data packets from various sources. By removing redundant information, the data aggregation mechanism extends the communication rate as well as reduces the energy consumption. From this mechanism can integrate the data packets exploiting aggregation function into a single unit transmit. For example standard deviation, average, median, maximum, minimum and sum, etc. [11]. It would provide maximum reduction in transmission as well as a reduction in communication cost, network delay, bandwidth utilization, and energy consumption.

In this case study, primary intention is to provide a comprehensive survey study in the state of the art that is carried out by several research studies. From the existing study can say that there is a requirement to introduce and design optimal routing protocol to perform a secure data aggregation. The remaining part of the investigational study is structured into multiple sections; Sect. 2 provides the different routing strategies and design challenges for secure routing protocols in WSN routing. Section 3 illustrates the data aggregation scheme with existing algorithms. The related work is described in Sect. 4 followed by various security schemes for data aggregation described in Sect. 5. Section 6 gives the research gap followed, and the conclusion of the study is written in the Sect. 7.

2 Routing Strategy and Design Challenges in WSNs

In sensor network deployment process, routing is the most significant constraint which always gains more priority to the research challenges. Routing scheme utilizes convergence pattern to transmit the data from source to cluster head or sink node through multi-hop or single hop links. Usually, in multi-hop networks sensor nodes contain limited communication capacity which not allows for direct communications. Thus the result, WSN routing scheme requires the reliable route to forward packets based on sensor capacity, network characteristics, and other resource constraints (e.g., speed, memory, bandwidth, and energy, etc.).

However, there are two significant components which are involved in routing which responsible to manage the network traffic also; protocol scheme and another one is routing matrix [13].

The protocol based scheme mainly focuses on transmission policy, routing information storage, shortest path discovery, data forwarding and their characteristics, etc. while, the routing matrix based on protocol scheme and primary goal is select a path/route between the available nodes and it returns an optimal rout if there are multiple routes. There are several parameters involved in making routing decisions energy consumption, signal strength, hop count, etc. [14].

In WSNs, routing will be established based on two significant schemes, i.e. address centric and Data-centric. In the conventional WSNs, sensor nodes consider the address of the next node to be forward the data packet and address centric protocols will not provide an effective routing since there is an absence of global addressing scheme (i.e., IP in the WSNs). In this scheme, a sender node totally depends upon the address of the sink node along with the shortest path that is named as End-to-End routing strategy. While in the data-centric routing scheme the sender node forwards the data packet to the sink node but routing nodes responsible for seeing the content of the traveling packet and perfume some data aggregation routing functions on data placing at multiple sources. The significant fact of the data-centric routing scheme is that a packet is forwarded if it is desirable for the receiving node (or next node) [15].

Modifications or reconfiguration of network topology is a very complex issue which highly effect on network routing. Also, a communication link may fail if the energy level of the nodes becomes lower than the required threshold for maintaining the network links. Therefore, by considering this issue, a concept of virtual network topology is presented in [16]. This study mainly addresses the concept of energy efficient routing scheme for WSNs which improves performance in the network-lifetime. In [17] authors introduced a solution approach for data-aggregation and routing problem in WSNs and showed that proposed clustering algorithm and data aggregation scheme could provide significant results in energy consumption. Additionally, have introduced a combined approach of grid-based routing scheme and aggregator node selection scheme which enhances the performance in network lifetime, during incurring the acceptable levels of the time period under data aggregation.

Data aggregation with secure routing scheme receiving the more attention to the researchers which could be helpful in the designing of secure WSN. From the case study have found that there are multiple approaches already exists to represent the secure routing protocols which are the essential for data aggregation process to transfer the data packet from source to the sink node. Therefore in the next section have to discuss about data aggregation scheme in WSNs.

3   Data Aggregation Scheme in WSN

The concept of aggregation is to collect the data from the different sensor nodes by removing the redundant data [18], and data-aggregation schemes are classified into various categories [19] such as tree-based, cluster-based, and hybrid approach.

In a tree-based approach, data aggregation performs after the formation of the tree structure, i.e., routing formation. The tree structure is originated from the sink node by selecting suitable sensor nodes to behave like an aggregation point (represented in Fig. 2). The data is aggregated at intermediary nodes and passed to the header node (i.e., sink node). Considering into account the level of connectivity of sensor nodes to direct the aggregation strategy in order: to select the sensor nodes with the highest position of connectivity as header node and lowest position of connectivity as a leaf node. Also find the shortest route among the header node and sink node and reduce the data forwarded inside the network, This approach is well applicable for the applications that involve in network data-aggregation, example; monitoring of environmental conditions, where a large amount of data is received from the sink and gives the useful information. The limitation of this approach is packet loss any level due to connectivity or node failure and high cost of managing the tree structure in a dynamic environment.

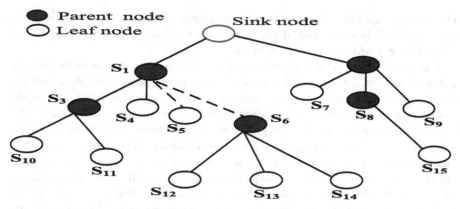

Fig. 2. Tree-based data aggregation policy

In clustering based approach, a network is grouped into clusters [20] (shown in Fig. 3). The particular sensor node, i.e. or cluster-head is selected to receive inside the cluster, pass the gathered information to the header node. The cluster heads can collaborate with directly to the sink node through long distance transmission or other cluster heads [21, 22]. In [23] Heinzelman et al. proposed a LEACH protocol which offers an energy balancing usage in the aggregation process. In this approach, few nodes are elected as heads on the basis of overall signal strength and indiscriminately turn this process between the sensor nodes within the network. Another energy efficient clustering approach is proposed by [24] which reduces the energy consumption rate during the cluster head election process also reduce the network control overhead. The objective was to distribute the equal amount of energy to improve the network lifetime. Data Aggregation (EA-FSDA) [25] has used Fuzzy Logic based scheme.

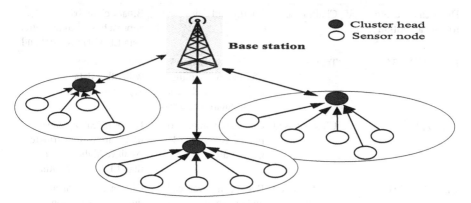

Fig. 3. Cluster-based data aggregation policy

A hybrid based approach is the combination of tree and clustering mechanism. In this, sensor nodes are grouped into two categories (i.e., tree and cluster), and the network is configured as sub regions implement one of these methods. In [26] authors introduced a hybrid approach where, a cluster based data aggregation policy is utilized to improve its robustness. Whereas in case of low loss rates, a tree-based scheme is utilized since of the efficiency which compresses the data.

However, there are several algorithmic approaches has been introduced by different authors to resolves the issues during the data aggregation process. Such algorithms are a tree-based shortest path and nearest source algorithm greedy algorithm [27], directed acyclic graph based approach [28], opportunistic data aggregation method for WSNs [29], anti-colony algorithm [30] and packet routing in network aggregation algorithm. Additionally, an algorithmic genetic approach is utilized to balance the energy while data aggregation in WSN. A scheduling algorithm is another important factor, which can affect the performance of the merging process. Most of the work done earlier to set up algorithms has been very specific to end2end end delays and power consumption problems. Data consolidation, a time reduction problem, was solved NP-hard and time measurement algorithm was introduced at [31].

The following Table 1 summarizes the different data aggregation routing algorithms.

Table 1. Summary of data aggregation algorithms

Algorithm	Topology	Objective	Characteristics
LEACH [23]	Cluster-based	Latency, network lifetime and delay	Randomly rotation of cluster heads, balance the energy usage among the sensors
PEDAP-PA [33]	Tree-based	Maximize the Network lifetime	Achieves double performance improvement as compared to LEACH and PEGASIS
Hierarchical chain based routing algorithm [34]	Chain-based	Energy and delay	Binary chain based approach is 2^3 times better than LEACH protocol and
EADAT [32, 34]	Tree-based	Increase the network lifetime by counting alive nodes at the end of the simulation process	There is no comparison with other data aggregation schemes
HEED [23]	Cluster-based	Counts the number of iterations until the 1st node death	Hypothetically, header nodes are well distributed. Achieve higher accuracy than LEACH algorithm
CLUDDA [35]	Cluster-based	Reduce the overhead and dynamic aggregation	Cluster communication during transmission Maintain the query cache at cluster heads

(continued)

Table 1. (*continued*)

Algorithm	Topology	Objective	Characteristics
MLDA] [36]	Tree-based	Increase lifetime schedule	The node with high residual energy Solves the time complexity problem
Greedy algorithm [37]	Chain-based	Minimum energy usage during network construction	Selection of appropriate route based on network density and location of sink node

4 Related Work

This section discusses the different forms of research work being carried out towards data aggregation, routing and safeguarding the communication system in WSN.

From the existing studies have seen that authors emphasized adopting optimization techniques to secure the communication channel. For example; in the study of [38] D. Qin et al. investigated a trust-based approach for secure routing with the aim of achieving reliable and effective results during data transmission. Primarily, the study analyzed the behavior of the sensor nodes based on their performance and usage of energy and evaluated their network performance by establishing the optimal route from source to sink node. This study represented the optimized routing mechanism by adopting semiring theory. However, the existing approach has witnessed the usage of swarm intelligence, optimization to find the cluster heads after reducing the energy, distance, and delay [8]. After the cluster heads identification, the algorithm finds the routing path to forward the message using cluster head to base-station. In various wireless real-time sensor applications, the user wants to access real-time information from the sensor node. In this regard, prior to obtaining the user authentication required to verify from a secure authentication method. As in real-time wireless real-time applications, user privacy plays a major role, and the authentication system for such a location must be anonymous. Therefore, Gope et al. [9] designed a unique authentication process for the WSN real-time application without compromising on other anonymous support. This approach focuses on achieving anonymity in the communication system. Abubakar et al. [10], proposed a Trust based cross-layer framework, which provides minimal protection against security attacks. The authors have introduced a series of cross-cutting rules that use multiple parameters for the exchange of multi-player data to reduce the effects of network security threats. In WSNs, routing is the most important operation to deals with data delivery to the base station. Recently, a trust-based routing mechanism is introduced for security enhancement and improves the data delivery performance among nodes. Many such routing approaches are proposed for secure communication against routing attacks.

Ishmanove et al. [39] evaluate current research and investigate open research challenges of safe routes in WSNs. Ren [40] explained that a trust-based scheme of trust is based on two factors such as the use of force and the acquisition of an attack. In various security attacks, black hole attacks are very common, which greatly affects data collection. The proposed solution can detect and avoid dark holes and improve data security [41]. From this approach can safely improve the security of the data route effectively and can improve network life time. WSNs have been heavily targeted by dangerous Byzantine invaders since their low power of calculation, limited power, powerful topology, and other factors. Byzantine intolerance is an age-old problem in the field of error tolerance and there is a wide range of system in the information system presented. Xu et al. [42] introduced an advanced version of the Byzantine algorithm for large WSNs with two imperial structures. The algorithm also includes elliptic curve cryptography and a digital signature algorithm that can withstand the onslaught of time and energy. Hamadi et al. [43] investigated a flexible network protection management algorithm to disable the performance of data delivery for wireless nerve networks. The work done by Mohammed et al. [44] has established secure and reliable routing routes in a multi-hop wireless networking system. The machine introduced combines payment and trust methods and reliability systems with a power-based protocol to improve route reliability and stability. In this way it can move nodes not only equally to transmit other packets but also can maintain route stability. And the author has designed "Reliable Shortest Route" and "Available Best Route" and listed them according to the above and the stability of the route. Implementation results have shown that the proposed system could increase the rate of delivery packs due to the establishment of stable routes. In [45] and [61] authors introduced a secure data-aggregation scheme by integrating the LEACH protocol with "Energy-efficient and Secure Pattern-based Data Aggregation protocol." This routing mechanism is suitable for cluster-based WSN. Always there is a tradeoff between power and defense. The prime challenge was to minimize the energy efficiency in WSN protocol which facilitates the efficient energy for security by comparison of other protocols under evaluation. Tang et al. [46] proposed the secure and reliable cost-based routing protocol. In this author considering the cost aware base routing protocols which address the high message delivery requirements.

Mohammadi et al. [47] analyzed the various dimensions of WSN security challenges and presented the wide variety of wireless sensor networks routing attacks and categorized them. The proposed mechanism classifies and differentiates the WSN's routing attacks based on features of WSNs routing layer, attacks, and attackers properties like as WSNs thread model, routing attacks nature, their strategies and effects. In this study, the prime focused on WSN security and entire work is splits into 3 folds which involve WSNs security, the threat model of WSN and routing attacks. What the authors also discussed about detection and defensive mechanism against routing attacks can help the security manager to manage the WSNs routing attacks more effectively. Long et al. [48], proposed a novel of the Tree-based routing scheme to preserve the source location privacy and maximize the network lifetime in WSNs. The study outcome of this approach has proven to possess an enhanced network lifetime. The prime objective is proved the high energy consumption and creates the redundancy diversionary routing scheme in non-hotspot areas with abundant energy. Therefore from a Tree-based routing scheme can achieve privacy preservation and WSN lifetime maximization. Juan.et al. [49] published an extended scheme of routing independent of any control message vehicular communication of nodes by introducing Watchdog nodes. The focus of this paper is to develop a secure routing protocol. As a solution, author utilizing the watchdog nodes and neighboring vehicles which can exchange and forward the packets by intended next hop. This mechanism is applied to VANET environment making this scheme capable of transferring the data packet in hostile scenarios where malicious nodes selectively transmit the data in the manner to cause packet losses. Therefore, in low-dense scenarios, the proposed secure routing protocol is very efficient due to lack of neighbors and enhanced version of prior legacy scheme till suffers from the influence of attackers which obtained maximum packet delivery ratio of about 50 percent. Selcuk et al. [50] presented the secure protocol mechanism based on synchronization factor for securely synchronizing the events in the network, without transferring synchronized control messages. The secure source based protocol provides the efficient a powerful en-route filtering method, where malicious messages can filter the form network. The author has indicated that the proposed legislation is able to achieve the harmonization event as quickly, accurately, and humbly as possible. This protocol is suitable for WSN systems where there is no need for complete synchronization and is able to provide a 7.24 μs clock accuracy of the delivery method given the current sensor technology that is more efficient than other previous methods such as GPS devices and twice as good as other power efficiency.

Zhan et al. [51] implemented a routing framework on the basis of trust factor securing communication in dynamic WSN. This trust-based scheme provides the trustworthy and energy efficient route. The major goal is to secure the WSN against the spiteful attacks in multi-hop routing mechanism which can identify the theft during routing information. The presented routing protocol achieves the high throughput, efficient energy, adaptability, and scalability. One more contribution of this paper is to accomplish comparatively low-overhead. While working on security, there is less emphasis on energy efficiency in algorithm construction. One the work carried out by Liu et al. [52] have presented on such energy-efficient technique that could be integrated with the security system in order to retain a good balance between energy efficiency and security performance. The authors have used a probabilistic Topology-Control for WSNs. The topology control is an efficient phenomenon which can increase the energy efficiency as well as improve the communication capacity in WSNs. In this novel, the author designed a communication model using probability theory. From the experimental results, they conclude that network energy efficiency could be increased by up to 250% and average node degree could reduce by 50%. Kellncr et al. [53] discussed various security challenges of the wireless sensor network with specially focused on the network layer. The prime goal was to provide a secure routing scheme for WSNs through the network. Therefore authors investigated the different types of security attacks on routing layer of wireless sensor networks like information disclosure, physical attacks, DoS attacks, Sybil attack, etc. The technique also highlighted the four most important related areas for secure routing were investigated and discussed involving cryptography, key-establishment, trust, and secure localization.

Lu et al. [54] presented a communication scheme for strengthening the authentication system considering the channel capacity of the nodes. The scheme has targeted to filters the injected false data in WSNs. From the comparative analysis outcomes, the proposed mechanism achieves high fidelity. For the purpose of the solution, they studied the random features of the WS transmission mode graph and estimated the probability of K neighbors. In addition, they have developed a custom JAVA simulator that demonstrates the effectiveness of the proposed method in terms of En-routing filtering and false positives. Gu et al. [55] designed a secure protect WSN's final communication policy The main idea was to pre-distribute different key numbers in different locations. Based on this approach, high-resolution protocol options were selected for the comparison of links with low-resilience while routing to sink node. It also applied the alternative routing path over high-resilience links for managing of the good balance between End to End secure communication links. Furthermore, they highlighted the various kinds of countermeasures against the security attacks. Shu et al. [56] has published the randomized multipath routing algorithm for the collection of secure data in WSN. The author has explored the four distributed mechanisms to propagate the information shares: such as i) purely random propagation, ii) directed random propagation, iii) random propagation of non-recursive form and iv) multicast tree assisted random propagation. Single-hop neighborhood information is applied in the first scheme whereas double-hop neighborhood information is applied in the second scheme which improves the energy efficiency. From the third method can achieve the same effects but also can record all traversed nodes to ignore traversing them again in the future. The fourth method propagates the shares in sink direction and makes the message delivery process more efficient. The author evaluated these dispersive routes by avoiding black holes and conducted the asymptotic analysis process for the worst case of packet interception and energy efficiency under "Purely Random Propagation (PRP)" scheme. Based on the analysis results, the author estimated the tradeoff between random propagation parameters and secret sharing parameters. The technique optimized all those parameters for minimizing of end-to-end energy efficiency for different security constraint. Tscha et al. [57] presented a routing mechanism based on source location privacy for WSNs of multiple sensors. The technique has used greedy-based approach for enhancing the location privacy. It is a Hybrid approach, where next hop node is selected in one of 4 modes; 1) Greedy, 2) Random, 3) Perimeter, and 4) retreat modes. P. De et al. [58] presented a Disease theory framework for analyzing the spread of malware attacks on a network of broadcasters. A structured framework can capture the local and temporary interactions of the distribution process. The first objective was to illustrate the process of communication between used and not exposed areas and to address three major broadcast processes such as i) Trickle, ii) Firecracker, iii) Flood. In this study the author used a mathematical model to analyze the process of spreading malware across various multihop streaming systems. Create this operating system captures behavior based on the evolution of broadcast protocol. Maarouf et al. [59] introduced a security solution using a trust-based information system. The scheme represents a system tracking feature to solve the problem of active monitoring in WSN. This program provides a possible way to reduce node monitoring activity. Finally, performance features are calculated in the form of a percentage of the ON-node average number of node monitoring activity. Ren et al. [60] demonstrated an integrated security structure to provide complete protection against data confidentiality, access, and authenticity. In this study the author has developed a new model of location-based data security in WSN. The entire offer is divided into four folders as the first proposed novel framework for effective local key management. Second, the proposed location-based system provides an end-to-end security guarantee. Third, the suggestion scheme had the potential to filter out false data in the face of popular data injection attacks. Ultimately, this approach provides high-quality data access by dealing with all interference attacks and forward transmission options. Performance parameters are analyzed with respect to storage capacity, computer calculations, and over-performance communication and energy saving. Roy et al. [61] have presented the greedy routing protocol for designing of secure routing algorithm and also designed a suitable encryption algorithm. According to this algorithm, each forwarded data packet is encrypted with the help of different keys. The analysis of curve based greedy routing algorithm shows that comparison parameters between Direct-Diffusion and LEACH protocol and stated that the proposed algorithm has less complexity by the comparison of existing methods.

The paper [62] and [63] explored an investigational study of secure data routing and aggregation techniques over WSNs. In [63] authors proposed a cross-layer scheme for optimizing routing with secure data aggregation, where algorithms provide a minimum cost, improved load balance or high security. Authors showed that cross-layer approach is well suitable for node identification, route adjustments and data aggregation which supports for large-scale WSNs. Additionally, both studies highlighted the energy consumption problem during data aggregation.

5 Security Schemes for Aggregation Routing

This section illustrates current research progress in the data aggregation process for WSNs which includes three major authentication mechanisms such as i) Key management scheme, ii) Certification and iii) Routing security.

5.1 Key Management Scheme

In current years, researchers have found various key management schemes and these schemes are categorized concerning their characteristics. According to the cryptography system, they classified the key management scheme into the symmetric and asymmetric scheme. Based on node key distribution methods, they categorized into the random key-management scheme and deterministic key-management scheme, and on network topology based; they divided into distributed and hierarchical key management scheme and so on.

- **Symmetric and Asymmetric key management scheme**: In sensor networks, the key-management scheme can be categorized as symmetric key-management and asymmetric key-management. In the first scheme, the sensor node contains similar keys for both Encryption and Decryption method and contains few calculation and storage amount. Whereas, Asymmetric key management has been taken unsuitable for WSNs, due to its huge requirements of storage, computing, and communication capabilities of sensor nodes. However, asymmetric key management algorithm is applied for WSNs security. By comparing of both methods, symmetric key management scheme is more advantageous than the asymmetric method concerning computational complexity.
- **Random and Deterministic key-management scheme**: In random keystroke, sensory nodes derive their keys from the key pool in a random way. The main advantage

is the easy access to the keys and flexibility. In the process of managing the determinant key, the sensor nodes check the fixed probability of finding their keys and take advantage of the fact that they can easily find the correct key.

- **Distributed and Hierarchical key management scheme**: Depending on the network topology, WSN key management can be classified as key management distribution and successive key management. In distributed mainstream control, sensor nodes have the same power of calculation and communication, and key communication and referrals are performed collaboratively between sensor areas. In the Hierarchical system, the network nodes are divided into clusters, and each cluster is collected as a cluster head and standard sensory nodes.

5.2 Certification

In a networking scheme, certification of network security plays an essential operation that provides the identity authentication and message authentication. In the following sub-section, discussing these two certification methods as well as briefly discussing basic methods of encryption; i.e., Symmetric and asymmetric method.

- **Identity Authentication**: one of the important characteristics of WSN is to provide a secure and fast access mechanism when every node accesses the self-organizing network. Recently, researchers developed the different certified authentication issues on encryption method. The symmetric encryption method is one of the primary characteristics of WSNs. However, the symmetric encryption method contains a lesser amount of computational efficiency than the asymmetric method because of the limited amount of nodes energy. The major advantage of symmetric cryptosystem has a strong calculation in authentication. Although, a research study shows that, if an amount of computation and storage-load is more, asymmetric keys also can be applied for WSNs.
- **Message Authentication**: Message authentication is nothing but to authenticate the received message from the sender side. This can be accomplished from a digital signature or symmetric method. Typically, there are two major categories in message authentication processes i) point to point authentication method and ii) broadcast authentication method. The second authentication method is a common method applied for message transmission in order to save resources in WSNs. Most commonly used protocol for broadcast authentication is TESLS protocol.

5.3 Routing Security

In WSN, routing is essential for data transmission and data aggregation process. In Multi-hop networks, WSNs have special characteristics, an i.e., aspect of routing security and need for depth research. The typical routing algorithms are broadly classified as i) Data-centric, ii) Location-based, and iii) Hierarchical-structure based routing protocol.

The data-centric routing protocol specially designed for WSNs which solves the data redundancy problem and generates the fused data from the nodes cooperation and increases the efficiency of data transmission as well as conserves the network energy. In location-based routing protocols, almost every node can use the location information and makes the route option without the need to save a route table. Examples for location-based routing protocols are; i) "Greedy Perimeter Stateless Routing" *and ii)* "Geographical Energy Aware Routing" protocols. In the Hierarchical structure based routing protocol, the sensors nodes are divided into multiple clusters, and each cluster contains a cluster node, controlling the communication between the nodes. After this, each cluster-head will transfer the data entered to the gateway-node which reduces traffic and control the node power. "Low-energy Adaptive Clustering Hierarchy (LEACH)" and "Threshold sensitive Energy Efficient Sensor Network Protocol (TEEN)" are the commonly used routing protocols. The next section highlights about research gap found towards the data aggregation mechanism in WSN.

6 Research Gap

This section discusses the existing research gap towards data aggregation with security.

- Secure data aggregation and transmission is one of the significant challenges to be considered during the designing of large-scale WSNs. In several applications, sensor nodes are placed at open places which are vulnerable to physical attacks that may compromise with security keys. Secure data-aggregation is the challenging task if the aggregator node and other sensors are malicious. Therefore, there is need of trust-aware routing scheme to perform a secure data-aggregation mechanism for large-scale WSNs.
- Energy demand during data aggregation; increasing of network lifetime in WSN is the major constraint, which pays more attention. Continuous energizing of node impossible since its expense. Therefore, in the low energy wireless networks, the power battery or energy harvesting sensors are required to maintain the network lifetime for future performance.
- The standards for wireless sensor networks use a first/second radio power model, which means that small improvements in energy efficiency should also improve data transfer quality and data-integration performance. This practice should be included in the performance appraisal of any research work that focuses on energy efficiency in WSN.
- Most of the existing works have talked about the usage of secure routing protocols for WSNs but without considering multi-layer security performance. In addition, some of the research spaces tested in studies related to data integration processes are less effective in a different network, higher technical complexity, no measurement, and no coping problems.
- From the high-security aspects, need to design an optimized routing strategy which ensures multi-level secure data aggregation scheme for resting any lethal attacks that significantly drains the energy of the sensor nodes.
- Some of the research papers illustrated that secure aggregation routing is one of the challenging issue assisting in transmission and communications in WSN, but it should be noticed that clustering and tree-based scheme uses security agreements such as LEACH, PEGASIS, HEED, etc., which are no longer valid and all are reported for major attacks. Existing security strategies used in WSNs are designed only to

detect similar networks and not different sensory networks. Therefore, the adoption of the previous level of security route in futuristic sensor network applications is not effective against malicious attacks.

7 Conclusion

In the proposed survey study, have discussed the different aspects of wireless sensor networks, routing strategies, different challenges, and design issues during the deployment of sensors in large-scale heterogamous network environments. This study mainly focused on secure data transmission and aggregation scheme also overviewed on various algorithmic concepts like DFS tree algorithm, DAG, OPAG, anti-colony algorithm and Greedy based algorithms, etc. In the review of the literature, the section has discussed different security routing scheme as well as data aggregation approaches. In the result have found research gap towards secure data aggregation with optimal routing scheme.

Therefore, in the future, there is essential to design an optimized routing protocol that ensures multi-level security in aggregation of data in WSNs. Also to develop a potential model to ensure trust and reputation computation over futuristic reconfigurable sensor networks to resist any lethal attacks.

References

1. Sohraby, K., Minoli, D., Znati, T.: Wireless Sensor Network Technology, Protocols, and Applications. Wiley, Hoboken (2007)
2. Seema, A., Reisslein, M.: Towards efficient wireless video sensor networks: a survey of existing node architectures and proposal for a Flexi-WVSNP design. IEEE Commun. Surv. Tutor. **13**, 462–486 (2011)
3. Tavli, B., Bicakci, K., Zilan, R., Barcelo-Ordinas, J.M.: A survey of visual sensor network platforms. Multimed. Tools Appl. **60**, 689–726 (2012)
4. Kumar, S., Dhull, K., Arora, P., Luhach, A.K.: Performance of energy conservation models, generic, micaz and micamotes, using AODV routing protocol on a wireless sensor network. Scalable Comput. Pract. Exp. **20**(4), 631–639 (2019)
5. Karlof, C., Wagner, D.: Secure routing in wireless sensor networks: attacks and countermeasures. Ad Hoc Netw. **1**, 293–315 (2003)
6. Qin, D., Yang, S., Jia, S., Zhang, Y., Ma, J., Ding, Q.: Research on trust sensing based secure routing mechanism for wireless sensor network. IEEE Access **5**, 9599–9609 (2017)
7. Bhatt, M., Sharma, S., Luhach, A.K., Prakash, A.: Nature inspired route optimization in vehicular adhoc network. In: 2016 5th International Conference on Reliability, Infocom Technologies and Optimization (Trends and Future Directions) (ICRITO), pp. 447–451. IEEE, September 2016
8. Choi, J., Bang, J., Kim, L., Ahn, M., Kwon, T.: Location-based key management strong against insider threats in wireless sensor networks. IEEE Syst. J. **11**(2), 494–502 (2017)
9. Gope, P., Lee, J., Quek, T.Q.S.: Resilience of DoS attacks in designing anonymous user authentication protocol for wireless sensor networks. IEEE Sens. J. **17**(2), 498–503 (2017)
10. Umar, I.A., Hanapi, Z.M., Sali, A., Zulkarnain, Z.A.: TruFiX: a configurable trust-based cross-layer protocol for wireless sensor networks. IEEE Access **5**, 2550–2562 (2017)
11. Singh, A.P., Luhach, A.K., Gao, X.Z., Kumar, S., Roy, D.S.: Evolution of wireless sensor network design from technology centric to user centric: an architectural perspective. Int. J. Distrib. Sens. Netw. **16**(8), 1550147720949138 (2020)

12. Saleh, S., Basurra, A.: Collision guided routing for ad-hoc mobile wireless networks. Ph.D thesis, Department of Computer Science, University of Bath, October 2012
13. Maratha, P., Gupta, K., Luhach, A.K.: Improved fault-tolerant optimal route reconstruction approach for energy consumed areas in wireless sensor networks. IET Wirel. Sens. Syst. 10(3), 112–116 (2019)
14. Ardakani, S.P.: Data aggregation routing protocols in wireless sensor networks: a taxonomy. arXiv preprint arXiv:1704.04588 (2017)
15. Al-Karaki, J.N., Kamal, A.E.: Efficient virtual-backbone routing in mobile ad hoc networks. Comput. Netw. 52(2), 327–350 (2008)
16. Al-Karaki, J.N., Ul-Mustafa, R., Kamal, A.E.: Data aggregation and routing in wireless sensor networks: optimal and heuristic algorithms. Comput. Netw. 53(7), 945–960 (2009)
17. Fasolo, E., Rossi, M., Widmer, J., Zorzi, M.: In-network aggregation techniques for wireless sensor networks: a survey. IEEE Wirel. Commun. J. 14(2), 70–87 (2007)
18. Rajagopalan, R., Varshney, P.K.: Data-aggregation techniques in sensor networks: a survey. IEEE Commun. Surv. Tutor. 8(4), 48–63 (2006)
19. Younis, O., Krunz, M., Ramasubramanian, S.: Node clustering in wireless sensor networks: recent developments and deployment challenges. IEEE Netw. J. 20(3), 20–25 (2006)
20. Villas, L.A., et al.: DRINA: a lightweight and reliable routing approach for in-network aggregation in wireless sensor networks. IEEE Trans. Comput. 62(4) (2013)
21. Ozdemir, S., Xiao, Y.: Secure data aggregation in wireless sensor networks: a comprehensive overview. Comput. Netw. 53, 20222037 (2009)
22. Heinzelman, W.R., Chandrakasan, A.P., Balakrishnan, H.: An application-specific protocol architecture for wireless micro sensor networks. Trans. Wirel. Commun., 660– 670 (2002)
23. Younis, O., Fahmy, S.: HEED: a hybrid, energy-efficient, distributed clustering approach for ad hoc sensor networks. IEEE Trans. Mob. Comuput. 3(4), 366–379 (2004)
24. Swathi, Y., Chitnis, S.: Energy aware fuzzy logic secure data aggregation (EA-FSDA) technique for wireless sensor networks. Int. J. Eng. Adv. Technol. (IJEAT) 8(6) (2019). ISSN: 2249-8958
25. Manjhi, A., Nath, S., Gibbons, P.B.: Tributaries and deltas: efficient and robust aggregation in sensor network stream. In: SIG-MOD, Baltimore, MD, USA, pp. 287–298. ACM (2005)
26. Krishnamachari, B., Estrin, D., Wicker, S.: Impact of data aggregation in wireless sensor networks
27. Motegi, S., Yoshihara, K., Horiuchi, H.: DAG based in-network aggregation for sensor network monitoring. In: Proceedings of the 2005 Symposium on Applications and the Internet (SAINT06) (2006). 0-7695-2262-9/06
28. Chen, Z., Shin, K.G.: OPAG: opportunistic data aggregation in wireless sensor networks. In: 2008 Real-Time Systems Symposium (2008)
29. Liao, W.-H., Kao, Y., Fan, C.-M.: Data aggregation in wireless sensor networks using ant colony algorithm. J. Netw. Comput. Appl. 31, 387–401 (2008)
30. Chen, X., Hu, X., Zhu, J.: Minimum data aggregation time problem in wireless sensor networks. In: 1st International Conference on Mobile Ad-hoc and Sensor Network–MSN, pp. 133–142 (2005)
31. Fotso, D.B.F.: Efficient data aggregation and routing in wireless sensor networks. Ph.D diss., Télécom ParisTech (2013)
32. Tan, H.O., Korpeoglu, I.: Power efficient data gathering and aggregation in wireless sensor networks. SIGMOD Rec. 32(4), 66–71 (2003)
33. Lindsey, S., Raghavendra, C., Sivalingam, K.M.: Data gathering algorithms in sensor networks using energy metrics. IEEE Trans. Parallel Distrib. Syst. 13(9), 924–935 (2002)
34. Ding, M., Cheng, X., Xue, G.: Aggregation tree construction in sensor networks. In: 2003 IEEE 58th Vehicular Technology Conference, vol. 4, no. 4, pp. 2168–2172, October 2003

35. Chatterjea, S., Havinga, P.: A dynamic data aggregation scheme for wireless sensor networks. In: Proceedings of the Program for Research on Integrated Systems and Circuits, Veldhoven, The Netherlands, November 2003

36. Kalpakis, K., Dasgupta, K., Namjoshi, P.: Efficient algorithms for maximum lifetime data gathering and aggregation in wireless sensor networks. Comput. Netw. **42**(6), 697–716 (2003)

37. Du, K., Wu, J., Zhou, D.: Chain-based protocols for data broadcasting and gathering in sensor networks. In: International Parallel and Distributed Processing Symposium, April 2003

38. Qin, D., Yang, S., Jia, S., Zhang, Y., Ma, J., Ding, Q.: Research on trust sensing based secure routing mechanism for the wireless sensor network. IEEE Access **5**, 9599–9609 (2017)

39. Ishmanov, F., Zikria, Y.B.: Trust mechanisms to secure routing in wireless sensor networks: current state of the research and open research issues. J. Sens. **2017** (2017)

40. Ren, J., Zhang, Y., Zhang, K., Shen, X.: Adaptive and channel-aware detection of selective forwarding attacks in wireless sensor networks. IEEE Trans. Wirel. Commun. **15**(5), 3718–3731 (2016)

41. Liu, Y., Dong, M., Ota, K., Liu, A.: ActiveTrust: secure and trustable routing in wireless sensor networks. IEEE Trans. Inf. Forensics Secur. **11**(9), 2013–2027 (2016)

42. Xu, J., et al.: Byzantine fault-tolerant routing for large-scale wireless sensor networks based on fast ECDSA. Tsinghua Sci. Technol. **20**(6), 627–633 (2015)

43. Al-Hamadi, H., Chen, I.R.: Adaptive network defense management for countering smart attack and selective capture in wireless sensor networks. IEEE Trans. Netw. Serv. Manage. **12**(3), 451–466 (2015)

44. Mahmoud, M.M.E.A., Lin, X., Shen, X.: Secure and reliable routing protocols for heterogeneous multihop wireless networks. IEEE Trans. Parallel Distrib. Syst. **26**(4), 1140–1153 (2015)

45. Rahayu, T.M., Lee, S.-G., Lee, H.-J.: A secure routing protocol for wireless sensor networks considering secure data aggregation. Sensors **15**(7), 15127–15158 (2015). Puliafito A. (ed.) https://doi.org/10.3390/s150715127

46. Tang, D., Li, T., Ren, J., Wu, J.: Cost-aware secure routing (CASER) protocol design for wireless sensor networks. IEEE Trans. Parallel Distrib. Syst. **26**(4), 960–973 (2015)

47. Mohammadi, S., et al.: A comparison of routing attacks on wireless sensor networks. J. Inf. Assur. Secur. **6**, 195–215 (2011)

48. Long, J., Dong, M., Ota, K., Liu, A.: Achieving source location privacy and network lifetime maximization through tree-based diversionary routing in wireless sensor networks. IEEE Access **2**, 633–651 (2014)

49. Martinez, J.A., Vigueras, D., Ros, F.J., Ruiz, P.M.: Evaluation of the use of guard nodes for securing the routing in VANETs. J. Commun. Netw. **15**(2), 122–131 (2013)

50. Selcuk Uluagac, A., Beyah, R.A., Copeland, J.A.: Secure SOurce-BAsed Loose Synchronization (SOBAS) for wireless sensor networks. EEE Trans. Parallel Distrib. Syst. **24**(4), 803–813 (2013)

51. Zhan, G., Shi, W., Deng, J.: Design and implementation of TARF: a trust-aware routing framework for WSNs. IEEE Trans. Dependable Secur. Comput. **9**(2), 184–197 (2012)

52. Liu, Y., Ni, L., Hu, C.: A generalized probabilistic topology control for wireless sensor networks. IEEE J. Sel. Areas Commun. **30**(9), 1780–1788 (2012)

53. Kellner, A., et al.: A survey on measures for secure routing in wireless sensor networks. Int. J. Sens. Netw. Data Commun. **1**, 17 (2012)

54. Lu, R., Lin, X., Zhu, H., Liang, X., Shen, X.: BECAN: a bandwidth-efficient cooperative authentication scheme for filtering injected false data in wireless sensor networks. IEEE Trans. Parallel Distrib. Syst. **23**(1), 32–43 (2012)

55. Gu, W., Dutta, N., Chellappan, S., Bai, X.: Providing end-to-end secure communications in wireless sensor networks. IEEE Trans. Netw. Serv. Manage. **8**(3), 205–218 (2011)

56. Shu, T., Krunz, M., Liu, S.: Secure data collection in wireless sensor networks using randomized dispersive routes. IEEE Trans. Mob. Comput. **9**(7), 941–954 (2010)
57. Tscha, Y.: Routing for enhancing source-location privacy in wireless sensor networks of multiple assets. J. Commun. Netw. **11**(6), 589–598 (2009)
58. De, P., Liu, Y., Das, S.K.: An epidemic theoretic framework for vulnerability analysis of broadcast protocols in wireless sensor networks. IEEE Trans. Mob. Comput. **8**(3), 413–425 (2009)
59. Maarouf, I., Baroudi, U., Naseer, A.R.: Efficient monitoring approach for reputation system-based trust-aware routing in wireless sensor networks. IET Commun. **3**(5), 846–858 (2009)
60. Ren, K., Lou, W., Zhang, Y.: LEDS: providing location-aware end-to-end data security in wireless sensor networks. IEEE Trans. Mob. Comput. **7**(5), 585–598 (2008)
61. Roy, S., Conti, M., Setia, S., Jajodia, S.: Secure data aggregation in wireless sensor networks. IEEE Trans. Inf. Forensics Secur. **7**(3), 1040–1052 (2012)
62. Yang, Q., Zhu, X., et al.: Survey of security technologies on wireless sensor networks. J. Sens. **2015**, 9 (2015). Hindawi publication corporation
63. Talele, A.K., Patil, S.G., Chopade, N.B.: A survey on data routing and aggregation techniques for wireless sensor networks. In: 2015 International Conference on Pervasive Computing (ICPC), pp. 1–5. IEEE (2015)
64. Mishra, M., Gupta, G.S., Gui, X.: A review of and a proposal for cross-layer design for efficient routing and secure data aggregation over WSN. In: 2017 3rd International Conference on Computational Intelligence and Networks (CINE), pp. 120–125. IEEE (2017)

Comparative Analysis of Internet of Things (IoT) Security Models

Tamanna Siddiqui and Saif Saffah Badr Alazzawi[✉]

Aligarh Muslim University, Aligarh, UP, India

Abstract. Nowadays the internet of Things (IoT) is among the most trending technology to make the world better and smart. But IoT technology is not fully matured yet and there are so many security challenges faces while implementing (IoT) in real life that must be overcome like Improper tools upgrades, lack of competent and robust security agreements, user unawareness, and active appliance monitoring. In this paper, we explore the background of IoT cyber security and privacy measures; identify many security and privacy issues. Different methods used to protect parts of systems and systems based on IoT. Currently existing security solution, excellent models privacy required, suitable for different layers of IoT-operated applications. In this work, we proposed a comparative analysis of various IoT security models like Amazon Web Services (AWS), Trust model in IoT-enabled Vehicular Networks, and Autonomous IoT/IIoT Security Models. Along with proposed its solutions and future scope and impact of these security challenges on our social, economical and commercial life.

Keywords: IoT · Security models · Cybersecurity · Security threats · Cloud computing · Internet and communication technology (ICT)

1 Introduction

The word Internet of Things (IoT) related to the idea of connected devices through sensors with the help of the Internet. The enormous use of IoT devices for multiple purposes like smart homes, communication, education, business and transportation hike its popularity in the world and it will lead soon in near future. Now, it is easily possible to communicate through the wireless and remote location with the help of IoT. The IoT was introduced in the early '90s and it was known as computing or embedded computing the Internet. In the year 2011, there was a drastic switch in technology from traditional ways to automation like smart home, smart grid and smart meters which helped the organization to market research and business decisions. IoTs also developed the living standard of the people from automation. It also connected things, Humans, systems and knowledge [1]. Moreover, the privacy and security challenges can be faced due to the unrestrained in this field like no password privacy, devices evaluation failure, malicious data access and use of IoT devices in a casual way. All these vulnerable things increase the risk of getting hacked, manipulation and data theft. Lack of security and policies of IoT considered it as the most vulnerable field by security specialist and researcher. Researcher and security

© Springer Nature Singapore Pte Ltd. 2021
A. K. Luhach et al. (Eds.): ICAICR 2020, CCIS 1394, pp. 186–196, 2021.
https://doi.org/10.1007/978-981-16-3653-0_15

eminent have developed many security algorithms and protocols to safe IoT devices from theft but security strategies are not properly mentioned and followed [2]. On the other side, hackers developed different malware and infected worms to attack devices they try to theft vital data generated by companies' employee or individuals who share significant information [3]. That is why people face security challenges while sending data. Security threats can be reduced by developing high-security defence mechanisms against threats if they can be detected by organizations experts. Many organization currently using IoT based devices [4]. It has created a competitive environment among multiple business tycoons. Data collection manipulation and improvement are highly accepted through IoT devices in data-oriented companies which created major issues in privacy and security. It is necessary for companies to higher experts handle such kind of breaches and create an inclusive security measure and polices to protect the essential data and items of the company with sustainability. Like IoT smart home connected to the local network is the source for vulnerability to hackers it can violate the personal data business information and other important things which may lead to a big loss to a person or organization, It is a dynamic era every second of life technology is changing and due to which it is very difficult to programmers and developers to protect devices, data from hackers and crackers. According to L. Tawalbeh [5], 5G technologies which are now one of the new technologies is going to come in the market and it will play a vital role in IoT applications and implementation. This technology has a short length of propagation with high volume and bandwidth that may increase the more devices and tower to propagate in same region in wireless mode. It will be beneficial to users but it also has privacy and security risks such that a new area may poses illegal access to channels all these risks must be managed. Our work is to give through explanation of IoT applications, advantages and abilities. Next to creating a well planned security network with applications our suggestion is that it is better to avoid such kind of problems and take possible safety measures. Our work will create direction to users, organizations to apply policies, awareness of theft to end users and all others that are part of IoT development program.

The rest of the paper is organized as follows: The next Sect. 2 presents the related work in IoT security models, in Sect. 3, presents the overview of the existing security models, Sect. 4 analysis and discussions, Sect. 5 future scope and Sect. 6 conclusion and results.

2 Related Work

As we know, the Internet of Things (IoT) has started converting multiple products like homes, appliances, customers, organizations its working procedure in a smart way. In recent years, IoT occupied the place of much traditional work and help in do in an efficient and effective model. According to S. S. B. Alazzawi, T. Siddiqui, and N. A. Khan [6], wireless sensor network has played an important role in IoT security and find its vulnerability on the results they have developed a trust and reputation security model which can try to address the limitation in the wireless network. And the major problem of risk and challenge of cybersecurity of IoT products, hackers and crackers are continuously targeting the devices to find the loophole and vulnerable positions to attack from there. T. Siddiqui and S. S. Badr Alazzawi [7] says that cybersecurity risks in IoT devices can be managed by tools and techniques which can provide safeguard against the vulnerabilities of multiple devices like gateways, mobile applications, and appliances. According to R. Ankele, S. Marksteiner, K. Nahrgang, and H. Vallant [8] the huge development of IoT in the industrial field make has opened a gateway to the future production and growth of industrial field IoT security is a major issue in the current scenario will change by using new technology that will bring automation in many industries and all these development and highly used IoT products can bring many security risk and threats, cyber-attacks can increase and traditional methods are not completely helpful to defends such attacks. According to Leach, A. K., Dwivedi, S. K. & Jha, C. K [9]. E-commerce is the best system for business and its Service Oriented Architecture (SOA) gives an autonomous platform. And its security is one of the major challenges due to poor planning and designing of E-commerce system it also affects the hike in the business [10]. According to A. K. Luhach and R. Luhach [11], the SOA can give an analysis of the security can prevent. Nowadays, IoT can be used in our houses, cities, and medical fields IoT based four layered communication can enhance the security at every layer [12]. IoT also helps to communicate in various physical devices to enhance the development of Information and Communication Technology (ICT) [13]. F. Ahmad, A. Adnane, F. Kurugollu, and R. Hussain [14] says that a Vehicular Ad-hoc NETwork (VANET) is one of the most important and used technology in today's world, now vehicle can share its data which is generated from many sources in real-time monitoring bases and it requires a secure environment so that the data is protected its integrity remains to maintain its integrity they have developed a Trust Models for Safety Applications in IoT-enabled Vehicular Networks which can simulate the results and protect the data generated by the vehicle. According to M. binti Mohamad Noor and W. H. Hassan [15] the security of any person using IoT devices must be maintained and in recent years the research on security on IoT devices has gained momentum with the tools and techniques.

3   Overview of the Existing Security Models

The current IoT models that are widely used in the market are based on shared security systems, covering a huge base of services, in some cases they cover too much and have the site depend on them to a degree where the security becomes very predictable as the actions taken by the models are easily predictable, therefore specialized security models are required an trusted by many corporations and site owners as they allow for the indispensable option of customizing their security with the help of third-party programs which make the resulting model much more specific and tailored for the client rather than for a general populace. There are various security model exists for IoT devices security, they have tried to find the better solutions of threats and risks of security, attacked by multiple sources. Among many we have mentioned few of them given below:

3.1   The Amazon Web Service Model

The first model tackles the problem of how to reduce operational burden on a security system in a rapidly expanding infrastructure online. Proposed in the AWS or Amazon web services, this security model secures the infrastructure which supports the cloud services of the infrastructure and helps them maintain a reliable and shared security throughout the infrastructure without putting too much load or operational burden while minimizing the human interference to a minimum.

The model AWS model divides the different aspects of security into different 'responsibilities', this allows for the shared work on all the different responsibilities while putting the lowest burden on the security system. The customer-related objects which include data, IDs, system information, both side encryptions and networking information are included in the 'responsibility for security 'in' the cloud, meaning a person or another third party protection system can be implemented on those objects. While the AWS cover the responsibility for security 'of' the cloud these include the region parameters, the zones with the availability of the service, the edge locations for the hardware devices and the abilities of computation, storage, database and networking are handled in the software aspect.

This classification makes the system highly customizable to the needs of a business and able to adapt to a wider host rather than a very specific no. of them. Other than the extremely adaptive approach of AWS, they have other compliances for the security in the physical and hardware aspects such as temperature maintenance for the smooth operation of servers and other hardware.

The system is quite flexible as well as it can move the incoming traffic on a server to a different server in case of failure, allowing for rapid recovery from errors which might occur due to the lack of availability of servers.

The security is handled by the implementation of different rule sets such as ACL (Access control lists), by providing secure access points (HTTPS), FIPS (Federal Information Processing Standard Publication).

The design extremely faults tolerant and hence can cope with the demands of an ever-increasing network. The AWS is separate from the Amazon corporate network and hence relies on an SSH- public key authentication through a bastion host. The system, however, relies on so many middle steps for authentication and agreements that the learning curve for the implementation is quite steep, it does not provide enterprise-grade support, this needs to be bought separately.

Despite being so complex and steady the system has faced many high profile outages in recent history. Another factor is that the AWS does not support multi-cloud which is limiting for the IT industry as in the system's base it is intended for the security 'of' the cloud rather than the security of the main cloud and its supplementary cloud.

3.2 Trust Model in IoT-Enabled Vehicular Netwokrs

This model sprouts out of the necessity for clear, concise and accurate information needed for the self-driving vehicles which require proper information to make better decisions in real-time to avoid any sort of accidents from happening. This requires that the vehicles be provided proper data which was free of any unnecessarily added information which might tamper with the whole outcome of the information provided by the other nodes. Therefore every node is given a trust score which is evaluated base on the analyzed information sent by that node.

The paper discusses these trust models:

3.2.1 Eigen Trust

This trust model uses two different variables which are global and local reputation which is determined by the information sent by that node and calculated as such.

Local Trust between two nodes (q, r)

$$\underset{qr}{\mathrm{L}} = satisfied\,(q, r) - unsatisfied\,(q, r)$$

The local trust is normalized and the value of 'i' obtained is put into the Global Equation which yields the global reputation the Eigenvalue of the nodes will be the same in the entire network which promises consistency.

3.2.2 Peer Trust

Peer trust works based on these-

- No of transactions performed by the nodes
- Feedback of nodes regarding the information
- The credibility of the node giving that information
- Context factor.

The equation for the peer trust model is

$$\mathrm{T(i)} = \alpha \sum_{n=1}^{l} (i)\mathrm{S}(i, n)\mathrm{CR}(\mathrm{p}(i, n))\mathrm{AF}(i, n) + \beta \mathrm{xCF}(i)$$

The credibility that is derived from the nodes or CR(j) takes the intersect of both node's transactions into consideration.

In simpler terminology, the peer trust system works on a cross-examination factor for the information of two nodes with overlapping transactions to determine the credibility.

3.2.3 BTRM-WSN

Also known as Bio-inspired trust and reputation model for wireless sensing networks. This model works based on ant colony optimization algorithm. That allows us to find good/ shortest and feasible path from one location to another. This running on a wireless network instructing the vehicles is an amazing possibility as it uses the nodes to provide the best path from one location to another based on their trust and reputation.

3.3 Autonomous IoT/IIoT Security Model

From the above-listed models, we can see a pattern as there are areas where they excel and areas where they are vulnerable or just inept to expand more than their initial abilities, therefore there is a cusp of qualities and points to keep in mind which are needed to check and design a security system for IoT technologies keeping in mind their applications, uses and future applications. The paper "Requirements and Recommendations for IoT/IIoT Models to automate Security Assurance through Threat Modelling, Security Analysis and Penetration Testing" records these necessities intensely proposing several of the requirements and recommendations for the process.

The parameters are to be considered with the final result in mind and the types of attacks that might follow up in consideration of the service that is being offered.

Eg. The previously stated Eigen trust model deployed for the feeding of proper information from nodes to each other can be attacked to alter the information and cause accidents/ delays which might be the major intent of attackers, therefore, the system implemented was the trust model which excels at detecting any attacks that change the values in the transactions to accomplish its goals, therefore a system that detects changes in values was the ideal security for its security, this makes the directly affecting the system very difficult. Passive attacks however won't affect the system directly so they are not prioritized in the security model.

The AWS model also does this by limiting itself to a single cloud and not being multi-cloud and having strict compliances and authorization protocols which result in very controlled access rather than going multi-cloud and allowing for more access points for attacks to be carried out as the parameter for the AWS was the security of the cloud and preventing any threat to reach the cloud rather than protect the contents inside the cloud.

The approach of Threat Models plays a vital part in this area, knowing which threats are prone to attack the system brings a clearer picture of the parameters needed. Therefore rather than simple generalized protection, a specialized model for protection can be put in place. The models which emerge from the previously mentioned methods need to go through security analysis and penetration testing.

The models need to be analyzed for the features they offer and the methods they use to offer those features, encryptions used and other features are tested for their effectiveness. In the penetration phase testing the models need to go through several simulated attacks on them of the desired type of attack.

Eg. A model made for preventing phishing needs to go through several phishing attacks simulated on it, which test its integrity, encryption, packet safety, integration with the desired technology and error-proof backend design, etc.

In the end, a proper analysis of the model-based upon the listed factors is needed:

- Network properties
- Hardware properties
- Software and Operating system Properties
- Security Properties
- Performance properties

The system also should be competent to make sure convenient data authority across users. To keep the privacy of multiple users while handling the huge amount of data, data analytics algorithms and cryptographic techniques are required. These are the recommendations for the development of IoT/IIoT Models to automate security assurance through threat modelling security analysis and penetration (Table 1).

Table 1. Comparative analysis between trust models for safety applications in iot-enabled vehicular networks

Attack type	Eigen trust	Peer trust	BTRM-WSN
Authentication attack	Effective only if the impersonating node tries to attempt an active attack. Passive attacks eg. Eavesdropping is undetected	Effective against all authentication attacks as the impersonating system compromises the credibility and hence the system can detect them	Not effective if the impersonating node replicates the information that is normally sent and then mixes malicious information with it
Availability attack	Extremely effective as it gathers trust from neighbouring nodes and is hence able to identify an availability attack being performed	Effective as the system cross-references the instances and hence can differentiate the node that the attack is being performed on by comparing it to its cross-referenced node	Extremely effective as an availability attack results in the destruction of trust due to availability of packets and hence the system detects it, However wormhole attacks and hello flood attacks are extremely effective against this system
Confidentiality attack	Not effective as it is passive in nature and hence goes undetected	Not effective as it is passive in nature and hence goes undetected	Not effective as it is passive in nature and hence goes undetected
Integrity attack	Effective as the integrity attack mostly changes the trust value and hence gets detected	Effective as the cross-referencing of the information reveals the change in integrity and hence the attack gets detected	Effective as the packets transferred will have an integrity difference when compared to other packets and hence get detected

4   Analysis and Discussion

This paper presents a literature review of comparative analysis of various IoT based security model, this review paper is very supportive because it brings important information of several IoT-based security techniques used in multiple models of computer science field on a single platform to better understand the field and this is the important contribution of our paper, as we know from the above study combining both IoT and cyber security can make the system more productive, efficient and create various new challenges in the field of computer science which can draw the attention of scientists and researchers to convert those challenges into opportunity. We have reviewed many security-based techniques along with their technical aspects which are best in our knowledge. Table 2 has successfully demonstrated the comparative analysis of AWS, IoT-enabled Vehicular Networks and IOT/IIOT security models on the bases of Confidentiality, Integrity and Availability (CIA) triad and Future aspects.

Table 2. Comparative analysis based on CIA triad

Security model	Confidentiality	Integrity	Availability	Future aspects
AWS	Provides confidentiality due to its nature of being restricted to a single cloud rather than being a multi-cloud model	The integrity of the data being received in the cloud is safeguarded but only after the implementation of third-party models which might result in a breach of integrity itself	The data is available for the administrators however the normal user might not be able to access all the data	As the trends of web-based applications are increasing in near future its security will highly increase with model algorithms
IoT-enabled Vehicular Networks Eigen Trust	It is unable to identify the passive attacks such as the eavesdropping attacks. Therefore, it compromises confidentiality	The system is very good at detecting and dealing with integrity attacks	The data is readily available to all the nodes to be used. Hence the availability is good	Many companies are working on automated vehicle system and this model is to identify the passive attack so its compromisation will be removed with other ones
IoT-enabled Vehicular Networks Peer Trust	Does not offer confidentiality as it detects breaches after they have occurred and a node has been compromised	The integrity is well secured as the data is cross-referenced and checked to give it any credibility	The data is shared by and among all the nodes. Hence the availability is good	In near future, this type of model will detect breaches in the early stage of the attack so its confidentiality will not be compromised
IoT-enabled Vehicular Networks BTRM-WSN	Confidentiality is compromised similar to the other trust models	Integrity is well maintained due to regular checks performed by other nodes	Availability is good since the data is shared by all the nodes	This model shares the data to all the clouds so its confidentiality and integrity will maintain shortly

(continued)

Table 2. (*continued*)

Security model	Confidentiality	Integrity	Availability	Future aspects
IoT/ IIOT security model	It provides confidentiality to some extents as the other models	Integrity is not highly maintained due to the high generation of data	Availability is better data is highly generated and maintained by automated devices	As the industrial revolution is going to happen many companies and organization are going to automate their processes in future

5 Future Scope in IoT-Based Security

As we know, data generation through smart things is increasing rapidly on the cloud. Because we are surrounding with the IoT based devices like our offices, home, vehicles all are connected with the internet and if they will not secure, it is a threat to users. And require some important security measures. We expect in the next few years it will be based on the growth of security standards, user behaviour and education of IoT devices. We have proposed some following future scope:

- Future IoT devices systems will rapidly and properly respond to security attacks and vulnerable part of the device and prepare to ratify improvement system. The system must be able to identify the problems and weakness in the system and take proper precautions and security actions for various part of the system is also necessary.
- The system is also competent to make sure convenient data authority across users. To keep the privacy of multiple users while handling the huge amount of data, data analytics algorithms and cryptographic techniques are required.
- For the advance IoT systems, risk evaluation and risk management techniques will be required for the complete lifecycle and modern technologies to gather and process security-related figures to make active and online vulnerability analytics based on that data. We need some novel machine learning-based real-time risk assessment model. That can warn with maximum correctness and the minimum amount of false positives. Modern risk evaluation system and security rules are necessary to give warning earlier in future IoT devices.

6 Conclusion

We can conclude our research about the approach to tackle cyber security for IoT and what to expect and what to prepare for and from such systems in because it brings important information of several IoT-based security techniques used in multiple models of computer science field on a common platform to better understand the field. And this is one of the important contributions of our paper. The applications of IoT-based devices may not be just limited to corporations or businesses. If in the mentioned models, improvement can provide a much better environment even on consumer platforms, helping people to consolidate the internet, Identity and the individual rights for a person. Social services can avail improved truth models to circle out fake accounts and stop misinformation from spreading. The AWS if becomes able to provide the same level of safety on a multi-cloud level, it can ensure a safe environment for not only a single corporation but the whole business circle. From the above study combining both IoT-based devices and cybersecurity can make the system more efficient and create various new challenges in the field of computer science which can draw the attention of scientists and researchers to convert those challenges into opportunity. So there will be a great scope of security in IoT based devices.

References

1. Patel, K.K., Patel, S.M., Scholar, P.G.: Internet of Things-IOT: definition, characteristics, architecture, enabling technologies, application & future challenges. Int. J. Eng. Sci. Comput. **6**, 1–10 (2016)
2. Conti, M., Dehghantanha, A., Franke, K., Watson, S.: Internet of Things security and forensics: challenges and opportunities. Futur. Gener. Comput. Syst. **78**, 544–546 (2018)
3. Aldwairi, M., Tawalbeh, L.: Security techniques for intelligent spam sensing and anomaly detection in online social platforms. Int. J. Electr. Comput. Eng. **10**, 275–287 (2020)
4. Makhdoom, I., Abolhasan, M., Lipman, J., Liu, R.P., Ni, W.: Anatomy of threats to the Internet of Things. IEEE Commun. Surv. Tutorials **21**, 1636–1675 (2019)
5. Tawalbeh, L., Muheidat, F., Tawalbeh, M., Quwaider, M.: IoT privacy and security: challenges and solutions. Appl. Sci. **10**, 4102 (2020)
6. Alazzawi, S.S.B., Siddiqui, T., Khan, N.A.: Generalization of IoT applications: systematic review. Int. J. Sci. Res. Comput. Sci. Eng. Inf. Technol. **3**, 688–694 (2018)
7. Siddiqui, T., Badr Alazzawi, S.S.: Security of Internet of Things. Int. J. Appl. Sci. Res. Rev. **05**, 1–4 (2018)
8. Ankele, R., Nahrgang, K., Marksteiner, S., Vallant, H.: Requirements and recommendations for IoT/IIoT models to automate security assurance through threat modelling, security analysis and penetration testing. *arXiv* (2019)
9. Luhach, A.K., Dwivedi, S.K. Jha, C.K.: Applying SOA to an E-commerce system and designing a logical security framework for small and medium sized E-commerce based on SOA. In: 2014 IEEE International Conference on Computational Intelligence and Computing Research, pp. 1–6 (2014). https://doi.org/10.1109/ICCIC.2014.7238358
10. Satapathy, S.C., Joshi, A., Modi, N., Pathak, N.: Preface. Adv. Intell. Syst. Comput. **409**, v–vi (2016)
11. Luhach, A.K., Luhach, R.: Research and Implementation of Security Framework For Small And Medium Sized E-Commerce Based on SOA (2015)
12. Isha, Luhach, A.K., Kumar, S.: Layer based security in internet of things: current mechanisms, prospective attacks, and future orientation. In: Unal, A., Nayak, M., Mishra, D.K., Singh, D., Joshi, A. (eds.) Smart Trends in Information Technology and Computer Communications, SmartCom 2016. CCIS, vol. 628, pp. 896–903. Springer, Singapore (2016). https://doi.org/10.1007/978-981-10-3433-6_107
13. Isha, Luhach, A.K.: Analysis of lightweight cryptographic solutions for internet of things. Indian J. Sci. Technol. **9**, 2–8 (2016)

14. Ahmad, F., Adnane, A., Kurugollu, F., Hussain, R.: A comparative analysis of trust models for safety applications in IoT-enabled vehicular networks. IFIP Wirel. Days 2019-April, 1–8 (2019)
15. Mohamad Noor, M.b., Hassan, W.H.: Current research on Internet of Things (IoT) security: a survey. Comput. Netw. **148**, 283–294 (2019)

Study of Energy Efficient Routing Protocols for Adhoc-Wireless Sensor Networks

Rakesh, Payal, and Suresh Kumar[✉]

ECE Department, University Institute of Engineering and Technology (UIET), MDU,
Rohtak, Haryana, India
sureshvashist.uiet.ece@mdurohtak.ac.in

Abstract. Wireless Sensor Networks (WSN) comprise of a large number of deployed sensor nodes in a certain desired structure. These sensing nodes are generally of minimum cost, less power and different functionality with the capabilities of sensing the parameters, communicating and computing the desired data. Energy conservation is one of the important issues in WSN as DC batteries are employed as power source for the nodes and at times, it is not feasible to replace the nodes frequently. This makes saving of power vital so as to increase the node life span. To ensure the availability of the sensor network for longer duration and minimize the use of power resources, we need to focus on energy efficient routing protocols. This has led the WSN to be one of the hottest topics for researchers. Therefore, it becomes utmost essential to study the current protocols used in WSN with respect to their applications and limitations. In this paper we have made a consolidated effort to analyze the protocols. This will facilitate the development of new or modified routing protocols for optimum performance of AWSN for deployment in both static and mobile environments including hostile terrain.

Keywords: Ad-hoc Wireless Sensor Network (AWSN) · AODV · AEED · DYMO · Packet Delivery Ratio (PDR) · Total Packet Received (TPR)

1 Introduction

Adhoc WSN is being considered as fastest growing research areas in the modern digital world. WSN contains a collection of analogous, self-motivated nodes called sensor nodes. These nodes are having lesser power, fewer computational capacity and basic memory. These are connected by a wireless radio frequency medium. The basic function of sensor networks comprises collection of data from the environment and then sending it to the desired destination.

The routing process in WSN differs from conventional IP network routing, as it exhibits numerous exceptional characteristics [1]. The Routing Protocol (RP) for Adhoc WSN must have the ability to select best path for communication among the nodes while reducing the bandwidth and overheads to ensure proper routing and transmission time to converge after the topology changes. One of the significant concerns in WSN remains the network's energy efficiency.

© Springer Nature Singapore Pte Ltd. 2021
A. K. Luhach et al. (Eds.): ICAICR 2020, CCIS 1394, pp. 197–206, 2021.
https://doi.org/10.1007/978-981-16-3653-0_16

Due to bigger sized networks these days with more amount of information, energy consumed is also higher, thus leading to early death of a node. This led to the development of energy efficient RPs which reduces the amount of power used in data sampling and collection for extension of network lifetime.

The paper structure is organized as follows. Section 2 highlights the classification of RPs. Section 3 involves the latest research works in this area followed by Sect. 4 describing the paper conclusion with future outlooks.

2   Classification of RPs

There are different categories of RPs in wireless sensor networks such as proactive, reactive and hybrid RPs. They differ from each other based on the way of obtaining routing information as shown in Fig. 1 below.

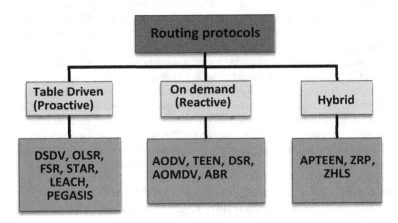

Fig. 1. Basic classification of RPs

2.1   Proactive RPs

Also called table driven protocols, they maintain routing information every time regarding the connectivity of every node in the network. A new list of routes and their destination is maintained time to time by circulating the routing tables in the network. At each node fresh attribute and sequence number is added for every route. Here the routing information is computed and shares the data packet volume between the source and the destination. Large bandwidth and more memory requirements of these types of protocols have made them suitable for wired networks only. DSDV, OLSR, FSR, STAR, LEACH and PEGASIS are some of the examples of proactive RPs.

2.1.1 Destination Sequence Distance Vector (DSDV)

Here routing table is being maintained by each node for all destinations. In each entry sequence number is given by the destination node. Full dump and packet update are used to carry all information about node whenever it detects a decisive change in the network. Updated messages bear the destination address, the number of hops to arrive at the destination and the route sequence number. Preferred routes are labeled with the most recent sequence number.

2.1.2 Optimized Link State Routing (OLSR)

Routes are always available at the time of demand in this protocol. It also facilitates reduction in overheads by using multipoint relays. As the time interval is brought to minimum it also helps in changing of topology faster. Hello and topology control are the two types of messages used. Hello is used for finding the link status, whereas the topology control is used for broadcasting for self and final destination node.

2.1.3 Fisheye State Routing (FSR)

This is a unicast and link state algorithm based routing protocol. It helps in minimizing the routing overhead and still maintains the existing network topology information. In FSR, link state table is maintained on receiving the information from the transmitting node. It used different time interval for different entries in the table updated. The frequency used for propagation of updated information is comparatively higher. It also helped in maintain the good order of scalability by not sharing all the updates with every node in the network. That means the information is shared need basis. Here the topology information is shared as event based and not periodically, thereby reducing the overheads.

2.1.4 Source Tree Adaptive Routing (STAR)

Path between the source node and base station is found using A* algorithm. Two list are used for this purpose i.e. Open and Closed list. Generally it arranges the nodes in tree structure. However, open list is used for the nodes that are to be checked and closed list keeps the details of already tested and checked nodes.

A* algorithm takes into consideration a distance-plus in conjunction with cost heuristic function of node n, when f(n) to specify the order for the visiting nodes. Heuristic function basically comprises of addition of two functions as given below

$$f(n) = g(n) + h(n) \tag{1}$$

Where, g(n) depicts the cost between source and current node n and h(n) specifies heuristic estimate regarding actual distance between n to destination.

2.1.5 Low-Energy Adaptive Clustering Hierarchy (LEACH)

This protocol has self-organizing and adaptive clustering properties. Here the fixed BS is positioned somewhat away from homogeneous nodes having the characteristics of energy constrain. One of the nodes assigned the role of cluster-head (CH) and it behaves like a base station. LEACH randomizes the rotation of CH to enable them sharing the power equally between the sensors for optimum energy consumption. By compressing data, this RP executes data fusion activity, resulting in reduced energy dissipation thereby increased network lifetime. Set-up phase and steady phase are the rounds executed by LEACH [2].

Clusters are formed in set-up phase, which leads to selection of CH for each cluster. Each node generates a random number from 0 to 1. In case the generated number is lower than threshold node [T(n)] results in nomination of that node as CH. T(n) is given by:

$$T(n) = p/1 - p[rmod(1/p)], \text{ n } G = 0 \tag{2}$$

Where, p specifies the % of nodes that are CHs, r specifies the current round and G denotes the set of nodes yet to be used as CH in the past 1/p rounds.

2.1.6 Power Efficient Gathering Sensor Information System (PEGASIS)

Every node has information about the other node. PEGASIS is based on the assumption that energy consumption is equal and life time is also equal for all. Greedy algorithm (GA) is used for forming the chain since each one knows about the other node. Transmission and reception of data are done between the nearest neighbor nodes only. The transmission is done with minimum power so that it sensed only by nearest neighbor node. Data is fused by each node in the received data frame while constructing the chain. Aggregated data to the Base Station (BS) is transmitted by the CH. The chain comprises of nodes located nearby and helps to maintain path towards base station. PEGASIS is superior to LEACH because it eliminates the overhead of dynamic cluster. Global information is available to every node and that is one of the greatest limitations of the protocol.

2.2 Reactive RPs

These RPs establish routes on demand. A route is created between the source and destination node on demand as per the need basis. A route discovery process is always generated in the network on getting a request. This process ceases to exist immediately once a route is found. Examples of demand RPs are AODV, AOMDV, ABR, DSR and TEEN.

2.2.1 Ad hoc on-Demand Distance Vector (AODV)

This routing algorithm facilitates in providing a route whenever requested by the source node Path-discovery process is initiated by source node as and when data is to be transmitted among nodes. It initiates a route request (RREQ) packet for broadcasting in the network to access the route to the destination. Nodes on getting this information update their status for the source node. That includes the source and destination (i) address (ii) sequence number (iii) the broadcast identifier. AODV applies the symmetric links for this purpose. Broadcast of Hello messages is done to infer any break in established link. Detection of link break in an active route results in propagation of a route error (RERR) message. Receipt of RERR, leads the source node to re-initiate the process of route discovery.

2.2.2 Ad-hoc on Demand Multipath Distance Vector (AOMDV)

AOMDV is a modified version of AODV. Here the source node has no predefined fixed paths to the destination. The source node follows the broadcasting of a RREQ packet in order to process route discovery. Receipt of a RREP packet indicates availability of route. In case of unavailability of route the process of broadcasting of RREQ packet takes place. In the process of route discovery cutoff problem may arise and will result in reverse path ignorance. This is due to suppression of duplicate PREQ by the intermediate nodes. Cutoff problem can be solved by sharing the same intermediate nodes in the multiple links disjoint and combining them in a single route till destination.

2.2.3 Associativity-Based Routing (ABR)

ABR basically performs its three basic functions, namely firstly Route discovery, secondly the Route reconstruction and finally the third one is Route deletion. During route discovery, route desiring node will broadcast BQ message to find a route till destination. Nodes receiving the query other than destination will put their addresses and association bearing QoS information in response to the query packet. In Route reconstruction, it may lead to either partial route discovery or invalid/valid route erasure/updates. This is mainly based on the movements of nodes in the new discovery. However the move executed by the source will result in a fresh BQREPLY process. In case discovered route is not required, a route delete (RD) is executed by the source node using broadcast to enable all nodes to update their information. The RD message is sent using full broadcast.

2.2.4 Dynamic Source Routing (DSR)

DSR is basically comprised of two elements firstly the discovery and secondly the maintenance of source routes. In discovery mechanism, route request is flooded by the wireless nodes. The source and destination is defined by the packet request sent for discovery. The target node always scans its own cache route before processing the reply. In case failure to get a route the target will be forced to initiate its own route discovery mechanism. DSR generally maintains records of all intermediate nodes. Complete routing path is put in a single data packet by the source node. In case the source node fails to found the routing path for the specified destination. Flooding leads to route discovery process by sending RREQ packet. The reply is route recorded within the existing RREQ packet. The superiority of this protocol is its inability to offer multiple routes by avoiding loop formation. However, larger end-to-end delay and scalability are its bigger limitations.

2.2.5 Threshold Sensitive Energy Efficient Sensor Network (TEEN)

TEEN is a routing protocol based on clustering. In this technique, the nodes are made to sense the surrounding environment regularly. In this case energy consumption is much larger during message transmission when compared to data sensing. This results in longer life of a network when transmission is minimum.

2.3 Hybrid RPs

The combined features of proactive and reactive protocols play a vital role in the hierarchal routing. In this protocol, intermediate nodes hold information regarding the network and its closest node. Zone radius refers to the zone size that is defined by the number of hops. Hybrid RPs cartels the advantages of proactive as well as reactive RPs and at the same time hybrid RPs overcome disadvantages of proactive and reactive RPs. These protocols suffer from certain drawbacks such as higher consumption of memory. APTEEN, ZRP and ZHLS are the examples of this type of protocols.

2.3.1 Adaptive Threshold Sensitive Energy Efficient Sensor Network (APTEEN)

This is modified and updated TEEN version. It facilitates the user in setting threshold values and decides on count time interval. In count time interval a node is made to sense and implement retransmission of the data if it fails to do so in specified time. This is hybrid protocol, capable of emulating both proactive and reactive network based on chosen threshold value and particular count time. However, it may lead to an additional complexity in the system.

2.3.2 Zone RP (ZRP)

This hybrid protocol exhibits higher efficiency in comparison to traditional routing because of lesser routing traffic. Here the network is divided in different sub zones. ZRP comprises of three protocols, namely (i) Intra zone Routing Protocol (IARP), (ii) Inter zone Routing Protocol (IERP) and (iii) Border cast Resolution Protocol (BRP). IARP is applied when a route falls within the zone and IERP is applied outside the zone. In case destination does not fall into the zone, it makes the source to broadcast a Route Request message among all the peripheral nodes.

2.3.3 Zone Based Hierarchical Link State (ZHLS)

ZHLS is mainly based on a hierarchical addressing scheme comprising of zone and node ID information. Based on the location in pre-defined zone map, the node is allotted zone ID. This map may be known to all existing nodes. In case there exists one physical link between two different zones the connectivity is executed using virtual link. ZHLS specifies two-level network topology structure namely, the node and zonal topology. Also, it specifies the two different levels of link state comprises of node level and zone level LSP. A node in general broadcast periodically. Node LSP has the node IDs of all neighbors falling in common zone and zone IDs of remaining zones. In case there is a break in the virtual link, broadcast of the zonal LSP is done by the gateway nodes throughout the network.

3 Latest Research Works Reported in Literature

The research across the world is going on in this area. Some of the latest one reported in literature are discussed further. *Tabbana, F.,* evaluated performance of 3RPs i.e. AODV,

DSDV and ZRP as a function of nodes from 10 to 100 and their speed ranging within 10 m/s to 90 m/s respectively. Every protocol has different results for different metrics. For Delay and Average Throughput, AODV is a more reliable than the other two protocols. DSDV performed superior than AODV for the evaluation parameters (i) End-to End delay, (ii) Packet Delivery Ratio (PDR) (iii) Throughput and (iv) Packet Loss for particular conditions. At higher node speeds, DSDV has been found to be performing better than AODV for PDR and Packet Loss Ratio but for dropped packets, ZRP performs best. Finally, application type selects a particular RP [3]. *Bhat, S.M. et al.,* measured performance of OLSR, AODV, DSR, LAR and ZRP RP both in static and mobility, where the nodes used with varying density from 25 to 250 nodes in the environment of Qualnet 5.0.2 network simulator. It was investigated that the reactive RPs AODV and DSR have been found to be better for their applications in terms of (i) average jitter and (ii) throughput. The location based Protocols (ZRP, LAR and OLSR) on the other hand, need enough time for establishing route discovery and maintenance. OLSR is convenient for random and irregular traffic among the nodes in large and dense mobile networks [4].

Sharma, D. et al., have used AOMDV RP for different numbers of node configuration and evaluated the optimum efficiency of MANET based scenario created for different transmission power for a configuration of 40 to 120 nodes. The authors found performance of AODMV superior to AODV for many performance metrics. The optimal performance of MANET was observed at 2.5dBm power. The authors brought out that their research work will help network element designers to select carefully various parameters like (i) node density, (ii) energy consumption (iii) optimum transmission power in order to reduce packet losses and for different sub modules [5]. *Kumar, S. et al.,* have considered AODV routing protocol to measure the performance of different energy models (i) Generic (ii) Micamotes and (iii) Micaz. It was examined that the energy consumption in Micamotes model has been reduced by 80.46% and 428.57% for transmission mode, 102.94% and 335.6% in receiving mode when compared to (i) Micaz and (ii) Generic energy models, respectively. Micaz energy model consumed lesser energy by 54.36% and 23.45% respectively than Micamotes and Generic energy models in idle mode. Micamotes is concluded to be the finest model in terms of energy saving in all modes [6].

Prabha, K., made a performance evaluation of AODV, DSR and Wireless RP (WRP) using two different scenarios, with nodes (50 and 100) and area sizes (1500 and 2000 × 1000 m^2). The WRP outperformed the other two protocols for different metrics used like routing overhead, AEED, data packets sent, throughput, data packets received and data packets requested for re-transmission. The author concluded that the performance of MANET RPs can be affected by the mobility pattern [7]. *Kumar, S. et al.,* employed AODV and DYMORP to investigate the performance of various energy conservation models (i) Generic, (ii) Micamotes and (iii) Micaz for Throughput, AEED and energy consumption in transmission and Reception mode. The Micamotes energy model using AODV RP consumed less energy up to 42.99% and 29.90% in transmit and 59.24% and 33.96% in receive mode. Further evaluations revealed AODV better than DYMO in terms of Throughput and AEED [8].

Daanoune. I. et al., proposed an improved LEACH RP for balancing the energy consumed by the sensor nodes and sustainability of network lifetime and concluded that the network lifespan is improved more than the original LEACH protocol [9]. *Mohammed, S. A. et al.*, investigated a technique for improvement in energy consumption to an optimum level to enhance network lifetime of WSN. The proposed technique was around 200% energy- efficient as compared to the basic LEACH [10].

Pitchaimanickam, B. and Murugaboopathi1, G., proposed a Hybrid technique of Firefly Algorithm in conjunction with Particle Swarm Optimization (HFAPSO). An improvement in network lifetime has been observed, thus resulting in rise in the number of the active nodes and minimum consumption of energy. The proposed methodology was found better in terms of throughput and Residual Energy (Er) than the firefly algorithm [11].

Sharma, N. et al., proposed energy efficient protocols for enhanced QoS in WSN. The performance metrics parameters (i) throughput and (ii) network lifetime were found improved by 10.00%, 26.00%, and 63.00% respectively. The authors suggested that future work can be focused on employment of WSN protocols in different environmental conditions [12].

Adil, M. et al., have employed several intellectual Energy Gauge Nodes (EGN) to measure the performance using different activities such as (i) Er, computation, (ii) identification of ordinary nodes energy levels, (iii) optimal route advertisement. The proposed infrastructure ensures that the nodes remain active for a maximum duration. The simulation results exhibits that the Throughput, Network Lifetime, Packet Loss Ratio (PLR), End-to-End (E2E) delay and energy consumption is effective as compare to the existing schemes [13]. *Bhola, J. et al.*, investigated that with the use of LEACH along with optimization (O-LEACH), an increment in the throughput and PDR of 17.44% and 7.27% respectively and reduction in energy consumption by 17.39% is observed. It was concluded the energy consumption rate is reduced by 64.97% as compared to the previous LEACH RP [14].

Luhach, A.K. et al., proposed Honey Bee Optimization based improved mobility Balanced Energy Efficient Network Integrated Super Heterogeneous (HBO-iMBEENISH) Protocol for optimized sink mobility. The protocol improved stability period by 33% and network lifetime by 916 rounds over iMBEENISH protocol due to optimized sink movement in the network [15]. *Maratha, P. et al.*, proposed a fault tolerance strategy to prevent packet loss by changing the battery threshold. This will notify the sink regarding the dying nodes earlier. The proposed work has enhanced the network lifetime by 9% compared to its competitor approach [16].

Singh, A.P. et al., carried out a detailed review focusing on the progression in architectural designs and developments, the pros and cones and future fields of research in WSNs. The authors suggested using evolutionary and other optimization techniques for selection of appropriated service among numerous available alternatives [17]. *Kumar, S. et al.*, have made a performance investigation of AOMDV RP in a designed AWSN scenario using different number of nodes. The research has been focused on determining the optimum power required for transmission. The optimal performance has been obtained at 75 nodes with 2.5 dBm power [18].

As far as concern in routing is that most of the current routing conventions work for stationary sensor hubs and the sink. However, for circumstances like battlefield where layout of nodes need to be flexible, and hence, new and modified routing techniques are necessary to overcome portability overhead and changed topology in constrained power situations.

4 Conclusion

In spite of many applications of WSNs, it becomes necessary to transmit information properly keeping in mind utilization of power; network lifetime and network limited resources. Routing and transmitting the traffic data up to the last base station in compliance with minimum energy is the most considerable difficulty with these networks. In this study, various RPs were analysed for energy efficient Adhoc WSNs. Then, their features and characteristics have been highlighted. Each protocol when used for different scenario situations shows definite advantages and drawbacks. Although, these protocols perform well in terms of energy conservation. But QoS needs to be addressed to assure exploitation for optimum energy consumption to execute the ensured data transfer rate and reduced delay. This era is rapidly growing but still there are many challenges which need more attention of researchers in the future, especially to meet the dynamic and battle field requirement, where the node network has to function in hostile environments. Future research can be focused on the integration of WSN with wired networks (i.e. Internet) for RPs.

References

1. Kaur, P., Kad, S.: Energy-efficient routing protocols for wireless sensor network: a review. Int. J. Sci. Technol. Res. 6(12), 92–96 (2017)
2. Brar, G.S., Rani, S., Song, H., Ahmed, S.H.: Energy efficient direction-based PDORP routing protocol for WSN. IEEE Spec. Sect. Green Commun. Netw. 5G Wirel. 4, 3182–3194 (2016)
3. Tabbana, F.: Performance comparison and analysis of proactive, reactive and hybrid routing protocols for wireless sensor networks. Int. J. Wirel. Mob. Netw. (IJWMN), 12(4) (2020). https://doi.org/10.5121/ijwmn.2020.12401
4. Bhat, S.M., Shwetha, D., Devaraju, J.T.: A performance study of proactive, reactive and hybrid routing protocols using qualnet simulator. Int. J. Comput. Appl. 28(5), 10–17 (2011)
5. Sharma, D., Kumar, S., Arora, P.: Performance evaluation of MANETs with Variation in transmission power using ad-hoc on-demand multipath distance vector routing protocol. In: International Conference on Communication and Electronics Systems (ICCES), pp. 363–368 (2020)
6. Kumar, S., Dhull, K., Arora, P., Luhach, A.K.: Performance of energy conservation models, generic, micaz and micamotes, using AODV routing protocol on a wireless sensor network. Scalable Comput. Pract. Exp. 20(4), 631–639 (2019). https://doi.org/10.12694/scpe.v20i4.1563
7. Prabha, K.: Performance assessment and comparison of efficient ad hoc reactive and proactive network routing protocols. SN Comput. Sci. 1, 13 (2020). https://doi.org/10.1007/s42979-019-0015-y

8. Kumar, S., Dhull, K., Sharma, D., Arora, P., Dahiya, S.: Evaluation of AODV and DYMO routing protocol using generic, micaz and micamotes energy conservation models in AWSN with static and mobile scenario. Scalable Comput. Pract. Exp. **20**(4), 653–662 (2019). https://doi.org/10.12694/scpe.v20i4.1563
9. Ikram, D., Baghdad, A., Ballouk, A.: An enhanced energy-efficient routing protocol for wireless sensor network. Int. J. Electr. Comput. Eng. **10**(5) (2020)
10. Mohammed, S.A., Aly, K.A.E., Ghuniem, A.M.: An enhancement process for reducing energy consumption in wireless sensor network. Int. J. Emerg. Trends Eng. **8**(6), 2765–2769 (2020). https://doi.org/10.30534/ijeter/2020/89862020
11. Pitchaimanickam, B., Murugaboopathi, G.: A hybrid firefly algorithm with particle swarm optimization for energy efficient optimal cluster head selection in wireless sensor networks. Neural Comput. Appl. **32**(12), 7709–7723 (2020)
12. Sharma, N., Singh, B.M., Singh, K.: QoS-based energy-efficient protocols for wireless sensor network. Sustainable Comput. Inf. Syst. **100425** (2020)
13. Adil, M., et al.: An efficient load balancing scheme of energy gauge nodes to maximize the lifespan of constraint oriented networks. IEEE Access, **8**, 148510–148527 (2020). https://doi.org/10.1109/access.2020.3015941
14. Bhola, J., Soni, S., Cheema, G.K.: Genetic algorithm based optimized leach protocol for energy efficient wireless sensor networks. J. Ambient Intell. Hum. Comput. **11**(3), 1281–1288 (2020)
15. Luhach, A.K., Khamparia, A., Sihag, R., Kumar, R.: Honey bee optimization based sink mobility aware heterogeneous protocol for wireless sensor network. Scalable Comput. Pract. Exp. **20**(4), 591–598 (2019). https://doi.org/10.12694/scpe.v20i4.1553
16. Maratha, P., Gupta, K., Luhach, A.K.: Improved fault-tolerant optimal route reconstruction approach for energy consumed areas in wireless sensor networks. IET Wirel. Sens. Syst. **10**(3), 112–116 (2019). https://doi.org/10.1049/iet-wss.2019.0152
17. Singh, A.P., Luhach, A.K., Gao, X.Z., Kumar, S., Roy, D.S.: Evolution of wireless sensor network design from technology centric to user centric: an architectural perspective. Int. J. Distrib. Sens. Netw. **16**(8) (2020). https://doi.org/10.1177/1550147720949138
18. Kumar, S., Sharma, D., Payal, M.: Evaluation of AOMDV routing protocol for optimum transmitted power in a designed ad-hoc wireless sensor network. In: Sharma, M.K., Dhaka, V.S., Perumal, T., Dey, N., Tavares, J.M.R.S. (eds.) Innovations in Computational Intelligence and Computer Vision. AISC, vol. 1189, pp. 100–108. Springer, Singapore (2021). https://doi.org/10.1007/978-981-15-6067-5_13

IoT Based Smart Transport Management System

Vartika Agarwal and Sachin Sharma[✉]

Department of Computer Science and Engineering, Graphic Era Deemed to be University,
Dehradun, India
sachin.cse@geu.ac.in

Abstract. Currently, vehicle to vehicle communication is an important application and thrust area of research. In this paper the author highlighted the workings, executions, implementations and the application of the Internet of Things (IoT) in transport management and vehicle to vehicle communication systems. The main advantage of this Industry 4.0 based IoT technology is that it helps us to reduce road traffic and accidents. The limitations of GPS like accuracy, precision, effective analysis, etc. has led to the evolution of Mobile based V2V communication which is more effective, error proof, result oriented and smart. For proper analysis of traffic vehicle to vehicle communication is established. Random Data from vehicles taken by numerous sensors. Any car coming in its variety could effortlessly share the data by either of two cars nearby. With the help of vehicle to vehicle communication we can provide a path of emergency vehicles to reach the destination quickly. Based on the V2V application, Red and Green signals can be marked on the path as per traffic density and the emergency vehicle can take the shortest, fastest and low density route. Similar such examples are elaborated in the current research manuscript that will help the researcher in effectively finding the research gap for further advancement, analysis, innovation and optimization.

Keywords: Anisotropic magneto resistive sensor · RFID · Ultrasonic sensor node · Wifi · Traffic management module · Traffic density monitoring module

1 Introduction

Transport management systems is the need of today. No. of vehicles on roads are increasing day by day [1]. Every person has their transportation due to the increasing no of vehicles risk of accidents are also increasing [2]. Traffic congestion makes a great impact on productivity and economic growth. After a lot of research, many solutions have been proposed using IoT [3]. Some communication is using RFID, Lifi or many other technologies. Purpose of such model is to predict and control traffic flow [4]. The transportation problems in urban areas are very significant. Traffic congestion can have an effect on the lives of people in cities. Governing bodies such as International Telecommunications Services (ITS) are responsible for following the policies and agreements of operators and service providers in the transport management networks. The implementation of IoT

© Springer Nature Singapore Pte Ltd. 2021
A. K. Luhach et al. (Eds.): ICAICR 2020, CCIS 1394, pp. 207–216, 2021.
https://doi.org/10.1007/978-981-16-3653-0_17

technology into the transport management system would make it easier for regulatory bodies and users to reduce the number of incidents and to direct the route effectively. The new installations of IoT devices can be performed as per their specifications along the highways. The transport management system consists of traffic signs activated by IoT, flash lights for the route direction, security cameras, and multiple sensor numbers. In the transport workers' time map, monitoring and traffic conditions are required for easy maintenance of the highways and roads. IoT has a wide variety of applications in the industry and innovative methods for networking.

Fulfilling the growing demand for user services is one of the major challenges of the transport management system. Vehicle mobility in rapidly growing metropolitan areas could have an effect on the IoT services provided by the public transport system. In the transport management system, an effective vehicle tracking system and road map visualization with directions using IoT devices play a major role. In the transport management system, the IoT applications take care of data collection and IoT sensors gather different information and exchange it with the central cloud server.

2   Traffic Congestion Control System

Sensor array is used by traffic congestion control system. Such sensor is used to measure traffic density and then send this information to the phone via bluetooth. Work of android phone is to collect information about traffic density and send to the server [5, 6]. This server analyzes these traffic by extracting data to detect traffic and manage such traffic signal. After it information about traffic density to central server transfer from phone to server through internet [7].

3   Traffic Density Monitoring Module (TDMM)

Ultrasonic sensor is used by this model. This model is used to detect the length of vehicle queue. This model use microcontroller. Microcontroller is used to receive data from ultrasonic sensor. It also has a Wi-Fi module which is used to send data to traffic management module. Limitation of this system is that no experimental result has been found to verify the accuracy of system [8, 9] (Fig. 1).

4   Traffic Message Channel (TMC)

Major Drawback of GPS is that we can't find exact route. So concept of Traffic message channel was evolved. Main work of TMC is to transmit information about current traffic. If roads are blocked. TMC suggest an alternative route for vehicle. But congestion could occur on an additional route too if many vehicles uses TMC. To overcome such drawbacks, concept of vehicle to everything technology was evolved [10].

5   Traffic Management Module (TMM)

It is attached to the LED and connected to a microcontroller (Fig. 2).

Relay module: Relay module works like an electromagnetic switch which is responsible for any traffic congestion.

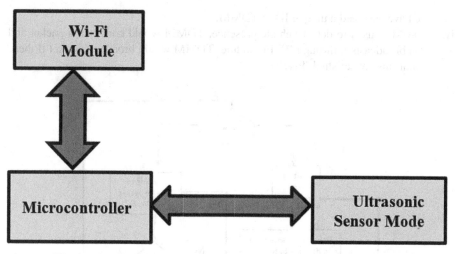

Fig. 1. Diagrammatic representation of traffic density monitoring module.

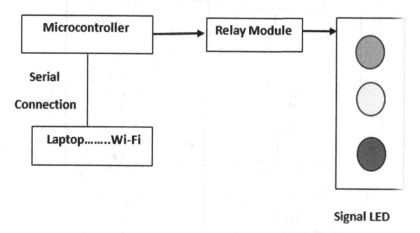

Fig. 2. Working of Traffic Management Module (TMM).

6 Working of Traffic Density Monitoring Module

i.   We have used USN (Ultrasonic Sensor node) for detecting the vehicle presence.
ii. We detect the presence of vehicle if measured distance is less then reference distance. We can symbolize measured distance by d_m and reference distance by d_r.

Reference distance (d_r) = width of road
Measured distance $(d_m) = C * (T_r - T_s)$
Where,
C = speed of sound waves
T_r = Time of reception.
T_s = Sending time of emitted signal of ultrasonic sensor.

iii. We have assigned a unique ID to TDMM.

iv. TDMM is used to detect vehicle presence. TDMM would construct a packet and then broadcasts it through Wi-Fi module. TDMM would broadcast packet if these conditions are satisfied (Fig. 3).

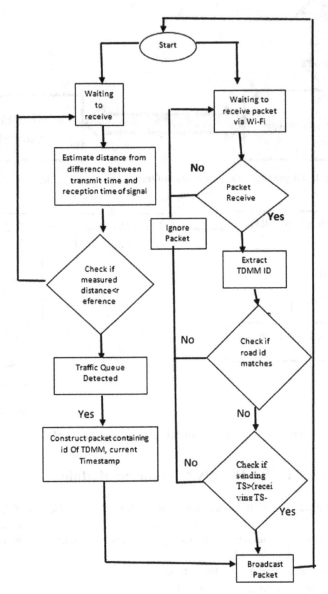

Fig. 3. Diagrammatic representation of detecting vehicle presence in queue.

a. $T_p > T_c - T^{th}$ where T_p = Timestamp value and T_c = current timestamp and T^{th} means threshold time value

b. Unique Road id of local TDMM is equal to the road id of remote TDMM.

The following algorithm is used for traffic congestion

i. We have to find out timestamp value (Tp) of packet and we have to compare these values with current timestamp (Tc). We should ignore if Tp < Tc-tth, where T^{th} is threshold time. Otherwise

ii. Check id of TDMM and then divide all received packets on the basis of road id.

iii. There are 3 TDMMs on each road having traffic congestion density.

   a. Zero TDMM means traffic queue is smaller.
   b. 1st TDMM means traffic queue length lies between first and 2nd TDMM.
   c. 1st and 2nd TDMM both indicates traffic queue length is between the 2nd or 3rd TDMM.
   d. TMM find out the operation time of traffic signal add this into microcontroller.

7   Case Study: 1

The purpose of this case study is to discover the vehicle-to-vehicle contact impact. For research, the subset of I-5 in the orange country is used (Fig. 4).

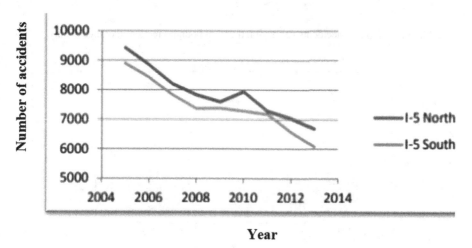

Fig. 4. Annual accident data on I-5.

California Highway Patrol report tells that no of vehicle involved accidents in the state of California is very high, it has gone down significantly in last seven years (Table 1).

The data of accident shows a decreasing trend on I-5 in northbound and southbound directions as discussed in Fig. 5 and Fig. 6.

Table 1. An accident comparison between 2005 and 2012 in California.

	Year 2005	Year 2012
Persons injured	292,798	226,544
2 Persons killed	4,304	2,995
Mileage death rate	1.31	0.92
Injury collisions	198,708	159,696
Fatal collisions	3,822	2,758

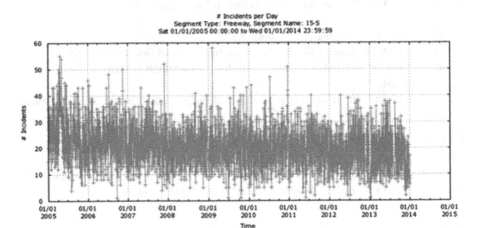

Fig. 5. Number of accidents per day on the northbound direction in orange county.

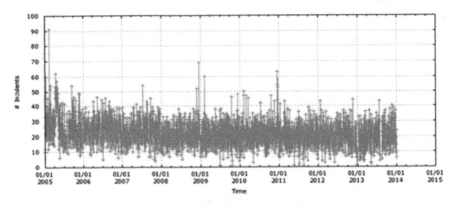

Fig. 6. Number of accidents per day on the southbound direction in orange county.

In Fig. 7, we can see that large no of accidents occurred on freeway mainlines and rest 31% occurred either on or off ramps.

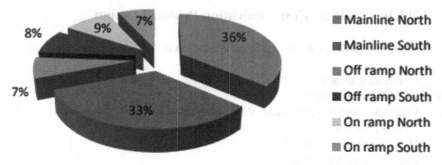

Fig. 7. Location of accident on I-5.

The number of accidents decreased when new technology was evolved. These systems warn driver about collision.

8 Case Study: 2

A significant number of injuries are minimized by the use of V2V technology. In 2012, there have been 1120 vehicle collisions. There is description from these accidents are as follows:

$$373 = \text{rear end}, 241 = \text{hit object}, \text{sideswipe} = 165.$$

We can see type of accident are mentioned in Fig. 8. Rear end collision occurred when there is any collision occurred with leading vehicle. rear end collision represents 34% of accidents. Sideswipe accidents occurred when there is not enough visibility. It represents 15% of accident. Hit objects are done by automated emergency braking system. It represents 12% of accident.

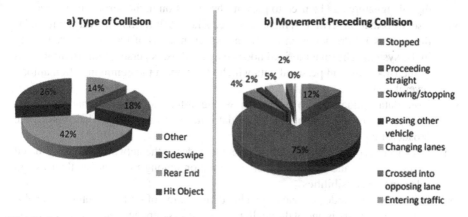

Fig. 8. Diagrammatic representation of movements before collision and accidents occurred due to this movement in 2012.

9   Vehicle to Vehicle Communication Protocol Design

A new communication protocol can be established in the following steps:

i.   Object identification
ii.   Information gathering
iii.   Study the current and standard V2V communication protocols
iv.   Design protocol
v.   Handling the constraint
vi.   Phase of implementation
vii.   Prototype version
viii.   Test phase
ix.   Phase of validation
x.   UAT Phase

V2V Communication Security

i.   Secured Scalability: The security is the main factor in vehicle to vehicle communication model. Information sharing is in encrypted or decrypted form.
ii.   Authenticated Connections: The connection between vehicles should be authenticated.
iii.   Service availability: The promised services by service providers should be secured and available to user 24×7.
iv.   User data confidentiality: It involves users data information confidentiality during communication by using encryption and decryption techniques among multiple sensors and infrastructure bodies.
v.   User information integrity: It is required to provide correct user information to end nodes during message communication from one node to another. The encrypted digital signature can be used to prevent the alteration in the service messages.
vi.   User information privacy: It includes to keep the user information away from unauthorized users. Privacy is an important aspect in terms of increase the reliability in the system. The unauthorized nodes may steal users personal information such as their location and personal data which may impact the communication among several nodes.
vii.   User data validation: To avoid the wrong information dissemination among multiple users it is important to validate the authorized users data before the broadcasting.
viii.   Data access control: It includes all possible nodes in the network who are situated in the network and broadcast their information among them as per their assign roles and responsibilities.
ix.   Heterogeneous nodes traceability: The identification of multiple authorized vehicles in the network is one of the challenges. If any discrepancy found in the network, then network can revoke the access of that node in the future.

x.   User data error identification: It is related to avoidance of the multiple data error in the V2V communication network among multiple nodes. Data error identification may lead to guide the multiple nodes in right direction such as optimized destination route search.

xi. User liability validation: It is related to search the liable user in the network and define their accountability in the network to avoid the breach in the communication network.

xii. Services flexibility: It includes the flexibility in the V2V device communication and essential services for safety applications. This flexibility provides low delay in the network for emergency communication services.

xiii. Revoke the broadcasting of altered messages: It is related to the false message broadcasting abandonment in the network to avoid the high volume of false altered message alarming.

Components Used in V2V Communication

i. Nodes: The node should support GSM Module.
ii. Server: It is a web application and it is used to capture the event log in ITS network.

10   Conclusion

The big problems are traffic congestion now a day because the demand for vehicles is growing. Owing to increased vehicle demand, fuel consumption and the risk of heart attacks are also growing. Our future research objective is to apply some tests and techniques to verify the efficiency of the device. In the future, the potential effect of IoT applications on the transport management system will be assessed. The use of IoT applications in real-time would become a practical and necessary technique for sustainable traffic management. The need of protection in heterogeneous sensors data and the extraction of required information from them can be explored in future.

References

1. Chauhan, V., Patel, M., Tanwar, S., Tyagi, S., Kumar, N.: IoT enabled real-time urban transport management system. Comput. Electr. Eng. **86**, (2020)
2. Vattaparambil, S.S., Koduri, R., Nandyala, S., Manalikandy, M.: Scalable decentralized solution for secure vehicle-to-vehicle communication (No. 2020-01-0724). SAE Technical Paper (2020)
3. Syed, M.S.B., Memon, F., Memon, S., Khan, R.A.: IoT based emergency vehicle communication system. In: 2020 International Conference on Information Science and Communication Technology (ICISCT), pp. 1–5. IEEE, February 2020
4. Liu, X., Jaekel, A.: Congestion control in V2V safety communication: problem, analysis, approaches. Electronics **8**(5), 540 (2019)
5. Sharma, S., Sharma, A., Goel, T., Deoli, R., Mohan, S.: Smart home gardening management system: a cloud-based Internet-of-Things (IoT) application in VANET. In: 2020 11th International Conference on Computing, Communication and Networking Technologies (ICCCNT), pp. 1–5. IEEE (2020)

6. Sharma, S., Baig Awan, M., Mohan, S.: Cloud enabled cognitive radio adhoc vehicular networking (CRAVENET) with security aware resource management and internet of vehicles (IoV) applications. In: 2017 IEEE International Conference on Advanced Networks and Telecommunications Systems (ANTS), pp. 1–6. IEEE (2017)

7. Sharma, S., Ghanshala, K.K., Mohan, S.: Advanced spectrum management for next-generation vehicular communication: an AI approach. In: 2019 IEEE 10th Annual Information Technology, Electronics and Mobile Communication Conference (IEMCON), pp. 0632–0637. IEEE (2019)

8. Sharma, S., Muhammad, A., Mohan, S.: Cloud enabled cognitive radio adhoc vehicular networking with security aware resource management and internet of vehicles applications. U.S. Patent 10,659,528, issued 19 May 2020

9. Sharma, S., Muhammad, A., Mohan, S.: Smart vehicular hybrid network systems and applications of same. U.S. Patent Application 15/705,542, filed, 29 March 2018

10. Sharma, S., Ghanshala, K.K., Mohan, S.: Blockchain-based Internet of Vehicles (IoV): an efficient secure ad hoc vehicular networking architecture. In: 2019 IEEE 2nd 5G World Forum (5GWF), pp. 452–457. IEEE (2019)

Vehicular Ad Hoc Network: Routing Protocols

Yogesh Kumar[1], Isha[1(✉)], Arun Malik[1(✉)], and Ashish Kr. Luhach[2]

[1] Lovely Professional University, Phagwara, Punjab, India
{isha.17451,arun.17422}@lpu.co.in
[2] The PNG University of Technology, Lae, Papua New Guinea

Abstract. VANET (Vehicular ad hoc network) is a sub-branch or subclass of a mobile ad hoc networking. It is a new and growing technology which is works for vehicles. Safeness and security of all the passengers who are sitting inside the vehicles are the main motives of that technology. It enables the different modes of communications like Vehicles to infrastructure and Vehicles to vehicles by using different kinds of IEEE standards such as IEEE 802.11p. With the help of these standards, VANET is able to transfer the data packets or information to the vehicles because it is not sure that the drivers are aware of everything during the time of driving. In this technology, all the vehicles are considered as a node and the high mobility or movements of nodes create a major challenge or issue in transferring the data packets to the end devices. In this paper, on the basis of their strengths and weaknesses, various VANET routing protocols are evaluated and summarized.

Keywords: Protocols · Node · VANET etc.

1 Introduction

Vehicular Ad-Hoc Network or VANET is a technology in which all the vehicles act as a node and they create a mobile network. It can be allowing cars or any smart vehicles to connect to others which are in the range of 100 to 300 m with respect to the current vehicles. As any vehicles or cars drop out due to the signal spectrum and drop out of the current network, other vehicles may step in to link vehicles to each other in order to create a mobile internet.

Before that technology, to control their actions, drivers used their speech, motions, horns, and observation of each other's trajectory. In the second half of the 19th century, when the dramatic rise in cars found this difficult to maintain, traffic police took over the regulation and monitoring of traffic using hand signals, semaphores, and flashing lights. The 1930s found traffic controls being programmed and car signs were commonly implemented in the 1940s. In the 1960s, variable-message signs were adopted to provide drivers with data to respond to changing situations. Recently, with the help of wireless networking, drivers may share more details, such as traffic information and directions, with each other, helping to communicate more personalized and accurate knowledge. VANET tackles all these concerns relating to vehicle connectivity and on-going wireless communication studies.

© Springer Nature Singapore Pte Ltd. 2021
A. K. Luhach et al. (Eds.): ICAICR 2020, CCIS 1394, pp. 217–230, 2021.
https://doi.org/10.1007/978-981-16-3653-0_18

Now, Millions of civilians around the globe are killed by vehicular collisions or accidents. In developing several vehicular automation systems, protection is a predominant consideration. Significant importance is dedicated to reducing the risk of loss happening and improvising the efficiency of all device components. VANET has several independent nodes, consisting of smart setups that can move positions and are a wireless mobile device network that needs be linked to Wi-Fi or other mobile systems, self-configuring, infrastructure-less. The Vehicular Ad Hoc Network (VANET) is an ad hoc wireless network that utilizes traveling transports as nodes and is enabled to interact amongst them through a wireless network having features as consistent agility, quickly shifting topology, strong computing power, and flexible density of the network. VANET allows connectivity networks for infrastructure-to-vehicle (I2V), vehicle-to-infrastructure (V2I), and vehicle-to-vehicle (V2V). Vehicle-to-Networks (V2I) Communications is a wireless sharing of operational, safety resources within automobiles and road structures, mainly designed to circumvent crashes with power vehicles. The V2V framework is a network of kind, having complex wireless data transmission is used by neighboring vehicles, delivering relative proximity information to each other. This out-turns in pre-programmed connectivity and creating an ad hoc network while more vehicles are in the radio communications circle, enabling location, speed, and direction data to be transmitted.

2   Routings Protocols of VANET

The key aim of routing protocols is to reach a reasonable time to interact by consuming a minimal supply of network assets [5]. The routing protocol of five types are: routing based on topology, routing based on location, Geo cast routing, broadcast routing, and routing based on clusters. We have listed as according to the framework area and their accountability within (Fig. 1).

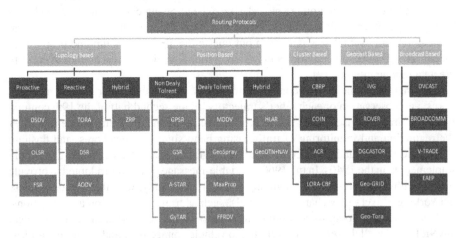

Fig. 1. Types of routing protocols

2.1 Based on Topology

In this routing protocols, every node makes a routing table for the saving of the address of another node, and at time the infrastructure of the network change then the routing table of each node gets refurbished according to the current network. It sends multiple types of messages like unicast, multicast, and broadcast. It can also be categorized as the Proactive, Reactive, and Hybrid routing protocol.

2.2 Based on Position

In this type of routing protocol the data will be transfer to one end to another end using the graphical coordinates of the nodes. It uses GPS devices to detect the position of the neighbor nodes. Any time an initial node or starting node wants to transfer the data to the end node or the target node, it just adds the location or the geographical coordinates of that destination or target node in the header of the data packets.

In the process of transferring packets, firstly find the location of the target node using the location in the header after the data will be sent to the target node. It is convenient for a frequently changing environment and no routing table is needed just as there is no need to maintain the routing table or route discovery. The downside of this protocol for routing is the GPS unit freezes in the tunnel and the positioning server also goes to into a state of deadlock.

2.3 Based on Cluster

In this routing protocols, specific types of nodes are in a group which is known as a cluster. In every group or cluster, there is one manager or cluster head. All the functionality of the cluster is managed by the cluster manager. Now, the communication between one or two clusters is directly done by the cluster manager. There are several clusters of this nature and connectivity is among numerous such clusters, their respective clusters are performed Heads-of-cluster. While broad networks may have strong scalability, It will be done, but the network overhead will be raised.

2.4 Based on Broadcast

In this routing technique information or the data will be transferred to all the nodes in the network with the help of broadcasting. Broadcasting is used when a single message is transferred to all the vehicles in the range. After that, the nodes are re-broadcast the receiving message to the other vehicles in the range, and so on. So this routing is reliable in nature but it consumes more bandwidth and most consider a drawback is it transfer many duplicate packets to the nodes which is the biggest reason for congestion and overloading.

It is mainly used for broadcasting information about traffic, weather updates, and emergency situations updates.

2.5 Based on Geo-Cast

It is basically location-based multicasting routing. In this routing protocol, the information or the data packets is delivered in a specific geographical region. Typically, it identifies a forwarding region through which it directs packet flooding in order to decrease overhead message and network congestion induced by them all overflow packets everywhere.

Mainly it is a multicast service but at the destination end, it performs unicast routing for forwarding the information or data packets. The data is only broadcast to the specific region, outside the region the data will be discarded.

3   Distance Sequance Distance Vector

It is a routing protocols which is based on routing information update mechanism. It is known as Destination Sequenced Distance Vector. It is the first proactive protocol proposed for an ad-hoc wireless network by Perkins and Bhagvat. This is the enhanced version of the Bellman-ford algorithm. It is a table-driven proactive type of protocol and each node in this protocol maintains the shortest path to the destination node. It exchanges the table entity with the neighbor at a regular time period (Fig. 2).

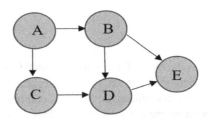

Fig. 2. Network of five devices

Like:

– A-B-E (Shortest Path)
– A-C-D-E
– A-B-D-E.

In this above scenario, if A is the starting node and E is the ending or destination node then the shortest path according to the DSDV routing algorithm is A-B-E.

Table Consist:

– Destination Identity Number
– Next hope Address
– Distance (Number of Hop)
– Sequence Number.

Route Broadcast Message consist:

- Destination Identity Number
- Next Hope
- Distance
- Recent Sequence Number.

Sequence number is Arbitrary in nature (Table 1).

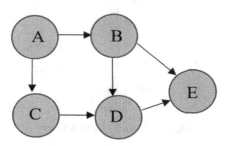

Fig. 3. Network of five devices

Table 1. Table of the Node A of Fig. 3 scenario.

Destination	Next node	Distance	Sequence no.
B	B	1	112
C	C	1	23
D	C	2	132
E	B	2	123

There are two ways to update a table in DSDV.

- Incremental Update
  When there is no major improvement in local topology, it is used. A single Network Data Packet Unit is required and the only entry that updates are shared with neighbor.
- Full Dumps Update
  It is used when local topology change significantly or the network data packet unit of the incremental update is more than one. The whole table that is updated is shared with a neighbor.

Table Maintenance in DSDV

- The information which is received by every node have the data of the most recent sequence number and that information is updated in the table.
- The node from the modified table determines the shortest way to meet the target.
- Every node has there owned a separate routing table for the shortest path information.

- After updating information in the routing table, the updated routing table id broadcast to its neighbor nodes.
- After receiving the new information, the neighbor node update that information in his table.

For Example (Table 2):

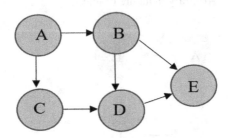

Fig. 4. Network of five devices

Table 2. Initial table of Node A w.r.t Fig. 4

Destination	Next node	Distance	Sequence no.
B	B	1	112
C	C	1	23
D	C	2	132
E	B	2	123

The above figure is the initial table of Node A. If Node B is disconnect for a moment so all the neighbors mark Node B distance as an infinity. But after some time Node B is connected After E then the whole table is changed. The old entry of Node B is discarded if the new entry of Node B has a larger sequence number as compare to the old one (Table 3).

Where RED box represent the old entry and the BLUE box is represent new entry of Node B.

New entry in only allowed when the sequence no. of old one is smaller than the new entry.

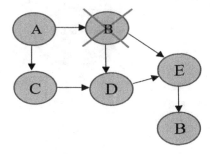

Fig. 5. Node B updating in network again.

Table 3. Tale update after Node B connect with the network again w.r.t Fig. 5

Destination	Next Node	Distance	Sequence No.
B	B	1	112
C	C	1	23
D	C	2	132
E	B	2	123
B	C	4	233

4 Dynamic Source Routing Protocol

It is a reactive routing protocol which is also known as on demand routing protocols. In this, when the sender wants to send the message to the end-user or its destination only that time the route discovered by the router for transferring the data to the destination. The mechanism is used in these routing protocols is source routing. Source routing is the routing in which the whole path to reach the destination is already known by the sender before sending the packets. If the sender knows the whole path then there is no need to maintain the route information by the intermediate node.

Phases of DSR Protocols

Route Discovery Phase

- RREQ Packet
  Sender broadcast the RREQ message packet to all of the nodes to find the route to reach the end or destination.

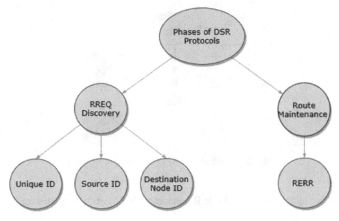

Fig. 6. Phases of DSR

- After receiving the RREQ packet by the destination node. The destination node generates an RREP packet (Route reply packet) and that packet has the whole information about the path of the sender to the receiver.
- RREP packet is unicast by the destination node in the network and it is only received by the sender node (Fig. 6).

Route Maintenance Phase

- RERR (Route Error Message)
  When any node is a disconnect to the network then the route maintenance phase sends a RERR message to the whole network and all the nodes in the network update this information in their routing table.

DSR uses Route-Cash: It is used to store the path for future use (Fig. 7).

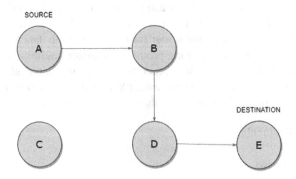

Fig. 7. Assumed Path of A to E

Let's Assume A discover the path to the E is,

A-B-D-E

Then the route cash store the path and in future A want to send any data to destination Node E then firstly A check the path in the route cash if there is any saved path to reach E node then A will follow the path otherwise A discover the new path.

For Example:

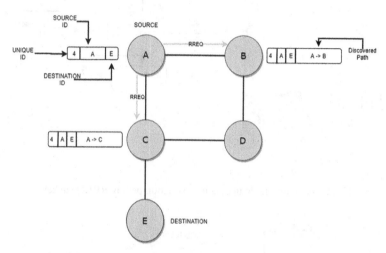

Fig. 8. Node A send RREQ request to neighbor node

In this above diagram, A is the starting node or source node so node A sends a Broadcast message RREQ to the whole network to find the destination node E. Initially A has Unique Identity, Source Identity, and Destination Identity (Fig. 8).

When the RREQ reaches the next neighbor node then it saves the path inside it. Like at node an RREQ message has a new portion of the discovered path in which it saves the path to reach the destination (Fig. 9).

This diagram shows that when Node A sends an RREQ packet in the network to find the optimum path to reach the destination.

At Node E we found two paths to reach Node E one is A-C-E and the second one is A-B-D-C-E. With the help of both paths, we reach the destination node but we are searching for the optimum path so the optimum path to reach the end E node is A-C-E (Fig. 10).

After finding the optimum path the destination node generates an RREP packet and unicast it in the network. Only the source nodes accept this RREP message. In this RREP packet, it has all the information about the optimum path to reach the destination (Fig. 11).

This is the final step in the process of finding the route in DSR protocol. In this Node A is receiving the Whole RREP packet and update that received path in its packet and follow this path to transfer the packet.

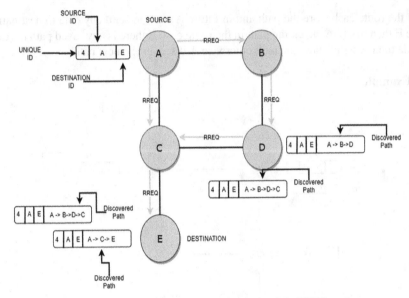

Fig. 9. Neighbor node update in destination path in RREQ packet.

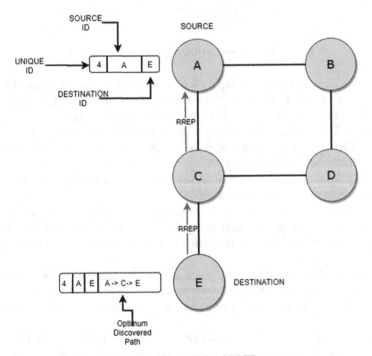

Fig. 10. Destination Node Send RREP message.

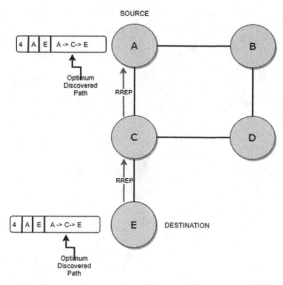

Fig. 11. Node A accept the RREP message and update the optimum path in its packet.

5 Zone Routing Protocol

It is a hybrid routing protocol which is the combination of both routing protocols Proactive and Reactive. Both the protocols in hybrid work differently, Proactive is used inside routing zones and reactive is used between routing zones. Any path to a destination inside the same local zone is rapidly created by IARP from the proactively cached routing table of the source. Therefore, if a packet's source and destination are in the same zone, it is possible to deliver the packet instantly.

Working

- Inside the zone, the destination node or end node were found, then the sender node transfers the data to the destination node directly.
- If the destination node or end node is not in the zone, then the source sends the RREQ message to the other node and its peripheral node.

Node 4 is the source node and node 9 is the destination node. And the peripheral node with respect to node 4 are 3, w.r.t node 3 are 2 and 5 so on (Fig. 12).

- If some of the peripheral nodes are present in the destination zone, then that node replies to the RREQ request with the RREP message and tell to the source node that he is in the destination zone and able to transfer the RREQ message to the destination node (Fig. 13).

Here node 10 is a peripheral node and present in the destination zone so it send RREP message to the source node.

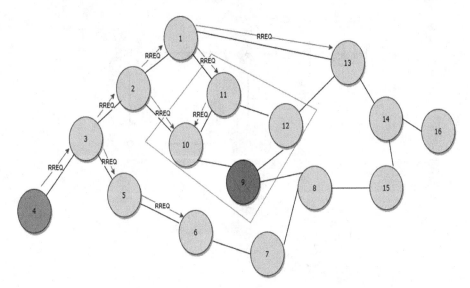

Fig. 12. Network of Inter or Intra domain connected devices.

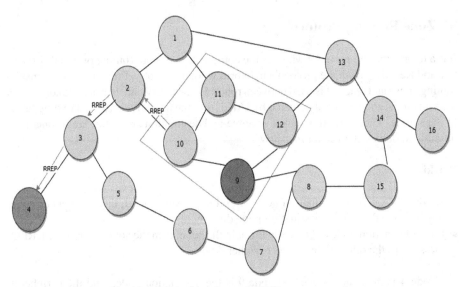

Fig. 13. Peripheral node send RREP to source node.

- If the peripheral node is not present in the destination zone, then that peripheral node further sends the RREQ message to its peripheral node and so on.
- At the end if one or more than one route reply is received by the source node ten in that case source node choose only one path or reply based upon some metric.

6   Conclusion

VANET is a significant looming area, source of research and field of progress that, with the aid of developments in mobile communication, results in advanced intra-vehicular communication. In this article, it is stated that the construction of VANET protocols is difficult because of the intense versatility of automobiles by contrasting and analysing the various routing protocols. Because the prevention of accidents between vehicles by minimising human error is one of the key benefits of utilising VANET systems, providing a safe link between nodes is also important. Research and creation of effective routing protocols in VANETs will be at the centre of crash prevention measures in the immediate future, and this will be a crucial part in the enlargement of autonomous vehicles. Considering considerations like safety, potency and adaptability of vehicular communication, routing protocols need to be developed.

References

1. Yadav, S., Rajput, N.K., Sagar, A.K., Maheshwari, D.: Secure and reliable routing protocols for VANETs. In: 2018 4th International Conference on Computing Communication and Automation, ICCCA 2018, pp. 1–5 (2018)
2. Patel, D., Faisal, M., Batavia, P., Makhija, S., Mani, M.: Overview of routing protocols in VANET. Int. J. Comput. Appl. 136(9), 4–7 (2016)
3. Sharma, S., Sharma, P.: Comprehensive study of various routing protocols in VANET. In: 2019 International Conference on Intelligent Computing and Control Systems, ICCS 2019, ICICCS, pp. 1272–1275 (2019)
4. Vats, S., Kumar, S., Shukla, S., Shankar, S.: VANET: a future technology. Int. J. Sci. Res. Publ. 7(2), 378–389 (2017)
5. Thalore, R.: A review of various routing protocols in VANET. Int. J. Adva. Eng. Res. Sci. 4(4), 237–243 (2017)
6. Laroiya, N.: Energy efficient routing protocols in VANETs. Adv. Comput. Sci. Technol. 10(5), 1371–1390 (2017)
7. Malathi, A., Sreenath, N.: A comparative study of clustering protocols in VANET. Int. J. Emerg. Trends Technol. Comput. Sci. 6(1), 11–20 (2017)
8. Marzak, B., Toumi, H., Talea, M.: Performance analysis of routing protocols in vehicular Ad Hoc network performance analysis of routing protocols in vehicular Ad Hoc network, November 2017
9. Sumayya, P.A., Shefeena, P.S.: VANET based vehicle tracking module for safe and efficient road transportation system. Procedia Comput. Sci. 46, 1173–1180 (2015). ICICT 2014
10. Altayeb, M., Mahgoub, I.: A survey of vehicular ad hoc networks routing protocols. Int. J. Innov. Appl. Stud. 3(3), 829–846 (2013)
11. Ben Jaafar, I.: A novel clustering algorithm based on agent technology for VANET. Netw. Protoc. Algorithms 8(2), 1–19 (2016)
12. García, D.L.: Inter-Vehicular Communication Systems
13. Kabir, M.H.: Research issues on vehicular ad hoc network. Int. J. Eng. Trends Technol. (IJETT) 6(4) (2013)
14. Jagga, S., Dey, I., Aparajit, A.: Performance analysis of DSR, STAR, ZRP routing protocols for a dynamic Ad-Hoc network. Int. Res. J. Eng. Technol. 4(2), 1428–1431 (2017)
15. Ghori, M.R., Sadiq, A.S., Ghani, A.: VANET routing protocols: review, implementation and analysis (2018)

16. Dashore, N., Singh, P.M.: Performance analysis of routing protocol in VANET **2**, 118–122 (2017)
17. Azees, M., Vijayakumar, P., Deborah, J.: Comprehensive survey on security services in vehicular ad-hoc networks. Proc. Int. J. IET Intell. Transp. Syst. **10**, 379–388 (2016)
18. Gupta, P., Chaba, Y.: Performance analysis of routing-protocols in vehicular Ad Hoc networks for CBR applications over UDP connections. Proc. Int. J. Eng. Comput. Sci. **3**, 6418–6421 (2014)
19. Hassan, A.S.A., Hossain, M.S., Atiquzzaman, M.: Security threats in vehicular Ad Hoc networks. In: Proceedings of International Conference on Advances in Computing, Communications and Informatics (ICACCI), pp. 404–411 (2016)

A Reluctant Checksum Scheme Based on the Inherent Characteristic of Wireless Networks

Nimmala Mangathayaru[1][✉], J. Ravi Kumar[2], and Ravindra Luhach[1,2]

[1] Department of IT, VNR VJIET, Hyderabad 500 090, Telangana, India
mangathayaru_n@vnrvjiet.in
[2] The PNG University of Technology, Lae, Papua New Guinea

Abstract. In this paper, we are describing concept to improve security of wireless sensor networks [1] using checksum one way function called hash code. Along with the security we are also performing file compression using compression techniques like zip input and output streams to reduce the storage cost. In existing technique security is provided using cryptography techniques but still attackers [5] can manage to get original data by hacking keys and eavesdrop (identify and alter packet) packet [7]. Cryptography techniques require heavy computation and can be hack by attackers. To improve security author is using reluctant checksum (hash code) [4] while sending data and only destination can decode and compare data. While sending data first corrupted data will be added to message and only source and destination may know how to get original data from corrupted data and message integrity will be checked using UMAC hash code. Sender will generate checksum code and send code with message to receiver and then receiver once again generate code on received message, if same hash code generated [4] then message was not eavesdrop or alter by attacker. By adding corrupted messages attacker will have no clue to identify which part of message is original and which part is corrupted and without getting original message attacker cannot alter packet and security[6] will be improve. Furthermore, we can add file compression concept to save the memory and processing time in our design with this the storage occupied by compressed file will be lesser than the original file.

Keywords: Security · WSNs · Open channel problem · Cumulative checksum · File compression

1 Introduction

Wireless sensor networks (WSN) pointed to the array of spatially distributed and dedicated sensors to track and record temperature conditions and to the structure of the data collected in a target field. The natural conditions such as sun, sound, pollution, stickiness, wind on are measured by WSNs. This is analogous to remote agencies expressly named in order to be able to provide sensor

© Springer Nature Singapore Pte Ltd. 2021
A. K. Luhach et al. (Eds.): ICAICR 2020, CCIS 1394, pp. 231–240, 2021.
https://doi.org/10.1007/978-981-16-3653-0_19

information centrally, since they rely on remote accessibility and unrestricted arrangement by businesses. Self-ruling Sensors are spatially diffused for the purpose of checking physical or environmentally friendly environments such as, for example, temperature, vibration, pressures, etc. Today's networks are two-way, with input obtained from relevant sensors and sensor operation controls. Military applications have convinced the development of remote sensor networks, for instance, the surveillance of the battle areas in many modern applications such as mechanical cycle observation and control, computer health tracking, etc. The WSN is made of "hubs" ranging from hundreds of hubs to thousands of hubs, with one or more sensors attached to each hub. A radio handset with an inner reception unit or combination with a reception external cable, microcontroller, an electrical circuit for interfacing the sensors and a power supply, usually a battery or type of implanted reaping energy are typically used for each of those sensor network centers. A sensor hub will fluctuate from a shoe box to the size of a grain of residue, but it currently does not appear to have the working "bits" of authentic minutes measurements. The cost of sensor hubs is often based on the complexity of the individual sensor hubs, varying from a few to several dollars. Size and cost constraints on sensor hubs contribute to contrasts of asset specifications, e.g. electricity, memory, device speed and speed of correspondence transmission. The geography of the WSNs will change from a simplistic star organization to a serious remote work organisation. The proliferation solution may be directing or flooding between the organization's leaps. From previous hardly time, we has seen fast infiltration about remote organizations at home as well as undertaking. Through expanded utilization of remote organizations [2], remote organization security gets more concern. Remote organizations are helpless against assaults what be much hard toward dispatch within wires space for toward the broadcast nature about remote channel [8]. That aggressors has simple admittance toward remote channel. Those be listen in as well as catch network outlines intended to further assaults, reason to open channel issue. Open channel issue be hard toward comprehend. Take WLAN [1] (remote neighborhood) for instance, WPA2 (Wi-Fi Secured Access 2) is generally utilized in light of the fact that it gives solid encryption. However, the assailants can in any case pick up unapproved admittance to WLANs by outline catching also, disconnected beast power assaults [6]. Especially, with the late advancements of elite figuring innovations, for example, illustrations handling unit (GPU) innovation as well as distributed computing innovation, likelihood about progress intended beast power assaults expanded drastically. Investigates displays the confirmation four-way handshakes casings about WPA2-PSK (PreShared Key) incorporate hash estimation about mystery key. The aggressor catches those casings as well as mounts disconnected word reference savage power assault. Quickened through GPU orelse distributed computing advancements, upon 130 million secret phrase blends be went for only 20 min. Organizations with no solid secret key assurance can be handily broken.

As aggressors can catch remote edges imperceptibly, and mount further disconnected savage power assault based on these casings, how to take care of open channel issue pulled in expanding consideration as of late. Mathematical channel decay multiplexing (ACDM) is an way to deal with take care of open channels issue throughout physical layer[6] spreadding range precode innovation. Within ACDM, code send vectors be resolved through solitary worth decay (SVD) about convolution network depicting the channel [8] between the transmitter as well as wanted beneficiary. Hence every possible transmitter– snoop channel can have an alternate multipaths structure, snoop's capacity toward identify as well as translate the transmissions be able to seriously decreased. iJam5 be other way toward deal with take care of open channel issue [2] at physical layer. Within iJam, the senders rehashes it transmits at multiple times. From every example within rehashed transmissions, the beneficiary haphazardly sticks for example for first transmission, or else the comparing test within reiteration. Hence, doesn't realize which sign example is stuck and which one is clean, it can't effectively decipher the information. ACDM as well as iJam tackle open channel issue for physical layer [6], however that type of methodologies requires much unpredictable remote equipment gadgets. A lot of time furthermore, endeavors are expected to grow such gadgets. Besides, such methodologies require the substitutions of remote gadgets that are broadly utilized. Fathoming open channel [8] issue without equipment adjustment be much alluring, what subject about the concept. This be generally acknowledged that cyclic excess check (CRC) checksum arrangement be utilized within information connect layer [6] outline intended to interchanges, regardless of whether wired orelse remote. CRC checksum be utilized intended to beneficiaries to recognize right casings through mistake ones. Regularly, right edges be conveyed to upper layers of correspondence conventions along with mistake ones be dropped. Within the articles, we make a questions upon this and since quite a while ago held plan guideline on the grounds that the busybodies additionally advantage from such office. The busybodies can catch right edges for additional beast power word reference assaults [5] and drop the mistake ones. On the off chance that the checksum of edges are secured and as it were the expected recipients can decipher it accurately, the busybodies can't recognize right edges from mistake ones. As edge mistake is unavoidable in remote organizations, outlines caught by busybodies contain both mistake outlines and right ones. In light of such blunder inclined casings, consequences of the accompanying disconnected beast power assaults [5] are deceitful. Along these lines, checksum assurance is a successful way to deal with tackle open channel issue. As thought about to approaches at physical layer[6], checksum insurance for information interface layer requires no equipment adjustment as well as able to be executed on generally utilized remote gadgets. In this article, a hesitant checksum plot named R-CS (hesitant checksum grouping) be planned. R-CS secures [3] checksum through ARQ (programmed rehash demand) about media access control (MAC) sub-layer.

Conventional CRC outline checksum succession be eliminated through DATA casing with two new checksums be utilized, cumulated checksum as well as shrouded checksum. Cumulated checksum be the restrictive OR (XORed) [4] aftereffect of CRC estimations of all casings effectively got through the proposed beneficiary. Concealed checksum is scrambled through cumulated checksum, that replace by conventional CRC checksum grouping by information outline. The sender know precisely the checksum about each casing. Along these lines, that be the cumulated checksum by XOR all checksum of the communicated outlines. The collector moreover keeps up cumulated checksum through XOR checksum [2] about total accurately got outlines. In the event that awful casings got, the recipient demands the sender to retransmit the casing until right edge got. Accordingly to the sender as well as beneficiary knows the cumulated checksum. Yet, to the snoops, that can't demand retransmissions of blunder outlines got. A solitary mistake casing should prompt disappointment within following the cumulated checksum. Every single ensuing edge can't be confirmed on the grounds that absence of cumulated checksum. As remote channel be inclined toward mistake, snoops can't catch all casings without mistake. R-CS be secure checksum toward addresses the open channel issue [5]. The commitments about article be twofold. Toward begin with, to about creators' information, that be the initial to contend generally utilized CRC outline checksum grouping isn't sensible from the point of view of remote security. Utilizing checksum unequivocally in information [2] connect layer outline makes open channel issue more genuine. It not just encourages the collector to deal with the edge successfully, yet in addition advantage the busy to catch right edges intended to further assaults. Second, a hesitant checksum plot R-CS be planned toward ensure the checksum. In view of the innate quality about remote channel, R-CS keeps the snoops through getting to the checksum about edges. In this way, the foes are under the danger of assaulting [7] the remote organizations dependent on mistake outlines. The achievement likelihood of such assaults is diminished significantly.

2   Literature Survey

2.1   Enhanced Protection Use of the Physical Layer

While regular cryptographic security systems are basic to the general issue of making sure about remote organizations, they don't straightforwardly use the novel properties of the remote space to address security dangers. The remote medium is an amazing wellspring of space explicit data that can supplement and upgrade conventional security components. In this article we contend that new security standards which misuse actual layer properties of the remote medium, for example, the quick spatial, ghastly, and worldly decorrelation properties of the radio channel, can improve secrecy and validation administrations. We plot some fundamental developments for these administrations, and afterward give a contextual analysis to how such techniques can be coordinated into a more extensive security structure for a remote organization.

2.2   GloMoSim: A Library for Large-Scale Wireless Network Emulation

Various library based equal and consecutive organization test systems have been planned. The paper portrays a library, called GloMoSim (Global Mobile framework Simulator), for equal reenactment of remote organizations. GloMoSim has been intended to be extensible and composable: the correspondence convention stack for remote organizations is isolated into a bunch of layers, each with its own API. Models of conventions at one layer collaborate with those at a lower (or higher) layer just through these APIs. The secluded usage empowers predictable examination of numerous conventions at a given layer. The equal usage of GloMoSim can be executed utilizing an assortment of moderate synchronization conventions, which incorporate the invalid message and contingent function calculations. The paper portrays the GloMoSim library, addresses various issues pertinent to its parallelization, and presents a bunch of trial results on the IBM 9076 SP, a circulated memory multicomputer. These trials use models built from the library modules.

2.3 Wireless Protection in the Physical Layer via Pre-coding Transmission via Dispersive Channels

Multi-layer security and data affirmation structures will get basic as potential assailants' assets keep on developing. Because of its developing use and clear weakness, remote correspondence is specifically need of security. As accessible computational force builds, transmitters will have the option to actualize advanced precoding to expand transmission security. We consider the security-improving ability of mathematical channel disintegration multiplexing (ACDM), a type of multipulse spread-range precoding for dispersive remote diverts that outcomes in symmetrical motioning at the recipient. In ACDM, the send code vectors are resolved from the SVD of the convolution network depicting the channel between the transmitter and wanted recipient. Since any potential transmitter-snoop channel will have an alternate multipath structure, the busy-body's capacity to recognize and interpret the transmissions can be seriously diminished. We create semi-expository formulae for the exhibition punishment experienced by a snoop utilizing the ideal direct MMSE beneficiary under the most pessimistic scenario presumptions that it has ideal information on the send code set and its own personal channel reaction. Utilizing sensible channel models, we exhibit that such a busybody encounters a critical presentation corruption, and show that this debasement is because of a mix of variety misfortune and between code impedance.

2.4 Wireless Protection Physical Layer Made the Channel Independent and Fast

There is a developing interest in actual layer security. Ongoing work has exhibited that remote gadgets can produce a mutual mystery key by abusing varieties in their channel. The rate at which the mystery pieces are created, in any case, relies intensely upon how quick the channel changes. Accordingly, existing plans have a low mystery rate and are mostly material to versatile conditions. Conversely, this paper presents another physical-layer way to deal with mystery key age that is both quick and free of channel varieties. Our methodology makes a recipient jam the sign in a way that actually permits it to interpret the information, yet

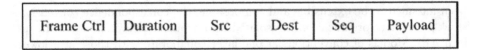

Fig. 1. DATA frame structure in R-CS

keeps different hubs from disentangling. Results from a testbed execution show that our strategy is altogether quicker and more exact than best in class physical-layer mystery key age conventions. In particular, while past work creates up to 44 mystery bits/s with a 4% bit difference between the two gadgets, our plan has a mystery pace of 3–18 Kb/s with 0% bit contradiction.

2.5 In the Face of a Military Interference with ARQ-Based Wireless Communication Networks

We explore the plan and execution of ARQ-based frameworks for remote highlight point (P2P) correspondence joins with amazing criticism directs within the sight of a key jammer over an added substance white Gaussian commotion channel subject to InterSymbol Interference (ISI). We characterize framework inactivity as the quantity of transmission endeavors at the transmitter to accomplish a fruitful exchange of an information parcel to the recipient. We endeavor to limit it by demonstrating this as an obliged advancement issue where the framework inactivity is limited with the end goal that the likelihood of effectively getting an information parcel at the recipient fulfills a recommended ensure. A game-hypothetical definition is given. Mathematical outcomes are introduced for delineation purposes.

3 Methodology

Step 1. S includes all Hsc and Hsh interne variables. Hsc is a combined inspection total and Hsh is a hidden inspection sum. Where, Hsc = 0 * 0. S then calculates secret DATAn checksum

$$Hsh = h1(Hsc, DATAn)$$

After that, S updated be cumulated checksum

$$Hsc = h2(DATAn)$$

Then compares toward usual wireless communications, FCS be ignores by DATA frame in R-CS

Step 2. R includes some Hrc, Hrh, and Hrtmp variables. Hrc is cumulated, Hrh is covered, Hrtmp stores temporary inspection sum. The Hrc flagship data is set to 0*0. When DATAn is obtained, R will measure the DATAn temporary check

$$Hrh = h1(Hrc, DATAn)$$

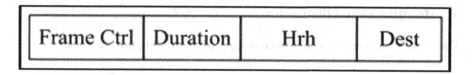

Fig. 2. ACK frame structure in R-CS

After that, ACKn gets from R toward S.

Step 3. When ACKn is obtained, S compares Hsh concealed internally and Hrh is hidden. If Hsh = Hrh, R will correctly receive DATAn. S transmits the frames continually, DATAn. If not, errors arise as should DATAn be retransmitted if Hsh+Hrh.

Step 4. On receives DATAn, R checks Seq fields toward determines either gotted frames be DATAn orelse DATAn+ 1. If Seq = n, that be retransmissions about DATAn, turns toward Step 2. Orelse, if Seq = n+ 1, there is no errors happen while DATAn as well as ACKn transmissions. R update the local variables.

$$Hrc = Hrtmp \bigoplus Hrc$$

When contrasted with conventional methodologies [4], the checksum about DATA outline be recognized toward S within ACK outline, rather than be conveyed the DATA outline. The foes can't get the checksum effectively through catching DATA outline. It goes without saying that moves controls from DATA edge to ACK contour is not measured as both a DATA contour and the corresponding ACK contour are registered by the controlsum. The vital advance aims at search sum protection with the combined inspection sum and the hidden inspection sum. The combined controls HSc, HRC be XORed [4], have essentially hit R as a result of all DATA outlines. The Hsc, Hrc and R sync retransmissions for error contours. Hrh is considered the secret search total along with Hsh. The encoded hate approximation of the latest DATA description is the shielded checksum. R communicates in the ACK contour Hrh during ordinary activities to validate justification for testing [8]. The search cycle [8] is easy because the Hsc and Hrc are synchronized with R. In any case, it takes a right combined check total to affirm that the captured DATA outline is accurate. This means that the opponent must not misinterpret the full contours of DATA. If you expect DATAn not to be correctly captured and any previous DATA contour has been right, you will affirm that DATAn is reduced by computerizing the concealed search total (4) and Hrh and the following ACK contour. Information casings be drops on the grounds that casing mistake [6]. However, from that point forward, that can't recognize mistake outlines from right ones due to lost synchronization of combined checksum.

4   Results and Discussion

The results was very effective when compared to existing systems.

S. no.	Type payload	Error size
1	Newtwork payload	29
2	or Error rate	8.6

In graph, we can see error rate (corrupted data) and packet rate. Apart from this we can compress the file while transmission to reduce the storage space with this the storage cost will be reduced. The below results shows the storage consumption before and after the file compression.

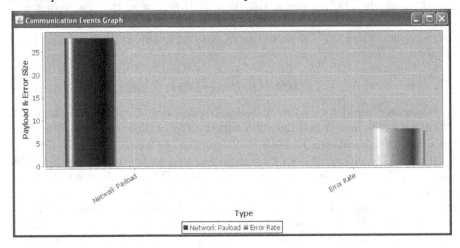

5   Conclusion

Within the paper, we planned a concept to improve security of wireless sensor networks [1] using checksum one way function called hash code and also reducing the storage cost for the transmitted data by compressing the file. In our planned work, While sending the data first corrupted data will be added to message and only source and destination may know how to get original data from corrupted data and message integrity will be checked using UMAC hash code. Our results shows that the compressed data length is lesser than the original data with this the storage cost reduced effectively.

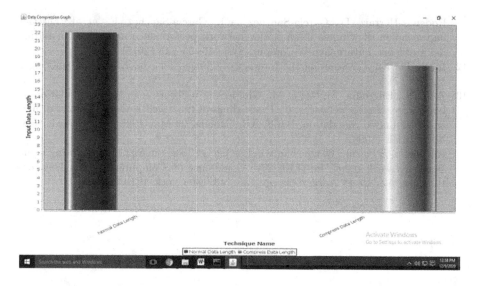

References

1. Mathur, S., et al.: Exploiting the physical layer for enhanced security [security and privacy in emerging wireless networks]. IEEE Wirel Commun. **17**(5), 63–70 (2010)
2. Gold, S.: Cracking wireless networks. Netw. Secur. **2011**(11), 14–18 (2011)
3. Li, S., Da Xu, L., Zhao, S.: The internet of things: a survey. Inform. Syst. Front. **17**, 243–259 (2015)
4. Sperandio, C., Flikkema, P.G.: Wireless physical-layer security via transmit precoding over dispersive channels: optimum linear eavesdropping. In: Proceedings of MILCOM 2002, Anaheim, CA, 7–10 October 2002, pp. 1113–1117. New York (IEEE)
5. Gollakota, S., Katabi, D.: Physical layer wireless security made fast and channel independent. In: Proceedings of IEEE INFOCOM 2011, Shanghai, China, 10–15 April 2011, pp. 1125–1133. IEEE, New York (2011)
6. KH, K.: Security attack based on control packet vulnerability in cooperative wireless networks. In: The Ninth International Conference on Networking and Services, Lisbon, 24–29 March 2013, pp. 123–128. Lisbon, Portugal. IARIA (2013)
7. Li, S., Da Xu, L., Wang, X.: On ARQ-based wireless communication systems in the presence of a strategic jammer. In: IEEE Global Conference on Signal and Information Processing, 2014, pp. 478–483. Georgia, USA. IEEE (2014)
8. Black, J., Halevi, S., Krawczyk, H., Krovetz, T., Rogaway, P.: UMAC: fast and secure message authentication. In: Wiener, M. (ed.) CRYPTO 1999. LNCS, vol. 1666, pp. 216–233. Springer, Heidelberg (1999). https://doi.org/10.1007/3-540-48405-1_14
9. Gollmann, D. (ed.): FSE 1996. LNCS, vol. 1039. Springer, Heidelberg (1996). https://doi.org/10.1007/3-540-60865-6
10. Hlavka, P., et al.: CRC64 algorithm analysis and verification 1. Prague, Czech Republic: CESNET technical report, December (2005)

11. Rodenas-Herraiz, D., Garcia-Sanchez, A.J., Garcia-Sanchez, F., et al.: On the improvement of wireless mesh sensor network performance under hidden terminal problems. Future Gener. Comput. Syst. **45**, 95–113 (2015)
12. Li, S., Da Xu, L.: Securing the Internet of Things, 1st edn. Elsevier, Cambridge, MA (2017)
13. Zeng, X., Bagrodia, R., Gerla, M.: GloMoSim: a library for parallel simulation of large-scale wireless networks. In: Proceedings of the Twelfth Workshop on Parallel and Distributed Simulation, Banff, AB, Canada, 29 May 1998, pp. 154–161. New York. IEEE (1998)
14. Rayanchu, S., et al.: Diagnosing wireless packet losses in 802.11: separating collision from weak signal. In: IEEE 27th Conference on Computer Communications, Phoenix, AZ, 13–18 April 2008, pp. 735–743. New York. IEEE (2008)

Security and Privacy

Anomaly Based Detection of Cross Site Scripting Attack in Web Applications Using Gradient Boosting Classifier

P. Sriramya[1]($\boxtimes$), S. Kalaiarasi[1], and N. Bharathi[2]

[1] Saveetha School of Engineering, Saveetha Institute of Medical and Technical Sciences, Thandalam, Chennai, India
[2] SRM Institute of Science and Technology, Vadapalani, Chennai, India

Abstract. Everything nowadays in operated and connected to the internet, this gives the attackers a great opportunity to steal the sensitive information of the users. Nowadays various kinds of attacks are there on the internet and attackers are continuously finding new ways to overcome the security. Proposed model would be able to detect the Cross-Site scripting attack using an Intrusion detection system. We will be using a modified dataset of KDD-CUP-99 to train our model. The Cross-Site Scripting (XSS) attack targets the web applications. The attacker targets the client side or the server side in this attack. The attacker injects malicious code into the application in the client side or targets the database in the server side. This proposed system focuses on the development that keeps track of the TCP packets parameters like service used, source bytes, destination bytes etc. which helps us determine whether the connection established is by a user or an attacker, thus it helps us detect the attack and prevent it. We have used Gradient Boosting Algorithm to detect the XSS attack and have compared the accuracy of the right detection of the attack with various other machine learning algorithms and have achieved high accuracy rate in the Gradient Boosting Classifier.

Keywords: Cyber security · Machine learning algorithm · Cross-site scripting attack

1 Introduction

The use of web-based technology has been increased exponentially in the past few years, this technology has been providing us different services such as e-commerce, social networking. But these technologies have also been under the radar of cybercriminals, these attackers exploit the code and steal confidential information of the users, they continuously find new ways of bypassing these security systems and exploiting the services. One such common cyberattack is the cross-site scripting attack. This is still on the list of top 10 attacks in OWASP [1].

© Springer Nature Singapore Pte Ltd. 2021
A. K. Luhach et al. (Eds.): ICAICR 2020, CCIS 1394, pp. 243–252, 2021.
https://doi.org/10.1007/978-981-16-3653-0_20

1.1 XSS Attack

It is the attack in which malicious scripts are injection into the website for malicious intent. The end user receives the malicious code through the web application compromised by the attacker. The end user would not be able to know if the script can be trusted or not since the user thinks that it is being received from a trusted source.

The attacker changes the code using modified tags and attributes. These malicious scripts can access session token, cookies and sensitive information of the end user. There are many flaws in a website that allows this kind of attacks, anywhere the web application takes an input from the user this script can be injected. Figure 1 gives a diagrammatic representation of step by step process of how XSS attack happens.

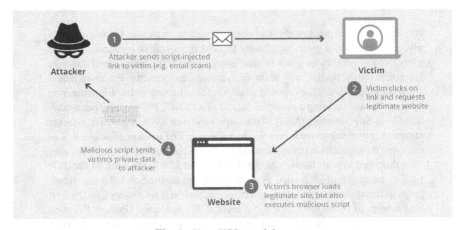

Fig. 1. How XSS attack happens

Stored XSS: In this attack the injected script is stored permanently in the compromised target such as the database, whenever the victim demands for any information from the database this script also gets transferred to the victim's browser from the effected server [2]. It is also called Persistent or type I XSS.

Reflected XSS: In this firstly the user is tricked into opening a link crafted by the attacker requesting malicious URL from the website, the server responds by providing a website which includes malicious string, the users browser executes this since it has been received from a trusted server, the sensitive information of the user is then transferred to the attacker [2].

There are ways in which we can stop XSS attacks to some extent; ways like encoding and obfuscation are used by the developers. We can filter the inputs received from the user to check if there is any malicious code there. We can encode the output data in the responses. In this paper we will propose an IDS framework that detects these attacks and prevents them.

1.2 Gradient Boosting Classifier

A gradient boosting classifier is a combination of multiple week classifiers that are combined to form a strong classifier for better results usually used with decision trees for improving the results [3].

Gradient boosting is one of the famous machine learning algorithms used to solve non-linear problems, it also reduces the chances of overfitting. The specialty of gradient boosting is that it reduces the chances of any errors in the result.

1.3 Intrusion Detection System

An intrusion detection system is similar to a wall of security that defends a network or a system. The intrusion detection system can be in the form of a software as well as a hardware that protects the vulnerable target from being compromised by the attacker. It continuously monitors the flow of traffic through it and informs the user if any unusual packet is detected.

Network based IDS: A network-based IDS detects malicious activities by monitoring the network traffic from attacks like denial of service, XSS [4].

Host based IDS: A host-based IDS monitors individual host networks for malicious activity. These are used for auditing purposes in a specific host [5].

2 Literature Survey

Cyber security attacks have been increasing day by day as the technology is getting advanced and new methodologies are being developed. These attacks can be prevented but there are always variations in the types of attack the victim is affected by and needs a solution.

XSS-based attacks are attacks based on JavaScript which have many attack vectors by which it can affect the victim. These attacks are differentiated into reflected, stored and DOM (Document object Model) based XSS [6].

To prevent XSS secure coding is necessary which includes escaping, input validation and sanitization.

Various XSS detection methodologies include IDS, Content analysis like string analysis, web query analysis and text filter, Input Validation and Pattern analysis. Also, JS parser and HTML parser are used to detect attack vectors in web page. Although these methods are good, they do not detect each and every type of attacks.

Also, while detecting XSS not only attack vectors are important but also sometimes they are encoded with URL encoder or base64 format and can bypass sanitization.

Due to widespread use of Artificial Intelligence XSS detection has become sophisticated. Many attack vectors can be monitored and tested using machine learning techniques [7]. Algorithms such as random forest, K neighboring, SVC, Linear SVC and gradient boosting are mostly involved in classification and detection of XSS. Of these depending on the data set some algorithms are beneficial as they have good accuracy and less false positive rate. The SVM classifier has a very low precision rate and does not meet the purpose of real world [8]. Researchers claim that the random forest algorithm has the highest accuracy but false positive rate is also high. The deep learning schemes can prove detection rates between 93% and 95%. It is excellent and false positive rate is very high.

There are various methods through which one can detect and prevent the XSS attack, some of the successful methods are analyzing the important features of the content of the web pages and the URL using classifiers, analyzing XSS related symbols using deep learning techniques and detecting the attack, using proper encoders for the HTML and java script, using machine learning techniques to detect anomaly, deep learning to protect the network traffic and detect unusual behavior.

There are a lot of issues in the existing system like less efficiency, less accuracy, more false positive rates.

3   Problem Statement

In this project we aim to detect the attack successfully and create a framework in the future which successfully stops the attacker from getting into the network, a framework similar to an intrusion detection system.

The dataset we are going to use is a modified KDD-CUPP 99 dataset which contains information of the connections established between the source and the destination, it has information of the TCP connection established and also the data of the network traffic. Some of the attributes are the flag type, source bytes, destination bytes, protocols used etc.

Using this particular dataset to detect the attack will help us analyze the behavior of different types of user and the actions performed by them in the network. This will allow us to stop the attacker and block him from the network permanently. This helps us in distinguishing between a legitimate user and a malicious attacker hence safeguarding the network.

In this paper we will explore various machine learning models and choose an appropriate model for detecting this type of attack with the parameters provided, we will be using recurrent neural network for decreasing the processing time and increasing the efficiency.

4   Description of the Proposed System

The proposed system detects both server-side vulnerability and client-side vulnerability. The server side is much easier to target than the client side since the web applications contain dynamical scripts and gives response to the users requests as per requirement of the user; it targets a much larger audience. There are two types in these. They are Reflected XSS and Stored XSS [15].

Reflected XSS attack (also known as Non-persistent attack) allows an attacker to inject a script into the search field or where there are parameters included in the website or application. This type of attack is mainly used to steal account information like, private information like cookies. The victim and the attacker have much more interaction in this kind of attack. This also allows browser exploitation since JavaScript code is also run inside the victim's browser [16].

Stored XSS attack (persistent attack) k targets social networking, e-commerce websites and other similar type of frameworks as they have a comment section where an attacker can post a malicious JavaScript which is stored in database and whichever person visits that website, the JavaScript loads and the attacker can have the cookies of the victim. This type of attacks originates from databases as it stores the script [14].

In client side attack the malicious code is injected and executed within the user's browser. The DOM based attack is executed in the document object model i.e. the data is not handled properly and attacker injects a payload which is stored in DOM. The client side is a major target for the DOM-based attack. This attack is very difficult to detect as it never sends malicious payload to the server, even WAFs can't see this attack.

The proposed system is composed of various parameters that are used to detect the anomaly. It uses the various signatures matching and behavior analysis techniques for the detection of the attack. Almost all the XSS attacks are detected, we have also compared the accuracy of different algorithms and choose the best one for detection.

4.1 Data Analysis

Before we start, we need to a proper dataset so that there are no disputes between values also we can have proper graphs and charts.

It is better to spend time analyzing data and build the data format, values and relationships which will help to understand observations in our outcome.

Exploratory Data Analysis is the approach of analysis before modelling which refers to the process of identifying anomalies, discover various patterns, testing the hypothesis. We take the help of various graphical representations to identify the relationship and dependencies between the parameters, all these initial investigations are important for optimal results.

It is called as Exploratory data analysis because you're building your knowledge base and understanding data on how well can it be used, which generate a lot of questions based on the model i.e. if it can work in particular way or not [9].

This process can be used to sanitize the data, to identify essential elements and filter out the non-required data. It is often performed with representative data sample.

4.2 Feature Selection

Feature extraction is the process of extracting important, non-redundant features from raw data. Suppose we have 5 text documents. Suppose there are 10 important words that are present in all 5 documents. Then these 10 words may not be contributing in deciding the labels for those documents. We can omit these words and create new features excluding those words.

TF-IDF technique: TF-IDF technique is a feature extraction technique based on frequency of features in documents. Suppose there is set of documents D (d1, d2, d3), TF (t, d) is term frequency = frequency of a term/feature value t in document d. Feature selection process tries to get most important features that are contributing to decide the label [10].

Univariate Feature Selection: This is a manual task. This involves checking the importance of every feature with our optimal goal. We then remove all the unwanted feature from our dataset, then check the variance of all features. The feature should bring a predictive power to the model that we build, hence we remove the features according to the value of the variance [11].

Pearson Correlation: This process gives us the best result out of the three processes. In this we calculate the dependencies between the feature and the parameter and then eliminate the features selecting only the important once [12].

4.3 Prediction

This dataset was released to create an intrusion detection system which can distinguish between bad connections and normal connection, protecting the network from unauthorized users. This dataset was first discovered by DARPA intrusion detection evaluation program in 1998, the KDD dataset was created in 1999 and it uses the modified version of the same.

Before starting our training and testing part we need to clean the dataset for this we have to remove the parameters that are not important and irrelevant to our ultimate goal, also we need to convert string values into numerical values using encoding algorithm. After these steps we have to correlate the parameters with each other to find the dependence between them. In the diagram given blow shows the various relations between the parameters.

After working with the dataset its time to work on the algorithms, we need to test different types of algorithm to find the perfect fit, for problems based on anomaly machine learning algorithms are better than deep learning technique [17]. We will use algorithms like decision tree classifier, K-Neighbors regression, SVC, linear SVC, random forest algorithm, gradient boosting classifier and voting hybrid classifier. Further in this section will be the explanation for each algorithm in detail.

5 Implementation

We use machine learning technique to identify weather an attack is XSS or not, for this we create a dataset and train the neural network model for finding an effective technique to detect the attack. Figure 2 shows the methodology of the proposed system.

5.1 The Dataset

The dataset created contains information from two classes that are the attackers and the real users. The dataset contains some major parameters such as the protocol used by the user, the service used and the type of flag. There are other parameters such as the source bytes, destination bytes, weather the logged I user is guest and other parameters related to the host.

The connection between the source and destination is either labelled as safe or an attack, a connection is basically a set of TCP packets that flow from source to destination. There are various time-based traffic features like the same host and same service features that tells the connection which have been using the same host and service for the past 2 s. There are host-based traffic features like the attacker will scan the host for more

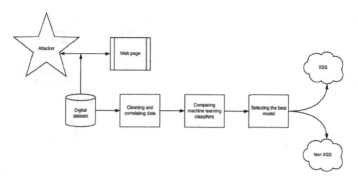

Fig. 2. Block Diagram of the methodology followed

than 2 s to find any open port or services, hence it is also possible to detect a malicious connection based on the features of host.

Now coming to content features which can lead us to the possibility of an attack, for example there are features like failed logins that tell us if the same user has failed to login more than once into the system, fi the user has logged in successfully they are assigned 1 or otherwise 0, if the user obtains the root shell they are assigned 1 or otherwise 0, number of root accesses are also calculated separately for each user, there are parameters that keeps track of the guest users as well.

The traffic features are computed using the two second time window, while the attacker plans to establish a connection to the host machine, they might experience errors while establishing these connections and these errors can be recorded service in the last two seconds, counting the number of connections to the same host in the past two seconds.

These parameters are correlated by machine learning technique and an efficient algorithm is selected to identify if the attack is XSS or not.

For tracking the attacker, there are parameters like SYN error, REJ error, number of connections established to the same [13].

5.2 Correlation

The string-based attributes are converted into numerical attributes using encoder, this is done because the machine cannot understand strings. After this the parameters are correlated to find the dependencies between them and also to select parameters that will be best for training our model and detecting the attack with maximum accuracy. This helps us save a lot of running time to identify and detect the attack and also improves the accuracy of finding the attack. Figure 3 give the focus on parameters that matter to detect the attack will improve our efficiency.

5.3 Performance Evaluation Metrics

To build the model we use some of the best algorithms like random forest, decision tree, linear SVC, K-neighbor's regression, gradient boosting to compare the accuracy

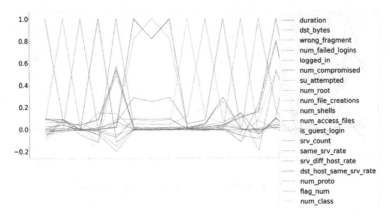

Fig. 3. Correlation of the parameters

between the techniques, we calculate the precision using Confusion matrix and compare them.

Figure 4 gives the confusion matrix belongs to the gradient boosting algorithm, as discussed earlier the matrix consists of four parts, the bar beside the matrix shows us the value of each part, the dark black color indicates that the precision is near perfect for this algorithm.

The value of voting classifier was very close to the gradient boosting algorithm, since they both are an ensemble model, they have higher accuracy than the rest of the algorithms, the gradient boosting forms an ensemble of the decision tree classifier to achieve the higher accuracy rate.

Fig. 4. Confusion matrix for gradient boosting technique

The gradient boosting technique is found to be the most accurate among all other techniques mainly due to the ensemble it forms of the various models. After testing all the efficient algorithms, the final model helped us in achieving the optimal results. Figure 5 give the comparative analysis graph of the accuracy of applied algorithms for which we can see that Gradient boosting Classifier has the maximum accuracy of 97% (Table 1).

Table 1. Comparing accuracy of applied algorithm

S.No	Accuracy	Algorithm
1	0.96385	Decision Tree Classifier
2	0.959858	K-neighbors Regression
3	0.945886	SVC
4	0.690397	Linear SVC
5	0.968507	Random Forest Regression
6	0.97006	Gradient Boosting Classifier

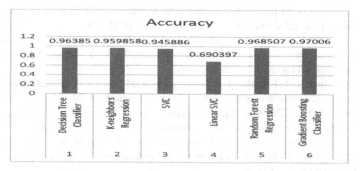

Fig. 5. Comparative graph of the accuracy of applied algorithms

6   Result and Conclusion

The XSS attack is successfully detected with the accuracy of 0.97 using gradient boosting classifier. This classifier is trained using anomaly-based dataset which distinguishes between a normal user and a malicious attacker. Hence the model is trained for behavioral analysis and detects the attack if any unusual behavior is found. Our model is based on the signature detection of various XSS attacks so the dataset we collected is trained with various algorithms and compared. We choose the one found best i.e. gradient boosting classifier. This selection is based on the accuracy and the number of false positive so that the detection is efficient. Hence, we can use these finding to detect and prevent XSS attacks in the future.

7   Future Enhancements

In future we would build a real time XSS prevention framework that protects the user from the attacker this real time system will act as a IDS for the users node as well as for the server, since both the server and the user are vulnerable to the attacker, by doing this even if the developer has not written the code securely the user will not be effected. We can also use deep learning to detect if some malicious content is being passed through the network, by doing this we can safeguard the network from being compromised. Machine learning can also be used to analyze the behavior of the users accessing the web pages and blocking the attacker from accessing it if any unusual behavior is detected.

References

1. Li, J.: Vulnerabilities mapping based on OWASP-SANS: a survey for static application security testing (SAST). Ann. Emerg. Technol. Comput. **4**(5), 1–8 (2020)
2. Kaur, D., Kaur, P.: Cross-site-scripting attacks and their prevention during development. IJEDR **5**(3), 106758 (2017)
3. Rahman, S., Irfan, M., Raza, M.: Performance analysis of boosting classifiers in recognizing activities of daily living. Int. J. Environ. Res. Public Health **17**, 35 (2020)
4. Yousufi, R.M., Lalwani, P., Potda, M.B.: A network-based intrusion detection and prevention system with multi-mode counteractions. In: International Conference on Innovations in Information, Embedded and Communication Systems (ICIIECS). IEEE Explore (2017)
5. Gassais, R., Ezzati-Jivan, N., Fernandez, J.M., Aloise, D., Dagenais, M.R.: Multi-level host-based intrusion detection system for Internet of things. J. Cloud Comput. **9**(1), 1–16 (2020). https://doi.org/10.1186/s13677-020-00206-6
6. Gupta, S., Gupta, B.B., Chaudhary, P.: Hunting for DOM-based XSS vulnerabilities in mobile cloud-based online social network. Future Gener. Comput. Syst. **79**, 319–336 (2017)
7. Ayeni, B.K., Sahalu, J.B., Adeyanju, K.R.: Detecting cross-site scripting in web applications using fuzzy inference system. J. Comput. Networks Commun. **1**, 10 (2018)
8. Nagar, P., Kumar, H., Tiwari, M.M.: Novel approach of intrusion detection classification deep learning using SVM. In: First International Conference on Sustainable Technologies for Computational Intelligence (2020)
9. Chong Ho, Y.: Exploratory data analysis in the context of data mining and resampling. Int. J. Psychol. Res. **3**(1), 109763 (2010)
10. Havrlant, L., Kreinovich, V.: A simple probabilistic explanation of term frequency-inverse document frequency (TF-IDF) heuristic. Int. J. Gen. Syst. **46**(1), 27–36 (2017)
11. Nair, R., Bhagat, A.: Feature selection method to improve the accuracy of classification algorithm. Int. J. Innov. Technol. Exploring Eng. (IJITEE) **8**(6), 25 (2019)
12. Schober, P., Boer, C., Schwarte, L.A.: MMedStat: Correlation Coefficients: Appropriate Use and Interpretation, vol. 126, no. 5, pp. 1763–1768 (2018)
13. Mahmoud, S.K., Alfonse, M., Roushdy, M.I.: A comparative analysis of Cross Site Scripting (XSS) detecting and defensive techniques. In: Eighth International Conference on Intelligent Computing and Information Systems (ICICIS) (2017)
14. Aliga, P.A., John-Otumu, A.M., Imhanlahimi, R.E.: Cross site scripting attacks in web-based applications: a critical review on detection and prevention techniques. J. Adv. Sci. Eng. (JASE) **1**(2), 25–35 (2018)
15. Fang, Y., Li, Y., Liu, L., Huang, C.: DeepXSS: cross site scripting detection based on deep learning. In: Proceedings of the 2018 International Conference on Computing and Artificial Intelligence, pp. 47–51 (2018)
16. Alghfari, F., Dan, W., Imran, A., Xiaoxi, W.: MLPXSS: an integrated XSS-based attack detection scheme in web applications using multilayer perceptron technique. IEEE Access **7**, 100567 (2019)
17. Luhach, A.K., Luhach, R.: Research and implementation of security framework for small and medium sized e-commerce based on SOA. J. Theor. Appl. Inf. Technol. **82**(3), 395 (2015)

Crypto Key Protection Generated from Images and Chaotic Logistic Maps

Kalyanapu Srinivas[1]($\boxtimes$), V. Janaki[2], V. Shankar[1], and P. KumarSwamy[3]

[1] KITS, Warangal, India
[2] VCE, Warangal, India
[3] SR University, Warangal, India

Abstract. Cryptography is a mechanism used for protection of valuable information from unacceptable users in the networking world. It's a challenging task to protect such assets from illegal users. This necessitated for the development of Cryptographic techniques to provide security as large volumes of digital data traveling through the shared media. These techniques range from traditional security systems to crypto image techniques. This brings forward to focus on cryptographic techniques that have strong algorithm and strong key. The strength of any crypto algorithm depends on the strongness of the crypto key used. Therefore, both the algorithm technique and key generation methodology are equally important. This motivated to propose and concentrate on a novel scheme that includes crypto key generation and crypto key protection where the protected key and its methodology cannot be traced by an ineligible user.

Keywords: Symmetric cryptography · Key generation · Images · Chaotic logistic maps · Key encryption (wrap)

1 Introduction

Improvement in telecommunications technology made the electronic data available via internet and utilize easily by communicating among the connected nodes/points. Organizations under different sectors like public, private, corporate, military, small & large businesses etc., are using these connected nodes/points for communicating large amounts of data. Therefore, to protect information there is a need to develop strong and better mechanisms.

Confidentiality, integrity, non repudiation, availability are the effective objectives of cryptographic schemes which are mainly designed to protect confidential information from malicious users. There are two categories of cryptographic schemes defined: schemes dependent on sharable key (symmetric systems) and schemes dependent on public private key (asymmetric systems). In symmetric key based crypto schemes, a key (sharable) is exchanged among communicating parties, a method for exchange of key is used, at both end parties same algorithm and key are applied. Example: DES, AES, IDEA etc., In Asymmetric key based crypto schemes, two keys – one key named public

© Springer Nature Singapore Pte Ltd. 2021
A. K. Luhach et al. (Eds.): ICAICR 2020, CCIS 1394, pp. 253–262, 2021.
https://doi.org/10.1007/978-981-16-3653-0_21

key, for the encryption and the other named private key, for decryption phase are used ensuring that both cannot be computed easily. Example: RSA, DSA etc.

The open internet environment facilitated the illegal users to access one's confidential information thereby exponentially increasing the count of threats. Now, there are no such competent enough techniques available or developed, for securing information. This made to focus for a crypto technique to have a strong algorithm with a strong unpredictable key. The algorithm strength depends on following characteristics: methodology in algorithm, key, length of key, key generation, randomness in key, protection of key and its transmission etc. Till date, most of the algorithms were dependent key with randomness generated from random number generators. Therefore it is viewed that key generation methods and key protection methods are equally important along with the algorithm used. This motivated to define and develop a novel technique for generation of keys with its protection.

The proposal was undertaken in two phases: In phase 1: methodology for key generation using images and Chaos logistic mappings and methodology for protecting the generated key (key wrapping) in phase 2.

2 Background Survey

A nascent field of research where images are used in cryptography is Crypto Image systems. This area has bought several challenges especially in key generation and key protection.

Key in any crypto algorithms - a stream of bits have been generated from bit generation schemes and used in various crypto applications. Images, having their own unique features and characteristics formed a source in generation of key.

Mobile pictures with chaotic logistic maps were used in the generation of true random numbers by Zhao, Liao, Xiao [2]. Initially a grey color image was generated from mobile picture, and later a binary image was obtained by applying diffuse technique. A stream of 16384 bits were generated by counting the blocks of divided ciphered image where each block is assigned with 0 (count of black pixels in block = even) or 1 and scanned in a particular order.

Kalyanapu Srinivas and Janaki [13] presented an new technique with images for generation of random numbers from extracted features of image, which were then used as single time password forming a strong factor during authentication.

Xuan Li, Guoji, Yuliang [4] experimented a method on images by applying chaos logistic maps in the generation of bit sequences. An colored image of desired size (M × N) was selected which was later converted into grayscale image. In this method, nine chaotic streams were generated using chaos logistic maps. By arranging the initial chaotic stream in an ascending order a new encrypted image generated was divided into 8 bit planes of size M × N which were scanned to get bit sequence. The other sequences are used to generate bit sequences by XOR operation resulting in bit sequence of $8 \times M \times N$.

Andrew, David, Alwyn [10] in their article described usage of face in generation of keys. In the first phase facial data was applied with wavelets transformation technique and then discretization where Face hash was the result. In the second phase, Shamir's secret sharing technique was applied to provide security.

The described above schemes are not successful in satisfying parameters of information security. Strength of key was also impacted by attempting to limit the key size. These necessitated and motivated to explore avenues by defining a new approach in order to achieve better security. Therefore, images in symmetric key generation technique using mathematical concept- chaos logistic mappings and protecting the generated keys were proposed. The mentioned approach is discussed in the next section.

3 Proposed Approach with Its Implementation

3.1 Basic Terminology

It is a challenging task to generate strong and secure key based on the importance of key and its role in crypto applications. Images in cryptography forms a new research field called Crypto image system where images are used in developing novel techniques. This session describes more novel method of key generation using chaos logistic mapping with images and key protection technique. Considering the properties of chaos logistic maps like dynamical behavior and measure of quantitative behaviour made it as a perfect choice for generating random sequence. The most important and basic property of both chaos logistic maps and images is a drastical change occurs in the generated output for a small change in single property. Therefore, these properties were considered in crypto key generation process of crypto algorithms. Pareek, Patidar, Sud described the properties of chaotic logistic mapping and Guoji, Li, Yu [4] described the properties of images that are satisfying properties of crypto keys, and were used in generation of streams of bits used as keys in cryptographic applications. Representation of the chaos logistic mapping was shown mathematically as

$$Y_{i+1} = r * Y_i(1 - Y_i) \tag{1}$$

for r (r = 1 to 4) being a system parameter with Y_i being the state variable.

3.2 Algorithm

In this section, chaos logistic mapping was applied to generate keys using colored RGB images was described. The inputs taken for the proposal are an image (*IM*), row size (*rsi*), column size (*csi*), number of selected points (*Pt*) on the image selected and specific size of key (l*n*) and generation of specific size of key is the output (l*n*).

Key Generation & Transformation Process-Sender Side

Input   :   **Image**

Output   :   **K (key)**

1. From a displayed set of images, an image (*IM*) was chosen and size of key
   (*In*), *rsi*, *csi* were given as inputs.

2. The *IM* was now resized to fixed size[*rsi csi*]

$$ResizedImg \leftarrow imresize(IM, [rsi\ csi]); \tag{2}$$

   A variable $|K_{en}|$ is assigned with desired size of key

$$|Ken| \leftarrow ln \tag{3}$$

3. Using mouse, on the selected contour of resized image certain count of points
   (*Pi*) were pointed and obtained point positions are assigned to a variable m.

$$m \leftarrow getposition(ResizeImg, Pi) \tag{4}$$

4. Using the pixel position the pixel values were computed and stored as shown.

$$Pce \leftarrow impixel(ResizedImg, m) \tag{5}$$

5. The matrix size was computed as shown and initial values from P_{ce} were selected and assigned as

$$P_{ce}\ i.e\ msize(P_{ce})$$

$$Y_0 = P_{ce}[k] \tag{6}$$

   //where k = 0: msize and l = k+1: msize

$$Z_0 = P_{ce}[l] \tag{7}$$

   //initial variables are encr_Y_0, encr_Z_0

6. Verification of the logistic mapping constraint was performed i.e the initial
   input values never be equal.

$$if\ Y[0]!=Z[0] \tag{8}$$

goto Step 6

   else

k = k+1;

goto Step 4

   end if

7. The defined chaos logistic map interval is [0-1]. Therefore, the initial input
   variable values are normalized.

$$Y[0]=Y[0]/1000; \tag{9}$$

$$Z[0]=Z[0]/1000; \tag{10}$$

   These initial input values are applied to two chaotic logistic mapping
   expressions in order to obtain the required bits

for(k=0; k<K_{en}; k++)

$$Y[k+1]=r*Y[k](1-Y[k]) \tag{11}$$

$$Z[k+1]=r*Z[k](1-Z[k]) \tag{12}$$

   //where Y, Z are state variables and r is called system parameter which
   //can have any value between 1 and 4 as per chaotic logistic map.

If Y[k] > Z[k]

$$A[k] = 0 \tag{13}$$

   else

$$A[k] = 1 \tag{14}$$

end if

end for

From a given set of images an image *(IM)* is selected. Using mouse a contour was selected based on the choice of user. The selected contour is used for pointing certain mouse clicks. From the selected clicks, the pixel values of the selected mouse clicks were identified and were represented in the form of a matrix $[P_{ce.}]_{PixQi}$(*Pi = number(selected points), Qi = values of Red,Green,Blue for each pixel*). From matrix, the initial values were assigned to the variables Y_0, Z_0. Later, the constraints of chaos logistic mapping were verified. Normalization of the values were performed in order to bring the values in the interval of [0–1]. At each iteration, the outputs are calculated taking the system parameter value in the range of [1–4]. Then comparison is done on the outputs of two logistic maps in ordet to generate the bits, thereby storing the bits in an array. This process is repeated until the size of the key was met $|K_{en}|$. The bit sequences thus generated forms keys can be used for any crypto applications.

Key wrapping or Key encryption is a technique to encrypt crypto key- an asset of encryption algorithms. It is designed for generating unpredictable keys with protective measures and key transmission in untrusting communications networks. The encryption of keys focus especially on n bit blocks of (n = 64) i.e. if the key size is longer than it is parsed into n sized blocks where n = 64 bits before the encryption begins. Therefore the only restriction in key encryption algorithm is placed on n which should be at least two. Overall security provided by key encryption is effected by the choice of key length which can be of n bits where n = 64, 128, 192, 256 etc. The key encryption process is described below.

Key Encryption Process
At this step, the following conventions are applied:

- K (Data key) - used for encryption of plain text. i.e. K = A[i].
- KWK (Key Wrapping Key) - used to multifold Data key (K).
- MK (Master Key) - used to multifold KWK.
- FW_K (Final wrapped) or multifolded key of K
- $MSB_m()$ and $LSB_m()$ - functions for the most significant bits and least significant bits of size m.
- ‖ - denotes concatenation operation.
- The length of a string X in bits is denoted |X|.
- Sequence of 0's and 1's represents a bit string.
- F(flag bit) - appended at the end of the key. If F = 0 no pad bits are added. If F = 1 pad bits of P_L (pad bit length) are added i.e. P_b (pad bits)–the number of bits to be added before F.

Input   :   **K, KWK**

Output   :   **MK, Final key FW$_K$**

1. Division of data Key (K) of length L into r sized n blocks

$$K \rightarrow K1, K2, K3........Kn \qquad L = |K|$$

If (L/r==0) //r=8,16, 32, 64 etc..

n=L/r   // n number of r bit blocks

else

$P_L=|P_b|$ //P_b are the 0 bits padded at the end of K
$n = (L \parallel P_L)/r;$ // P_L = length of padding bits padded after P_b

end if;   // n number of r bit blocks

2. Initialize Variables

KWK is assigned with k bits for k=16, 32, 128, ... a multiple of 8

3. Calculate Master key from K and KWK.

$$MK = LSB_m(KWK)\|MSB_m(K)\| LSB_m(K)\| MSB_m(KWK) \qquad (15)$$

//m-number of bits i.e $m=|KWK|/2$

4. The Outputs of the calculations are Final key (FW$_K$) and MK

$$FW_K=K1_r\|MSB_m(KWK)\|K2_r\|MSB_m(KWK)\|K3_r\|MSB_m(KWK)\|...$$

$$.........K(n-1)_r\|MSB_m(KWK)\|Kn_r\|MSB_m(KWK)\|P_b\|P_L\|F \qquad (16)$$

This process begins by taking the generated key (K) as input which is further divided into n blocks of size r as shown in step 1. Both P_L and P_b are padded to the final output where P_L is the length of the padded bits and P_b is the number of bits padded which depend on size of the key. Key wrapping key (KWK) of size n used to multi fold the key (K) at steps 2. Then at step 3, master key (MK) is computed using K and KWK. Final key is obtained by concatenating m - bits of each Key (K) blocks with m - bits of most significant bits of KWK and padding with P_b, P_L. A flag bit F is also padded at the end of final key which is used for the verification of P_b and P_L. This final encrypted key is further transmitted to the other end for decryption process.

Key Generation Process-Receiver Side
The decryption process at this end begins after decrypting the encrypted key. Therefore, initially the received encrypted symmetric key is decrypted by following the steps described below and then it is used for decryption process.

Input   :   **Final key FW_K, MK**

Output   :   **K, KWK**

1. Check Flag bit (F) and divide the Final key (FW_K) into number of m
   sized blocks

   If (F==0)   // Verification whether padding is done or not

   $$FW_K = K1_r \| MSB_m(KWK) \| K2_r \| MSB_m(KWK) \| K3_r \| MSB_m(KWK)$$

   $$\| \ldots\ldots\ldots K(n-1)_r \| MSB_m(KWK) \| Kn_r \| MSB_m(KWK) \qquad (17)$$

   else

   read P_L

   $$FW_K = FW_K - P_b \qquad (18)$$

   Outputs to

   $$FW_K = K1_r \| MSB_m(KWK) \| K2_r \| MSB_m(KWK) \| K3_r \| MSB_m(KWK) \| \ldots\ldots\ldots$$

   $$\ldots\ldots\ldots K(n-1)_r \| MSB_m(KWK) \| Kn_r \| MSB_m(KWK) \qquad (19)$$

2. From MK, derive the KWK which is used in multi-folding the original
   key K and calculate m

   $$MK = LSB_m(KWK) \| MSB_m(K) \| LSB_m(K) \| MSB_m(KWK) \quad (20)$$

   Outputs to

   $$m = |MK|/4.$$

   $$KWK = LSB_m(MK) + MSB_m(MK) \qquad (21)$$

3. Using KWK, derive the original Data key (K)

   $$K = FW_K - MSB_m(KWK) \qquad (22)$$

   $$\mathbf{K = K1_r \| K2_r \| K3_r \| \ldots\ldots\ldots\ldots\ldots\ldots K(n-1)_r \| Kn_r} \quad (23)$$

At the receiver end, after receiving the final key (FW) this technique is applied. First the flag bit (F) is verified, if F = 0 there are no padding bits i.e. P_b and P_L bits else P_L is computed in order to identify the P_b bits. These P_b and P_L are removed and the final key (FW) without padding bit is obtained. At step 2, KWK is computed using master key (MK). Later, using m-bits of MSB of KWK, the original key (K) is computed which is used for decryption process.

3.3 Experimental Evaluation

Example: At Sender: Wrapping Key

All values in this example are taken in ascii characters for convenience instead of stream of bits. Wrapping of key data with a 128-bit KWK is as shown

1. **Key (K): bed12207808941155068f738afgh3w5r**

   r=8   L=256(length of key K)   n=256/8=32 (32 number of blocks)

   F = 0(Flag bit) P_b = 0 (padding bits) P_L= 0(length of Padding bits)

2. Initialize variables

   KWK : fx8338f4dcc176fx |KWK|=16*8=128

3. Compute m and Master key M from K and KWK

   m=128/2 = 64   MK= dcc176fxbed12207afgh3w5rfx8338f4

4. FW_K=K1$_r$||MSB_m(KWK)||K2$_r$||MSB_m(KWK)||K3$_r$||MSB_m(KWK)||.........

   K(n-1)$_r$||MSB_m(KWK)||Kn$_r$||MSB_m(KWK)|| P_b||P_L||F

FW_K =	bfx8338f4	efx8338f4	dfx8338f4	1fx8338f4
	2fx 8338f4	2fx 8338f4	0fx 8338f4	7fx 8338f4
	8fx 8338f4	0fx8338f4	8fx8338f4	9fx8338f4
	4fx8338f4	1fx8338f4	1fx8338f4	5fx8338f4
	5fx 8338f4	0fx8338f4	6fx8338f4	8fx8338f4
	ffx8338f4	7fx8338f4	3fx8338f4	8fx8338f4
	afx8338f4	ffx8338f4	gfx8338f4	hfx8338f4
	3fx8338f4	wfx8338f4	5fx8338f4	rfx8338f4
	000000000 0			

At Receiver: Unwrapping of Padded Key

Input   :   **Final key FW_K , MK**

Output   :   **K, KWK**

1. Check Flag bit and divide the Final key (FW_K) into number of m sized blocks

   If (F==0) then

FW_k=	bfx8338f4	efx8338f4	dfx8338f4	1fx8338f4
	2fx 8338f4	2fx 8338f4	0fx 8338f4	7fx 8338f4
	8fx 8338f4	0fx8338f4	8fx8338f4	9fx8338f4
	4fx8338f4	1fx8338f4	1fx8338f4	5fx8338f4
	5fx 8338f4	0fx8338f4	6fx8338f4	8fx8338f4
	ffx8338f4	7fx8338f4	3fx8338f4	8fx8338f4
	afx8338f4	ffx8338f4	gfx8338f4	hfx8338f4
	3fx8338f4	wfx8338f4	5fx8338f4	rfx8338f4

2. From MK, derive the KWK which is used in multi-folding the original key K.

   MK= dcc176fxbed12207afgh3w5rfx8338f4   m= 256/4=64

   KWK = LSB_m(MK) + MSB_m (MK)

   KWK= fx8338f4dcc176fx

3. Using KWK, derive the original data key (K)

   i.e K=FW_k-MSB_m(KWK)

4. K=   bfx8338f4   efx8338f4   dfx8338f4   1fx8338f4

	bfx8338f4	efx8338f4	dfx8338f4	1fx8338f4
	2fx 8338f4	2fx 8338f4	0fx 8338f4	7fx 8338f4
	8fx 8338f4	0fx8338f4	8fx8338f4	9fx8338f4
	4fx8338f4	1fx8338f4	1fx8338f4	5fx8338f4
	5fx 8338f4	0fx8338f4	6fx8338f4	8fx8338f4
	ffx8338f4	7fx8338f4	3fx8338f4	8fx8338f4
	afx8338f4	ffx8338f4	gfx8338f4	hfx8338f4
	3fx8338f4	wfx8338f4	5fx8338f4	rfx8338f4)-

   (fx8338f4)

   K= K1$_r$||K2$_r$||K3$_r$||.....................Kn-1$_r$||Kn$_r$

   K= bed12207808941155068f738afgh3w5r

The approach begins with first, generation of keys where the pixel values of the mouse click points on selected contour of selected image are applied to chaos logistic mappings and secondly, the generated key is protected using proposed key encryption technique. At the other end, these techniques are applied specifically in symmetric key crypto systems.

4 Conclusion and Future Scope

The world of information security is rotating around the crypto key. Most of the security tasks in cryptography are composed of various components. One among them is crypto key. Therefore, in recent decades the focus of research was on crypto key generation and its protection. Experimentations are conducted with in key generation and its protection. Considering all the outputs of these into account, XuanLi-2011 [4] worked on generation of key using images and M. Islam, to transfer the information used images as keys. Several others also followed in protection of keys. An analysis on Wrapping of key was performed by Guillaume Scerri, Ryan Stanley-Oakes concentrating on the methodologies of securing the keys. Therefore, the focal point of this approach is to generate a crypto key which is strong, random, unique, unpredictable along with its protection.

References

1. Halevi, S., Krawczyk, H.: One-pass hmqv and asymmetric key-wrapping. Public Key Cryptography – PKC 2011, pp. 317–334 (2011)
2. Hu, Y., Liao, X.F., Wong, K.K., et al.: A true random number generator based on mouse movement and chaotic cryptography, Chaos, Solitons and Fractals, pp. 2286–2293 (2009)
3. Rogaway, P., Shrimpton, T.: Deterministic authenticated-encryption: a provable-security treatment of the key-wrap problem. In: Vaudenay, S. (ed.) EUROCRYPT 2006. LNCS, vol. 4004, pp. 373–390. Springer, Heidelberg (2006). https://doi.org/10.1007/11761679_23
4. Li, X., Guangzhou, Z., Zhang, G., Liao, Y.: Chaos-based true random number generator using image. In: International Conference. Published in Computer Science and Service System (CSSS), IEEE-2011, pp. 27–29. IEEE, Nanjing, China (2011)
5. François, M., Grosges, T., Barchiesi, T., Erra, R.: Image encryption algorithm based on a chaotic iterative process. J. Appl. Math. 3, 1910–1920 (2012)
6. Kester, Q.A.: Image encryption based on the RGB PIXEL transposition and shuffling. Int. J. Comput. Network Inf. Secur. 7, 43–50 (2013). https://doi.org/10.5815/ijcnis.2013.07.05
7. Odeh, A., Abu-Errub, A., Awad, M.: Symmetric key generation method using digital image. IJCSI Int. J. Comput. Sci. Issues Scopus Indexed J. 12(2), 254 (2015)
8. Venckauskas, A., Nanevicius, P.: Cryptographic key generation from Finger Vein. Int. J. Eng. Sci. Res. Technol. 2(4), 733–738 (2013). ISSN: 2277-9655
9. Gennaro, R., Halevi, S.: More on key wrapping. In: Jacobson, M.J., Rijmen, V., Safavi-Naini, R. (eds.) SAC 2009. LNCS, vol. 5867, pp. 53–70. Springer, Heidelberg (2009). https://doi.org/10.1007/978-3-642-05445-7_4
10. Andrew, B.J., Teoha, D.C., Ngoa, L., Gohb, A.: Personalised cryptographic key generation based on Face Hashing. Elsevier Computers and Security, vol. 23, pp. 606–614 (2004). www.elsevier.com
11. Srinivas, K., Janaki, V.: A study on image based authentication in automated security system. Int. J. Innov. Comput. Sci. Eng. 5(1), 64–69 (2015)

12. Patidar, V., Sud, K., Pareek, N.K.: A pseudo random bit generator based on chaotic logistic map and its statistical testing. Informatica, Scopus Indexed J. **33**(4), 441–452 (2009)
13. Srinivas, K., Janaki, V.: Crypto key generation from selected portion on an image with CRT. Int. J. Eng. Technol. (IJET) **9**(4), 2929–2940 (2017)
14. Srinivas, K., Janaki, V.: A crypto key generation from an image with application of CRT. Int. J. Pharm. Technol. (IJPT) **9**(2), 30174–30183 (2017)
15. Srinivas, K., Janaki, V.: Symmetric key generation algorithm using image based chaos logistic maps. Int. J. Adv. Intell. Paradigms. Inderscience Publishers (2018). ISSN (online): 1755-0394, ISSN (print): 1755-0386

An Efficient Fault Management in Communication Networks Using On Demand Link State Algorithm

K. Sashi Rekha[✉]

Saveetha School of Engineering, Saveetha Institute of Medical and Technical Sciences,
Chennai, India
sashirekhak.sse@saveetha.com

Abstract. Today's Internet backbone network offers enhanced performance to overcome loss, delay, and unavailability. In the occurence of failure of a component, the network becomes susceptible to problems like link faults, path faults, and router failure. Link failure causes looping, packet dropping, loss of data and unreliable network communication. So an efficient fault management implementation is vital to handle multiple link failures. Fault management is vital to get the network back to normal. To properly operate and maintain a complex network, the system as a whole, and each of its essential individual components, must work in tandem. In this proposed approach On-demand Link State (OLS) routing, with shared bandwidth technology is implemented for fault management, for handling multiple link failures. It guarantees the forwarding of loop free data to destinations in case of any number of network failures. The core idea of OLS routing is a blacklist, which carries information on downgraded links identified along the path that are to be avoided. This ensures uninterrupted data packet forwarding without packets getting dropped. Also, the shortest path to the destination is located, based on the state and cost of the link (Robertson and Nelakuditi 2012).

Keywords: Fault management · OLS · Link faults · Router faults and path faults

1 Introduction

This paper focuses on developing an algorithm for fault management in IP backbone networks that can handle multiple link failures to avoid loopbacks and packet dropping in case of link failures. The On-demand Link State (OLS) algorithm is implemented for handling multiple failures. The greedy and recovery approach is applied for packet transmission from source to destination. A packet is forwarded to the greedy mode, based on the least cost method. The cost is calculated using routing metrics and identifying the best path to the destination network. The formulation of the routing metrics, with route discovery and shared bandwidth, is described. The performance of the OLS routing algorithm is evaluated based on delay comparison, failure propagation and distance involved in the management of faults with various parameters (Bley 2007).

© Springer Nature Singapore Pte Ltd. 2021
A. K. Luhach et al. (Eds.): ICAICR 2020, CCIS 1394, pp. 263–271, 2021.
https://doi.org/10.1007/978-981-16-3653-0_22

2 Multiple Link Failures

The OLS routing algorithm, adopted in this work for handling multiple link failures, is presented in this chapter. Fault management methodologies, for the most part, efficiently identify single failures that cause looping and packet dropping. The OLS routing protocol can be efficiently used to handle multiple failures without looping and packet loss.

Looping normally occurs during data packet transmission. If a node fails and is not updated in the routing table, there is a continuous transmission of data from the sender to the degraded receiver. Packet loss occurs during network congestion, or when the packet fails to reach the destination. These two important issues are handled well by the OLS routing protocol, which ensures that packets reach their destination even if the network is congested or the link degraded (Johnson 2005).

The proposed approach is based on the restoration technique. The cost of the link for OLS routing, is calculated based on the routing metrics. Blacklist is carried by each packet with details of downgraded links encountered along its path. Each packet transmitted is updated with the link failure in the blacklist field, and the status of the packet is checked with the blacklist as well. This propels the packet towards the destination even when links or nodes fail (Maratha et al. 2019).

3 On-demand Link State Routing (OLS) Algorithm

The existing approach, Localized On-demand Link State (LOLS) routing, locates faults and protects against multiple link failures in IP networks. In this approach, the cost of the link is based on the labeled cost. In the proposed On-demand Link State (OLS) routing approach, the cost is calculated based on routing metrics. The link is said to be down if it is degraded. Under the OLS, each packet carries a blacklist and the next hop is decided on the basis of the multiple route information from the routing table maintained by each node. The node with the least cost is selected Kumar et al. (2019). Initially, theblacklist is empty. If there is a inconsistency a mid of the existing state and the advertised (blacklist) state of links along its path, degraded link will be added to blacklist adjacent to its next hop. The blacklist is reset to empty when the next hop has a shorter path to the destination. The OLS broadcasts details of the degraded link and gets the packet to its destination without looping (Mas and Thiran 2000).

3.1 OLS Handling of Multiple Failures

The network topology in Fig. 1, Based on the shared bandwidth the cost of the link is calculated and state of the link is advertised up. In the proposed approach of OLS, the shared bandwidth is calculated and used as a cost metric for the link. But currently, a dashed link is identified as a link with its state "down". Further, nodes adjacent to the dashed link will be familiar with its current failed state. Direction helps to discover next hop address for a packet and distance will be the cost spent to reach the destination.

A table is maintained by each node to calculate minimum distance from every node to other node. Minimum distance route is identified as the least cost route. The path to a

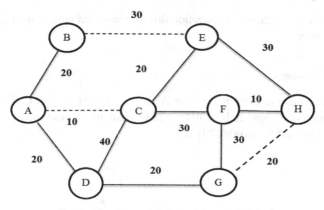

Fig. 1. Topology with dashed degraded links

destination is decided using the shared bandwidth, delay in transferring packets, number of users connected, cost, and hop count (Chao et al. 2001).

In Fig. 1, A is identified as source and H is the destination, a packet should be transmitted by identifying shortest path from A to H. But A to C link is degraded an alternate hop should be identified. The selected hop must be of least cost and loop free.

The cost calculated to reach H from A, B, and D is 50, 60 and 40 respectively. Since link A and C is degraded, the only permissible next hop is D. Again, at G, since the link from G to H is downgraded, the packet is transmitted through F. Now a packet from A is delivered to H successfully. Since the OLS approach includes the dead end details of a link in the packet so forwarding in-between routers is loop-free (Chen et al. 2004).

3.2   OLS Implementation of the Greedy and Recovery Approaches

Packets are switched between the greedy and recovery modes. Based on the least cost of the path evaluated, the packet will be forwarded to its destination. When a packet reaches a dead end in the greedy mode, it is forwarded to the recovery mode instead of being discarded. The packet carries a blacklist in the recovery mode. The blacklist has updates with specifics on downgraded links along the path, and a path that contains no downgraded links is chosen for the packet. If the packet arrives at a node with least cost the packet will be switched back to the greedy mode and the blacklist is reset to empty. Thus, the OLS propagates a linkstate only when required, which helps in loop-free packet forwarding to the intended destinations, despite the presence of degraded links (Cicic et al. 2009).

3.3   Routing Metrics

The routing metrics play a vital role in deciding the cost of the path for packet transmission from source to destination. In the proposed OLS algorithm, the cost of the path is decided based on the routing metrics with shared bandwidth, which does not apply to the existing algorithm. The proposed approach demonstrates improved performance in terms of the delay and failure propagation distance involved in fault management with various parameters.

3.4 Route Discovery

Let us consider the connections between A-B, B-C, C-E, C-D and C-F with allotted bandwidth limits of 20 bps, 20 bps, 30 bps, 25 bps and 40 bps respectively, as shown in Fig. 2 (Robertson and Nelakuditi 2012).

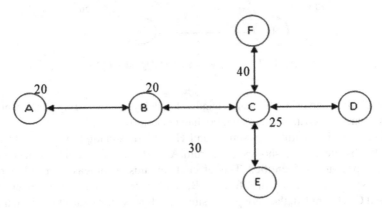

Fig. 2. Nodes connected with bandwidth limits

While making updates, the nodes measure the shared bandwidth limit, as shown in Eq. (1).

$$B_{sh} = \frac{B_{ln}}{N} \tag{1}$$

B_{sh}, the shared bandwidth; B_{ln}, the link bandwidth; and N, the number of users connected to a Node.

After the bandwidth is updated, the node that needs to transmit data checks the multi-route shared bandwidth. The node that shares the most bandwidth selects a route through that particular path. This helps in fast data transfer and increased throughput, measured in bits per second (Doerfler and Brightwell 2006).

3.5 Route Maintenance

Error message looping is averted by implementing the OLS, which uses route mainte-nance to share the error message when the link fails. The focus of the proposed OLS algorithm is to eliminate error message sharing and looping, apart from the blacklist in the packet header and the routing table maintained at each node.

The node affected by the failure is identified as problematic node. Table 1 shows the routing table of node A, featured in Fig. 1. At node A (for destinations B, C, and D), the routing table with the blacklist, shared bandwidth and hop count is as shown in Table 1.

Assuming that node A wants to transmit packets to destinations B, C, and D; the next hops would be B, D and D respectively. In connection with A to C, since the A-C link is downgraded, the immediate hop will be D. The bandwidth Shared for nodes A to B and C to D will be 10, 20, and 10 respectively. Based on the least cost with shared bandwidth, the path will be selected from source to destination (Doverspike and Cortez 2009).

Table 1. Routing table of node A

Destination	Next hop	blacklist	Shared Bandwidth	Hop count
B	B	Ø	10	1
C	D	A-C	20	2
D	D	Ø	10	1

3.6 Bandwidth Sharing and Path Selection

Based on the blacklist and routing table, the packet reaches the destination using the OLS, a scalable scheme for reliable forwarding. The path that offers the highest bandwidth will be considered for fast transmission of data packets and increased throughput (Appenzeller et al. 2004).

Therefore, bandwidth is shared for a link based on the number of users connected at each node. Consider the nodes connected by a wired link, as shown in Fig. 3. Consider that node A wants to send data to F. It can transmit the data through A—B—C—F (3 hops), or A—D—E—F (3 hops), or A—B—D—E—F (4 hops), or A—D—B—C—F (4 hops). It can choose an A—B—C—F (3 hops) or A—D—E—F (3 hops) path to transmit data. Now, as far as the 3 hop counts are concerned, we have two paths, A—B—C—F and A—D—E—F, both of which have an equal hop count and equal bandwidth. But we choose A—D—E—F because the number of connections at node D is 3, whereas node B has 5 connections. Since node B will have to share the link bandwidth with all the other existing connections, and node D has 3 links rather than 5 connected to it, node D is preferred to node B (Crochat et al. 2000).

The path is selected according to the hop count, bandwidth, and the number of connections. This connection information is made known to other nodes by means of control messages (Daniel and Sampath 2006). Initially, all nodes store the connection information which, when once updated, is not stored again (Singh et al. 2020).

3.7 On-demand Link State Routing Algorithm

Most of the fault management methodologies proposed efficiently identify single link failures but result in looping and packet dropping when it comes to multiple link failures. Given that the OLS routing protocol efficiently handles multiple failures without looping and packet loss, the proposed approach is based on the restoration technique as shown in the flowchart Fig. 4.

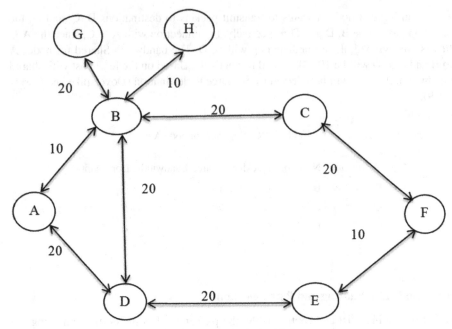

Fig. 3. Network of wired links

4 Performance Evaluation of the OLS

The proposed OLS algorithm is compared with existing LOLS, based on delay comparison, failure propagation distance and size of the blacklist packet.

4.1 Experimental Results

In the simulated IP network topology, the OLS guarantees loop-free forwarding of unnecessarily shared error messages, apart from dealing with multiple link failures. The dynamic IP network topology is connected with 15 nodes and data packet sizes of 500 kb initially.

4.2 Delay Comparison

The delay in fault management is compared, based on the existing and proposed approaches. Clearly, the delay encountered in the existing approach with a number of nodes shows a greater increase than in the proposed OLS approach.

$$\text{Packet Delay}_{[i]} = \text{Receiving time of Packet}_{[i]} - \text{Sending time of Packet}_{[i]} \quad (1)$$

$$\text{Total\_Delay of Packet} = \text{Total\_Delay} + \text{Delay}_{[i]} \quad (2)$$

The delay is expressed, based on the sending time and receiving time of the packet sequence, as shown in Eq. (1). The total delay is incremented each time, based on the delay value, as expressed in Eq. (2).

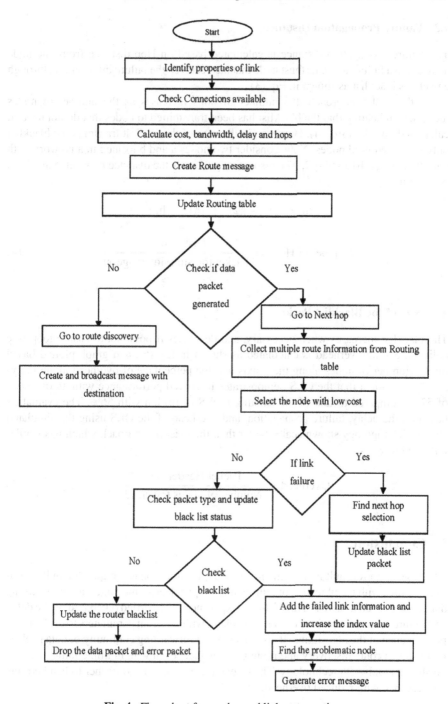

Fig. 4. Flow chart for on-demand link state routing

4.3 Failure Propagation Distance

The failure propagation distance is calculated based on Hop distance from one node adjacent to a failure to the farthest node that has received the failure information, through a packet's blacklist as shown in Eq. (3).

In the LOLS approach, the number of hops increases as the number of nodes increases, indicating that the blacklist has been transmitted to nodes that do not need it, calculated based on Eq. (4). However, in the case of the OLS, it transmits the blacklist only to the required nodes. Now, consider two nodes a and b located in a network with coordinates (g1, h1) and (g2, h2), respectively. If m, is the distance between a and b, m is given by

$$m = (g1 - g2)^2 + (h1 - h2)^2 \tag{3}$$

$$\text{Number of Hops} = \frac{\text{Distance(d)}}{\text{Packet transmission range(r)}} \tag{4}$$

4.4 Size of the Blacklist Packet

The blacklist increases when necessary, and decreases if possible, to ensure loop-free delivery. So the overhead is calculated as shown in Eq. (5), and graph plotted based on the number of nodes along the x-axis and the percentage of overhead along the y-axis. It is evident that the OLS demonstrates improved performance with an overhead of 52%, compared to that of the existing LOLS algorithm with 56%. The evaluation based on the delay, failure propagation, and overhead of the OLS using the simulated IP network topology shown scales better than the existing approach which has similar failure objectives.

$$\text{Overhead} = \frac{\text{Packet Header size}}{\text{Number of nodes traversed}} \tag{5}$$

5 Conclusion

OLS algorithm for fault management is based on restoration technique. It handles multiple failures with the objective of eliminating loopback error messages and transmitting data packets even if there is a link failure. Experiments are carried out, based on the delay and failure propagation distance of the problem, with different parameters to evaluate the performance of the algorithms. It also ensures the forwarding continuity of data packets by means of route discovery and route maintenance, even with multiple failures, based on shared bandwidth technology. The research can be extended further to handle route convergence with reduced overhead.

References

Bley, A.: Routing and capacity optimization for IP networks. In: Kalcsics, J., Nickel, S. (eds.) Operations Research Proceedings 2007. vol. 2007. pp. 9–16. Springer, Heidelberg (2008). https://doi.org/10.1007/978-3-540-77903-2_2

Johnson, A.: Bandwidth measurements in wired and wireless networks, Malardalen University Licentiate Thesis, Department of Computer Science and Electronics, Malardalen University, Vasteras, Sweden (2005).

Kumar, S., Dhull, K., Arora, P., Luhach, A.K.: Performance of energy conservation models, generic, Micaz and Micamotes, using AODV routing protocol on a wireless sensor network. Scalable Comput. Pract. Exp. **20**(4), 631–639 (2019)

Appenzeller, G., Keslassy, I., McKeown, N.: Sizing router buffers. Comput. Commun. Rev. **34** (2004). https://doi.org/10.1145/1030194.1015499

Singh, A.P., Luhach, A.K., Gao, X.Z., Kumar, S., Roy, D.S.: Evolution of wireless sensor network design from technology centric to user centric: an architectural perspective. Int. J. Distrib. Sens. Netw. **16**(8).https://doi.org/10.1177/1550147720949138

Maratha, P., Gupta, K., Luhach, A.K.: Improved fault-tolerant optimal route reconstruction approach for energy consumed areas in wireless sensor networks. IET Wireless Sens. Syst. **10**(3), 112–116 (2019)

Mas, C., Thiran, P.: An efficient algorithm for locating soft and hard failures in WDM networks'. IEEE J. Selected Areas Commun. **18**(10), 1900–1911 (2000)

Chao, C.S., Yang, D.L., Liu, A.C.: An automated fault diagnosis system using hierarchical reasoning and alarm correlation. Netw. Syst. Manage. **9**(2), 183–202 (2001)

Chen, M., Zheng, A.X., Lloyd, J., Jordan, M.I., Brewer, E.: A statistical learning approach to failure diagnosis. In: Proceedings of IEEE International Conference Autonomic Computing, pp. 1–8 (2004)

Cicic, T., Hansen, A., Kvalbein, A., Hartmann, M., Martin, R., Menth Gjessing, M.S., Lysne, O.: Relaxed multiple routing configurations: Ip fast reroute for single and correlated failures. IEEE Trans. Netw. Serv. Manage. **6**(1), 1–1 (2009)

Crochat, O., Boudec, J.L., Gerstel, O.: Protection interoperability for WDM optical networks. IEEE/ACM Trans. Netw. **8**(3), 384–395 (2000)

Daniel Jeske, R., Sampath, R.: Restoration strategies in mesh optical networks. In: 12th Pacific Rim International Symposium on Dependable Computing, pp. 147–153 (2006)

Robertson, G., Nelakuditi, S.: Handling multiple failures in ip networks through localized on-demand link state routing . IEEE Trans. Netw. Serv. Manage. **9**(3), 1–13 (2012)

Doerfler, D., Brightwell, R.: Measuring MPI send and receive overhead and application availability in high performance network interfaces. In: Mohr, B., Träff, J.L., Worringen, J., Dongarra, J. (eds.) EuroPVM/MPI 2006. LNCS, vol. 4192, pp. 331–338. Springer, Heidelberg (2006). https://doi.org/10.1007/11846802_46

Doverspike, R., Cortez, B.: Restoration in carrier networks. In: Proceedings of IEEE Workshop on the Design of Reliable Communication Networks (DRCN), pp. 45–54 (2009)

Application and Analysis of Phishing Website Detection in Machine Learning and Neural Networks

A. S. S. V. Lakshmi Pooja$^{(\boxtimes)}$, M. Sridhar, and G. Ramesh

CSE Department, Gokaraju Rangaraju Institute of Engineering and Technology,
Hyderabad, Telangana 500090, India

Abstract. Web Phishing asks the user to connect to a malicious website. The number one goal of this assault is to steal crucial statistics from the user. Intruder builds websites similar to those that look like the original website. It allows attackers to access Sensitive data such as username, password, details of debit cards etc. This paper aims to review many of the phishing detection strategies recently suggested for the website. This will also provide a high-level description of various forms of phishing detection techniques.

Keywords: Phishing website · URL · Machine learning · Neural networks

1 Introduction

In present days, As there are such huge numbers of individuals are monitoring utilizing web to perform different exercises like web based shopping Online mobile recharge, banking transactions, online bill instalment, banking transactions. Due to this client's large use, multiple security threats such as cybercrime are faced. There are several cybercrimes that are typically carried out Which includes spam, fraud, cyber terrorism and phishing. New cybercrime is a part of this phishing and is widely known nowadays. Phishing is an attempt at deception to obtain confidential client data. The website built by Phisher, for example, username, hidden word, banking information for different purposes, looks like the same as any real website and spoof client to get private customer data.Once innocent user hits the URL unknowingly it is cause for the attacks. For example, phishers sends an email to the user it appears to be from a trusted sender with a URL. Upon clicking the URL, the innocent user landed on the insecure Website.

The overall number of phishing web sites detected inside the 4th quarter of 2019 is 162, a hundred and fifty five, as shown by Anti Phishing Working Group (APWG). It is down from the 266,387 seen in quarter 3 and the 182,465 in quarter 2 and up from the 138,328 in 4th quarter of 2018 and 4th quarter of 2018 is slightly decreased when compared to 3rd quarter of 2018 was 151,014.

A. K. Luhach et al. (Eds.): ICAICR 2020, CCIS 1394, pp. 272–280, 2021.
https://doi.org/10.1007/978-981-16-3653-0_23

With 33% of overall phishing attacks, there were rises in the SAAS/webmail targeted sector and other sectors like payments with 21%, Financial Institution with 19%, cloud storage/File Hosting with 4%, eCommerce/retail with 4%.

As per the security threat studies, we can understand that in the forms of spam, phishing and malware delivery, there is a continuous rise in web attacks, which shows more effect on industry, educational institutions, the banking sector, etc.

Using a blacklist of malicious URLs generated by anti-virus enterprises is one approach to this answer.

The problem with this approach is that the blacklist cannot be designated, as new malicious URLs seem to pop up all of the time. Approaches are consequently wished that can automatically classify a brand new, previously unknown URL both as a phishing web page or as a valid one. Typically, these solutions are system-mastering procedures wherein a programme can categorise new phishing sites the use of a model built the usage of present assault training sets and different techniques for detecting internet-based attacks are:

- Static analysis
- Dynamic analysis
- Heuristic-based

Fig. 1. Processing cycle of phishing attack

2 Related Work

Various approaches are developed for identifying a harmful URL. Here are few approaches which have been used by researches for identifying a harmful or phishing URL. They are:

- Based on Machine learning
- Based on Neural Networking

(A) Based on Machine Learning

This approach works more effectively in larger datasets. In addition to that this removes the drawbacks of present approach and proficient in identifying zero day attack. It has proved that nearly 99% of data is accurate using machine classifiers. Output relays on training data size, collection of features, and type of classifier. This technique is constrained by the inability to detect when attackers use the compromised domain to host their website. In this place a whole lot of studies work has been carried out. For distinct classifiers, some paintings has been used to improve the accuracy of phishing internet site detection. Various classifiers are used: KNN, SVM, Decision Tree, ANN, Naïve Bayes, Component, ELM and Random Forest. Among some of these tree-primarily based DT and RF classifiers, as in keeping with my survey, the data set can be increased.

Any features or a collection of features are extracted from it by using ML techniques to classify phishing URLs. Two varieties of functions that can be extracted from URLs are commonplace, namely

- Host-based totally features
- Lexical traits

Host-primarily based characteristics perceive a website's features, such as the location of the website, by whom it operates and when the site was designed. In addition to that textual properties of URL are described by lexical features because URL Consists of textual content strings which may be break up into subparts like protocol, hostname and path and machine may additionally describe the persuasiveness of a site based totally on any aggregate of those additives.

In inclusion to URL-based applications, various types of applications are used in the detecting process of academic studies in machine learning algorithms. Features gathered from the studies for identifying phishing domains with machine learning techniques are listed. They are:

1. Based on URL features
2. Based on Domain features
3. Based on Page features
4. Based on Content features

1. Based on URL Features

URL is a primary thing a website analyzes to verify whether it is a phishing or not. There are certain points to distinguish the phishing domain URL. Features related to certain points are acquire while processing the URL functions which are mentioned below are based on URL.

Within the address, Digit count

- Complete Address Length
- Checking whether or not the URL is cybersquatted (www.adidas.com-www.Addidas. com)

Assessing whether or not a well-known brand name is included (apple-icloud-login.com).

2. Based on Domain Features

It has the function detecting the names of phishing domains. Unassertive area call queries, which we want to categorise as phishing or no longer, offer us with useful facts. Some useful domain related features are described under.

- Number of days completed after getting registered.
- Its name or its address for information processing in blacklists of well-known service names?
- Is the name of the licensee hidden?

3. Based on Page Features

Page primarily based capabilities utilizes the details about pages which might be rating services measured for trustworthiness. Below are some features which provides information about how secure a website is. They are:

- Global pagerank
- Country pagerank
- Position at the Alexa prime one million website.

Numerous page-based features provide us with data on the activity of the target site. Some of the characteristics are described below. It is not easy to acquire certain types of features. There are Some paid services to get certain kinds of features.

- Evaluates the range of regular, weekly or monthly website visits.
- It calculates Number of Page views per Visit
- It calculates average Visit duration of website.
- Domain Category.
- Web traffic share per country.
- Similar Websites etc.

4. Based on Content Features

By obtaining those form of functions needs energetic experiment to target domain. Page Contents are examined in order that we are able to identify whether or no longer goal area is used for phishing.

Some records regarding about pages being processed is listed under.

- Headings of the page
- Meta Tags
- Unseen Text
- Pictures etc.

We can collect information by analysing this data, such as:

- You want to login to the website.
- Website category
- Audience profile data, etc.

All features which are described above were used to detect a phishing site. In all cases, using these features may not be useful, and there are some disadvantages to using such functions. For example, it could no longer reasonable to apply any of the features consisting of primarily based on content capabilities to create a mechanism of fast detection that can evaluate the wide variety of domain names among 100,000 and two hundred. If we need to look at new registered domains, any other instance might be that Page-based totally capability is not very useful. Thus feature detection mechanism can use depend on the purpose of the detection mechanism. What functions Should be cautiously decided on to be used within the detection mechanism.

(B) Neural Network Based Approaches
Developing a practical deep getting to know version, designing the feedback required by the model, and filling out the features to complete the identification of the phishing internet site URL through the deep mastering version is the method of recognising faux domain names based on the deep getting to know version. For this sort of technique, the selection and design of the input model would have a direct influence on whether the model is successful. Currently CNN and RNN are the widely used models to detect phishing websites.

1. **Convolutional Neural Network:**
   Convolutional Neural Network (CNN) is a category of deep neural networks applied for picture processing studies. Compared to other algorithms for the image classification, CNN needs relatively little preprocessing. This learns features itself – a significant benefit in software development, which differ from other classifications pre-specified by conventional phishing detection researchers. Since it's far in particular meant for image category, it's far executed for phishing detection on embedded character-ranges. CNN networks include a layer of convolution, pooling layer and a fully linked community with non-linear activation characteristic.
2. **Recurrent Neural Network (RNN):**
   RNN is one form of Neural Network group, too. In RNN, the current step's input depends on the output of the previous step. But all inputs and outputs are not dependent on each other in neural networks, some instances such as when the next coming word of a sentence needs to be estimated, the previous words are needed, and then the previous words need to be remembered. Thus, with the aid of a Secret Layer, RNN came into being which solved this problem. Hidden State, which recalls some

details about a sequence, is the main and most critical feature of RNN. RNN has a "record" that gathers all data on what has been determined. It utilises the same values for and input as it performs the same task to produce the output on all inputs or hidden layers. Unlike other neural networks, this decreases the complexity of parameters.

3. **Long Short Term Memory (LSTM):**
   LSTM was designed by Hochreiter and Schmidhuber. They are special kind of RNN. It is mainly introduced to handle the situation RNN fails. RNN depends on the output of previous step for input of current step. So, it should remember all the inputs of the previous step. By introducing LSTM we can overcome this long-term dependencies.

LSTM consists of three gates. They are:

(i)   Forget gate
(ii)   Input gate
(iii) Output gate

- Forget gate: Forget gate decides what needs to be remember and it throws away unnecessary data.
- Input gate: Cell state is updated.
- Cell state gets multiplied by the forget vector which results in dropping a value in cell state and a pointwise addition is done which results in new cell state.
- Output gate: It comes to a decision what the next hidden country must be.

LSTM has capability of memorize the data for long period of time. It is used for predicting the data.

Search Strategy

It includes an overview of strategy that involved in searching for the details of the topic Phishing Website detection with different techniques.

Initially we prefer searching in IEEE Xplore to get papers published on phishing website detection in conferences and journals. Further, we proceed to read paper's title, abstract and keywords to find its relevance with our proposed work. Moreover, we read the content to find out related information about any phishing website detection system and its respective research work.

3   Results and Discussions

The different algorthims which are to detect a phishing website are reviewed individually. From the review of different survey papers.

References	Algorithm	Dataset	Accuracy
[8]	Convolution neural network (CNN) Long short term memory (LSTM) Recurrent neural nework (RNN)	Alexa and Phishtank website	97%
[10]	Neural network Deep belief network Backpropagation Technique	Not mentioned	Neural network-89% Deepbelief network-94% Random forest-91%
[11]	Neural network	UCI dataset Phishtank Website	96%

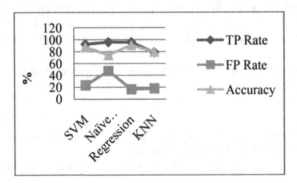

Fig. 2. Detection parameters.

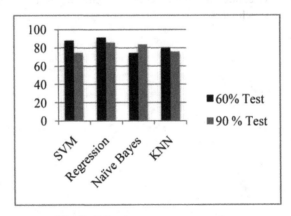

Fig. 3. Detection accuracy comparison

Figure 2 shows a comparison of TP Rate, FP Rate and Detection Accuracy of SVM, Naïve Bayes, Regression Tree and k-NN classifiers. Figure 3 shows detection accuracy parameters of the classifiers with 60% and 90% test split.

4 Conclusion

Phishing attack is the one of the most problematic cyber crime facing by a internet users.The usage of internet has been increased in the same way on the other hand threats from attackers also increased. In this paper, a survey of different type of phishing attacks which are faced by users and this survey brings a knowledge on different machine learning and deep learning techniques, there are many techniques which are used to reduce phishing attacks from attackers.

References

1. Shukla, Z., Zala, K., Kotak, R.: A survey of website phishing detection techniques. Int. J. Fut. Revol. Comput. Sci. Commun. Eng. **4**(1). http://www.ijfrcsce.org
2. Pujara, P., Chaudhari, M.B.: Phishing website detection using machine learning: a review. Int. J. Sci. Res. Comput. Sci. Eng. Inf. Technol. **3**(7), 2456–3307 (2018)
3. https://docs.apwg.org/reports/apwg_trends_report_q3_2019.pdf
4. Patil1, D.R., Patil, J.P.: Feature-based Malicious URL and attack type detection using multi-class classification. ISeCure ISC Int. J. Inf. Secur. **10**(2), 141–162. http://www.isecure-journal.org
5. https://randed.com/types ofphishing/?lang=en
6. https://towardsdatascience.com/phishing-domain-detection-with-ml-5be9c99293e5
7. Aung, E.S., Zan, C.T., Yamana, H.: A Survey of URL-based Phishing Detection. DEIM Forum 2019 G2-3 (2019)
8. Wang, W., Zhang, F., Luo, X., Zhang, S.: SPDRCNN: precise phishing detection with recurrent convolutional neural networks. Secur. Commun. Netw. **2019**, 2595794 (2019). https://doi.org/10.1155/2019/2595794
9. https://www.geeksforgeeks.org/introduction-to-recurrent-neural-network/
10. Verma, M.K., Yadav, S., Goyal, B.K., Prasad, B.R., Agarawal, S.: Phishing website detection using neural network and deep belief network. In: Sa, P.K., Bakshi, S., Hatzilygeroudis, I.K., Sahoo, M.N. (eds.) Recent Findings in Intelligent Computing Techniques. AISC, vol. 707, pp. 293–300. Springer, Singapore (2019). https://doi.org/10.1007/978-981-10-8639-7_30
11. Zhu, E., Chen, Y., Ye, C., Li, X., Liu, F.: OFS-NN: an effective phishing websites detection model based on optimal feature selection and neural network. IEEE Access, vol. 7, 04 June 2019
12. Shad, J., Sharma, S.: A novel machine learning approach to detect phishing websites. In: 2018 5th International Conference on Signal Processing and Integrated Networks (SPIN), pp. 425–430 (2018)
13. Peng, T., Harris, I., Sawa, Y.: Detecting phishing attacks using natural language processing and machine learning. In: Proceedings of the 12th IEEE International Conference on Semantic Computing (ICSC 2018), vol. 2018, pp. 300–301 (2018)
14. Bahnsen, A.C., Bohorquez, E.C., Villegas, S., Vargas, J., González, F.A.: Classifying phishing URLs using recurrent neural networks. Easy solutions research, Mind Lab Research Group, Universidad Nacional de Colombia, Bogotá

15. Pham, T.T.T., Hoang, V.N., Ha, T.N.: Exploring efficiency of character-level convolution neuron network and long short term memory on malicious url detection. Request permissions from Permissions@acm.org. ICNCC. https://doi.org/10.1145/3301326.3301336(2018)
16. James, J., Sandhya, L., Thomas, C.: Detection of phishing urls using machine learning techniques. In: 2013 International Conference on Control Communication and Computing (ICCC)
17. Kulkarni, A., Brown III L.L.: Phishing websites detection using machine learning. Int. J. Adv. Comput. Sci. Appl. **10**(7) (2019)

Author Index

Printed in the United States
by Baker & Taylor Publisher Services